THE
LOBBYING
STRATEGY
HANDBOOK

For my parents (who are kvelling in heaven)
And always for my husband

THE LOBBYING STRATEGY HANDBOOK

10 STEPS TO

ADVANCING

ANY CAUSE

EFFECTIVELY

PAT LIBBY & ASSOCIATES
University of San Diego

Los Angeles | London | New Delhi
Singapore | Washington DC

Los Angeles | London | New Delhi
Singapore | Washington DC

FOR INFORMATION:

SAGE Publications, Inc.
2455 Teller Road
Thousand Oaks, California 91320
E-mail: order@sagepub.com

SAGE Publications Ltd.
1 Oliver's Yard
55 City Road
London EC1Y 1SP
United Kingdom

SAGE Publications India Pvt. Ltd.
B 1/I 1 Mohan Cooperative Industrial Area
Mathura Road, New Delhi 110 044
India

SAGE Publications Asia-Pacific Pte. Ltd.
33 Pekin Street #02-01
Far East Square
Singapore 048763

Associate Editor: Kassie Graves
Editorial Assistant: Courtney Munz
Production Editor: Karen Wiley
Copy Editor: Melinda Masson
Permissions Editor: Adele Hutchison
Typesetter: C&M Digitals (P) Ltd.
Proofreader: Andrea Martin
Indexer: Jeanne Busemeyer
Cover Designer: Gail Buschman
Marketing Manager: Katie Winter

Printed in the United States of America

Library of Congress Cataloging-in-Publication Data

Libby, Pat.

The lobbying strategy handbook : 10 steps to
advancing any cause effectively / Pat Libby.

p. cm.
Includes bibliographical references and index.

ISBN 978-1-4129-9616-7 (pbk.)

1. Lobbying—United States—Handbooks, manuals,
etc. I. Title.

JK1118.L52 2012
324′.40973—dc23   2011020058

This book is printed on acid-free paper.

Contents _____

Acknowledgments _____

I have a notoriously bad memory. I joke that I'm a perfect match for my storytelling husband because he can repeat his favorites as often as he wants since I hardly ever remember the punch line. When I think back to the origins of the 10-step advocacy framework, I have to confess: I'm not entirely sure if I or someone else first laid out the 10 steps in this order. Initially I thought I was building upon work that originated at the Center for Public Interest Law at the University of San Diego, but when I called to ask Bob Fellmeth about it (he's the center's visionary director and a terrific advocate in his own right) and looked back at his training materials, we decided together that my construct was different. Bob, ever the great teacher and lobbyist, welcomed me to spread any and all good words on the subject. Parts of the framework seemed to grow out of some ideas taught by his center to which I give thanks.

Bob and I aren't the first people on the planet to develop a framework for teaching advocacy and for organizing advocacy campaigns. Great minds have devised constructs not only for teaching general advocacy (Arons, 1999) but also for teaching and conducting health advocacy campaigns (Flynn & Verma, 2008); legal advocacy (Srikantiah & Koh, 2010); social work/political advocacy (Hoefer, 2006; Moore & Johnston, 2002); international advocacy (Coulby, 2008); and others not referenced here. Most constructs refer to a series of steps as I do; however, none look exactly like the framework that is presented in this book. I am grateful to all of these people and others who have put thought into how to best share strategies for teaching advocacy and lobbying.

In addition to what I have written in these pages, I am extremely grateful to several dear colleagues and former students who contributed chapters to this book. They include:

Elizabeth Heagy, an amazing lobbyist in her own right and former President and CEO of the Center for Lobbying in the Public Interest. Liz wrote what I think is one of the easiest-to-understand chapters I've ever read on the rules for lobbying.

Maureen Carasiti and Ben McCue, former students who brought passion and high ideals to the causes they lobbied. Both wrote eloquent, riveting chapters about their respective experiences using the 10-step framework.

Howard Wayne, an amazing former California state legislator and my lobbying-course teaching partner for many years. Howard is an inspirational public servant who taught our students tons about the legislative process and made me think about it in new ways. Howard has written a great chapter describing how a bill works its way through the process and another chapter on monitoring legislation once it's passed. As you read them, you'll easily imagine that you're walking alongside him in the corridors of the state capitol.

John McNutt, who in characteristic generosity took the time to pen a terrific chapter on Internet advocacy—a topic he has written on extensively as one of the country's leading experts.

Brian Becker, another former student, who did a lot of great research for the book on the shape and function of state legislatures.

The book is that much better because of the collective wisdom from all of these amazing people.

There were also many current and former University of San Diego students who graciously agreed to share their lobbying experiences and proofread those parts of the book that included their stories. They included Gretchen Pelletier, Carolyn Smyth, Renee Scherr, Becky Lee Launder, Paige Simpson, Sarah Speed, Jeff McDonald, Jessica Towne-Cardenas, Darla Trapp, Maureen Guarcello, Jennifer Martin, Benny Cartwright, and Adina Veen. Jon Glasoe did a lovely job preparing a flowchart. Travis Degheri, Kelly Holmes, Frances Meda, and Annamarie Maricle were kind enough to share their press release, and Elaine Lewis did excellent research. All these students as well as the others mentioned above brought the 10 steps to life. Without them, there would be no book.

I also want to thank the terrific folks at the Center for Lobbying in the Public Interest and at the Alliance for Justice whose business is to guide and inspire people to create change. Melissa Mikesell, at Alliance for Justice, deserves special thanks not only for reviewing the draft manuscript but for helping me determine the book's title. Laura Stein deserves thanks too for reading many chapter drafts and for cheering me on. Kassie Graves, at Sage, has my undying gratitude for believing in me and this project. I would also like to thank the following reviewers for their thoughtful comments: Priscilla Allen, Louisiana State University; Louis Laster, University of Texas at Arlington; Warren Yoder, Jackson State University; Deborah Omokehinde, Wayne State University; and Susan Nakaoka, California State University, Dominguez Hills.

Finally and most important, I want to thank my husband, Mike Eichler, for inspiring me with his own example of an offbeat textbook that really works for students. As he once wrote and I'd have to agree, every day we have together is a true gift.

References

Arons, D. (1999). *Teaching nonprofit advocacy: A resource guide*. Washington, DC: Independent Sector.

Coulby, H. (2008, January). *INTRAC (International NGO Training and Research Centre) advocacy and campaigning course toolkit*. Retrieved March 24, 2011, from http://www.intrac.org/data/files/resources/629/INTRAC-Advocacy-and-Campaigning-Toolkit.pdf

Flynn, L., & Verma, S. (2008). Fundamental components of a curriculum for residents in health advocacy. *Med Teach, 30*(7), 178–183.

Hoefer, R. (2006). *Advocacy practice for social justice*. Chicago: Lyceum.

Moore, L. S., & Johnston, L. B. (2002). Involving students in political advocacy and social change. *Journal of Community Practice, 10*(2).

Srikantiah, J., & Koh, J. L. (2010). Teaching individual representation alongside institutional advocacy: Pedagogical implication of a combined advocacy clinic. *Clinical Law Review, 16*, 451–488.

Introduction _____

This book is for you and for people like you who aren't afraid of what they don't know.

It was written for you, a citizen of this fine country (or, perhaps, an aspiring citizen), on the assumption that you don't know much, or as much as you'd like, about how laws are made or public policy is shaped. It was written for you too if you have tried your hand at lobbying and are looking for some insight on how to build a more effective advocacy campaign without breaking your piggy bank. In short, this book is for you regardless of whether you are brand-new to this whole concept or have already dipped your toe into the advocacy ocean. It is for you as long as you're willing to roll up your sleeves, figure out what it's all about, and use your newly acquired skills to create positive change. Congratulations on buying this book, which is the first step in that process.

Before you continue reading further, I want to let you in on a little secret: You don't have to understand all of the intricacies of the legislative process to be a good lobbyist, just like you don't have to be a veterinarian to own a dog. In fact, you probably already have what you need: passion for your cause and good, hard facts about "it"—the "it" being the thing that needs to be funded or changed to make things better. Our elected officials, wise as they are, don't know everything there is to know about everything. That is why they rely on you, a real person doing real things out in the real world, to educate them about issues that are important. It really is that simple.

The goal of this book is to help you feel so comfortable lobbying that you'll do it! You can have a much more powerful impact on your work if you learn some basic and successful lobbying strategies such as those described in the pages that follow. Everyone who had a hand in writing this book will consider it a success if it inspires you to use the political system to advance the causes you work on day in and day out. Once you learn to lobby, you'll not only embrace it, but you'll wonder how you ever got along without knowing how. Mostly, you'll be amazed at what you can get done!

The framework in this book was devised during the past 30-plus years I have worked in the nonprofit sector. I thought carefully about the steps used to develop advocacy campaigns, built upon and refined those ideas, taught the framework to my students, watched them use it quite effectively, and decided that it was good enough to share with you. It's possible that when you try it out, you may have some ideas for making it even better. If so, please let me know and tell others too!

Most students who take a class to learn about lobbying have no idea how their local or state legislative processes work even though many are experienced nonprofit practitioners. Sometimes they're knowledgeable about one thing and not another—for example, they have lobbied their city councilor but have never set foot inside the state house. They arrive eager and nervous, passionate about an idea for an advocacy campaign, and fundamentally unsure about whether or not they'll be successful in the end. For the vast majority of these students, the semester includes their first-ever visit to the state capitol.

For all those reasons, it is awesome to see some of the ideas they propose at the beginning of the academic year become law by the end of the academic year (or, if not law, well on their way to becoming law). What's even better is that more often than not, their results, when successful, affect the lives of hundreds if not thousands of people. It's heady stuff. Of course, not all their efforts come to fruition, yet all of these students do have a chance to see how the system works "up close and personal." Several students will tell you their stories in this book so that you can see how their campaigns using the 10-step strategy evolved along the way. Their experiences will undoubtedly help shape and inspire your own work.

When you first begin to lobby, you'll draw on more experienced colleagues to help you find your way around city hall, county government, or your state capitol. Later that experience will give you the confidence to lobby on the federal level. In those early days much of what you'll learn will be through trial and error, and success will often be the result of luck (with a little charm thrown in for good measure). Things will eventually get easier once you understand the system, make a few allies, and figure out which strategies work best. This book is written to shorten your learning curve and increase your impact. The contributors to this book *are* those experienced colleagues who will help you as you go through the process of building and conducting a legislative campaign. Our focus is on lobbying at the *local* or *state* level to build your confidence to go on to bigger and better lawmaking at the national level.

Whether you call it lobbying or advocacy (so far, those terms haven't been defined for you!), it may seem like a mystery now, and it may even seem like a bit of a mystery after you've finished reading through to the end. Truthfully, the best way to learn is by doing. This book is designed to guide you through the process as you are engaging in the act. Please write to tell me what parts of the book were particularly helpful to you and which could have been clearer. That way, others can learn from *your* experience. And, if you're will-ing to share the details of your lobbying experience, we might agree to share your story with future readers!

Book Format

This book was written for *anyone* who wants to make change using our system of government. You don't have to be enrolled at a university to understand the concepts in it; honestly, you can learn about lobbying and become an effective advocate by reading the chapters and practicing what you've learned.

Although I've done most of the writing and taken the lead on begging, pleading, and cajoling the other contributors to write their parts, everyone associated with this book has a sincere interest in wanting you to learn how to be a successful advocate. Because of that, we've made an effort to write the chapters in such a way that it seems like we're sitting across from you with a cup of coffee talking through the steps while you're turn-ing the pages. We hope you'll find that style to be easy to read and even funny in parts.

In the book we're going to walk you through the following:

1. Why it's important to get engaged in lawmaking.

2. The legal dos and don'ts for nonprofit organizations that lobby.

3. How government budgeting works—specifically, the major policy quag-mires regarding taxes and spending that face our nation and states.

4. A bird's-eye view of how a bill gets passed that is so vivid you'll smell the scent of polished linoleum as you virtually walk the floors of the state capitol.

5. The 10-step lobbying campaign framework—a comprehensive strat-egy that people and organizations can use to change policy and law. The framework is the heart of the book. You'll read an explanation of how each step works and see how others have used it to lobby.

6. Several real-life examples of student-led advocacy projects that have used the 10-step framework to make an impact on state and interna-tional issues.

7. How Internet advocacy works best.

8. How to monitor the implementation of your bill once it gets passed.

As an added bonus, we've also included an addendum that describes how legislatures operate in different states across the nation.

Many of the examples in this book have to do with legislative campaigns that were conducted in California. The reason for that is I live in California and teach at the University of San Diego. Please don't let that geographical bias fool you into thinking that things work all that differently here than they do in other parts of the country. In fact, I learned how to lobby on the other side of the United States in my home state of Massachusetts where I did indeed drive a "cah." The basic structure of state legislatures is similar across the board; the 10 steps that comprise the advocacy framework are universal. Once you begin to understand how they work, I'm confident you'll be able to use them effectively.

1

Lobbying and Advocacy

What Does It Mean, and Why Should You Do It?

Pat Libby

To welcome you to the world of lobbying, this chapter will explain why people (in particular, people who work for social service agencies as well as other types of nonprofit organizations) don't do it, tell you about some amazing things that have happened in this country as a result of genuine grassroots activism, and, finally, introduce you to basic terms related to lobbying and advocacy.

Most of us who work for love or money (or both), on behalf of a cause, are believers. We believe we can make a difference. Whether we're working on behalf of animals, the environment, people in need, art, science, education, or what have you, we're committed—perhaps compelled by our ideals—to doing things that are larger than ourselves, things that make the world a better place.

Why, then, don't we lobby? What stops us from seizing the reins of government to work with officials at the local, state, or federal level to create laws that benefit the good of society? After all, if we step into the policy arena, don't we have a shot at creating change on a much greater scale?

People are often intimidated by the idea of lobbying. Some find it outright scary. Then there's all we don't know or forgot (let's face it—many of us snoozed through high school civics). We understand the basics of how government works, but the details are foggy at best. We don't have a grasp of what we're supposed to do (which we're embarrassed to admit). We don't want to look stupid. It seems so complicated. Sometimes, it even seems sleazy.

Second, we're afraid of getting into trouble. What if we violate some rule we don't know about or innocently misinterpret the law and the IRS takes away the tax-exempt status of the nonprofit with which we're affiliated?! What if our major funder finds out what we're doing and pulls the plug?! How can we find a minute in our crazy-busy lives to understand the regulations and explain them to our board members? What if they object? Aren't we already doing more than our fair share without having to rock the boat?

If you have these thoughts and feelings, you've got plenty of company. Study after study has shown that people who work for nonprofit organizations say that lobbying is important; however, they *don't do it* (or do much of it) for a variety of reasons.

In *Seen but Not Heard,* Bass, Arons, Guinane, and Carter (2007) report on the findings of the Strengthening Nonprofit Advocacy Project (SNAP)— a multiyear research project that was designed to discover how, and to what extent, nonprofits lobby. Their findings, based on a large-scale survey, telephone interviews, and focus groups with nonprofit staff, revealed a stunning contradiction: While nonprofits said that "public policy is essential to . . . their mission," most reported lobbying "at the lowest level" measured by the study (Bass et al., 2007, p. 17).[i] For instance, an astounding 63% of the more than 1,700 nonprofits surveyed confessed that they either "never" or "infrequently" "encouraged others to write, call, fax, or email policymakers."[ii] A second survey of more than 850 nonprofits conducted by the Johns Hopkins Nonprofit Listening Post Project developed in collaboration with the Center for Lobbying in the Public Interest (itself a nonprofit) echoed those findings. Those researchers, Salamon, Geller, and Lorentz (2009), reported that most nonprofits involved in advocacy "rely on the least demanding forms of engagement (e.g., signing a correspondence to a government official endorsing or opposing a particular piece of legislation or budget proposal)" (p. i).[iii]

As to why nonprofits lobby so sparingly, survey research directed by Jeffrey M. Berry of Tufts University revealed important clues. Berry and his colleagues quizzed randomly selected nonprofit leaders throughout the country about their organization's basic lobbying rights using eight simple yes/no questions. According to Berry, most "flunked the test."[1, iv]

In addition to being afraid, not fully understanding their lobbying rights, and not knowing how to lobby effectively, there are other theories about why

---

[1]Here are Jeffrey Berry's Lobby and Charities Quiz Questions (reprinted with permission). Can a nonprofit organization
1. support or oppose federal legislation under current IRS regulations?
2. take a policy position without reference to a specific bill under current regulations?
3. support or oppose federal regulations?
4. lobby if part of its budget comes from federal funds?
5. use government funds to lobby Congress?
6. endorse a candidate for elected office?
7. talk to elected public officials about public policy matters?
8. sponsor a forum or candidate debate for elected office?
   (The answers to all are yes with the exceptions of Questions 5 and 6.)

nonprofits have disengaged from the political process. Zeke Hasenfeld and Eve Garrow are among several academics who contend that many nonprofits—both in the United States and abroad—have become too closely aligned with government and, therefore, are less likely to challenge government.[v] They and others believe that as government increases its reliance on nonprofits to deliver services—particularly human services and health care—and those nonprofits rely increasingly on government for income, they are less likely to lobby for important changes that impact the people they serve. The Urban Institute tells us, for example, that in 2009, more than a quarter of the income received by human service nonprofits came directly from government.[vi] That cozy relationship means that nonprofits may be reluctant to speak up for fear of "biting the hand that feeds them." They may also be so involved in delivering services in a certain way (a way determined by the design of a government program) that they become blind to the bigger issues facing their clients or reluctant to advocate for innovative ways of providing services that may be more effective. In the act of taking government funds to operate programs, some human service nonprofits may morph into organizations that put a priority on protecting their own interests rather than advocating for the real needs of the individuals they serve. One can argue, as Hasenfeld and Garrow do, that this behavior is a consequence of "New Public Management" with its emphasis on corporate-like management practices and accountability of results.[vii] Others might claim "mission drift." Regardless of the reason, there is clear evidence that nonprofits across the sector are advocating at very low levels.

The deafening silence of nonprofit professionals and volunteers in political advocacy is resulting in the passage of new laws that undermine the personal and professional missions of those who work in the sector. For example, in October 2010, after a historic delay in passing the California budget (it was approved more than three months after the start of the state's fiscal year), legislators arrived at an agreement to close a nearly $19 billion budget gap (equal to more than 20% of the state's $87.5 billion budget) by cutting $4 billion from schools and health and human service programs. The state's public assistance program was a major target despite record unemployment levels that forced an increasing number of Californians onto welfare.[viii] Sadly, once the news was released, there was no public outcry on the part of organizations and people affected by the cuts. It was as if there was a collective shoulder shrug. This scenario wasn't unique to California; it was seen time and again in states across the country.

It can be argued that some nonprofit professionals, such as social workers, have a *moral* obligation to lobby. According to the National Association of Social Workers (NASW) Code of Ethics, social workers have "ethical responsibilities to the broader society." Specifically, the code states,

> Social workers should engage in social and political action that seeks to ensure that all people have equal access to the resources, employment, services, and opportunities they require to meet their basic human needs

and to develop fully. Social workers should be aware of the impact of the political arena on practice and should *advocate for changes in policy and legislation* [emphasis added] to improve social conditions in order to meet basic human needs and promote social justice.[ix]

The truth is that nonprofit leaders of all stripes *need* to be involved in the legislative process because otherwise the debate happens without them.

It's not just a matter of nonprofit professionals taking a backseat to advocacy when it comes to lobbying on behalf of the people they serve; nonprofits have also been noticeably absent in policy debates that have an impact on their own operations. A startling example of this was the lack of advocacy from nonprofits in the national health care debate. Nonprofits whose missions were focused on health care were, of course, fully engaged advocates; however, *all* nonprofits nationwide would inevitably find themselves affected by the outcome in important ways, yet few voiced their concerns.

Significantly, the health care law will directly impact thousands of nonprofits throughout the country. Those organizations that employ fewer than 25 full-time people where the average annual salary is less than $50,000 are eligible for a special payroll tax credit for health insurance. A whopping 65% of all nonprofits in America fall into that category.[x] That means that many small organizations that were struggling to provide decent benefits will now be covered by a law that they had no hand in shaping. What's more, those additional benefits might make a difference in the staffing patterns of smaller nonprofits: If more staff at those organizations have access to health insurance, a greater percentage may be able to stay employed there rather than leave for jobs at organizations that provide health benefits. While in this case it worked out just fine—those organizations that didn't participate in the health care debate ended up benefitting just the same—it's also possible that the outcome could have been even more beneficial if those organizations that had something to gain weighed in.

It hasn't always been this way. Advocacy by nonprofit leaders has had a major impact on our lives. If we take a quick walk through modern American history, we'll find some very important rights that wouldn't exist today without citizen activism that was led by community leaders. Many of these leaders harnessed the energy of other citizen activists by establishing nonprofit organizations to advance their cause. Let's take a look at what they accomplished by peering through the lens of the world that existed prior to these laws being established.

First, imagine living in a place where Black and White children were blocked from attending the same public schools or universities (despite a Supreme Court ruling to the contrary); where the country was so divided, the governor of a state (Arkansas) called for the National Guard to protect a public high school from integration by nine Black students; where parents of White students—not just in Little Rock, Arkansas, but in Boston, Massachusetts, and other places across the country—threw rocks at yellow school buses and screamed obscenities at elementary school children of color simply because they were going to their assigned public school; where the president of the United States had to send federal troops to protect a Black student who was attending a university in Mississippi where he had been accepted for admission; where drinking fountains were segregated by the skin color of the person who wanted to take a drink; where many restaurants refused to serve food to people who were not White, and could do so legally; and where people of color were required to sit in the back of a bus that also carried White passengers.

On June 11, 1963, Alabama Governor George Wallace said the following as he literally stood in a doorway to block two Black students from attending the University of Alabama: "The unwelcomed, unwanted, unwarranted and force-induced intrusion upon the campus of the University of Alabama today of the might of the Central Government offers frightful example of the oppression of the rights, privileges and sovereignty of this State by officers of the Federal Government."[xi] His opposition to federally mandated school integration was no surprise: During his inaugural address that previous January Wallace had proclaimed, "In the name of the greatest people that have ever trod this earth, I draw the line in the dust and toss the gauntlet before the feet of tyranny . . . and I say . . . segregation today . . . segregation tomorrow . . . segregation forever."[xii] In fact, the people of Alabama voted in Wallace for governor *because* of his stand against integration (views that he confessed to regretting quite deeply many years later).

As difficult as these facts are to believe, this was America prior to the Civil Rights Movement. It was an America in which many were frightened by the thought of people of different races "mixing" together. It was America until community leaders including Martin Luther King Jr., Medgar Evers, James Farmer, and Ralph Abernathy—the list is far too lengthy to name them all—and members of nonprofit organizations they represented such as the National Association for the Advancement of Colored People (NAACP), the Southern Christian Leadership Conference, the Congress of Racial Equality, and the Student Nonviolent Coordinating Committee organized to mobilize, protest, educate, and work with their elected officials to create the Civil Rights Act of 1964. The act outlawed segregation in schools and public places and prohibited discrimination based on race, religion, sex, or national origin, and its advocates went on to help create other important laws such as the Voting Rights Act, which followed in 1965. That act protects Americans against literacy tests, poll taxes (a fee one had to pay in order to vote), and other measures that existed previously in many places throughout the country that made it difficult for low-income people and people of color to participate in the electoral process.[xiii] The nation is a vastly different place because of the work of these individuals and organizations.

Ten years later, a community activist named Gale Cincotta, a feisty middle-aged widow with a high school education, drew attention to banks taking deposits from low-income communities in which they did not reinvest.

Cincotta and her colleagues gathered evidence of a pattern of discrimination where residents of low-income communities across the country (particularly residents living in predominantly minority communities) with steady jobs and good credit history were being turned down for home loans while their White counterparts with similar financial circumstances who lived in other neighborhoods were approved for loans. They dubbed this phenomenon "redlining," suspecting that banks were literally drawing red lines around the borders of poor neighborhoods they deemed too high-risk for making loans.

Banks were not skirting the law—this was then legal practice. However, people living in those communities felt that their neighborhoods—neighborhoods where they grew up, went to church, and played as kids; where their own kids played; where they gossiped about neighbors; and that they loved and wanted to own houses in—would never improve without loans for homes and businesses. They demanded that banks located in those neighborhoods—their neighborhoods—that took their deposit money had an obligation to lend there as well. Can you imagine having saved enough money to buy a home in the neighborhood you loved, yet a bank wouldn't give you a loan because it determined the neighborhood itself wasn't a good investment?

Cincotta and her neighbors were instrumental in establishing the Home Mortgage Disclosure Act of 1975, which not only proved their theory of unequal lending by requiring banks to disclose where and to whom they made loans but also set the stage for the establishment of the Community Reinvestment Act two years later. The Community Reinvestment Act of 1977 (commonly known as the CRA) was spearheaded largely by two nonprofit organizations founded by Cincotta: National People's Action (NPA) and the National Training and Information Center. Today the CRA plays a major role in ensuring that banks invest in communities where they take deposits. According to NPA, "Both of these laws are often referred to as the most important economic justice public policy for neighborhoods as they resulted in $4.7 trillion dollars being invested in low and moderate income communities across the United States."[xiv]

Then there's the simple matter of the air we breathe. Long before anyone heard the term *global warming*, Americans used to go about their daily lives seeing plumes of black smoke billowing out of factory smokestacks. It was a common sight. Buildings would be covered in soot from those emissions and from car exhaust. The gasoline that fueled cars contained dangerous levels of lead. In many places, it wasn't easy to take a deep breath—asthma and other respiratory illnesses were even more prevalent than they are today. The task of monitoring air quality was left to each state to decide. However, there was an unfortunate problem with that plan since air pollution travels across state borders.

In 1970, a U.S. senator from Wisconsin, Gaylord Nelson, hatched the idea of Earth Day. His idea was to work in collaboration with environmental organizations to organize events across the country that would raise the public's consciousness about the earth's precious and finite natural resources. As a result, that year, 20 million Americans participated in Earth Day events across the country. Those events are credited with paving the way for the passage of a broadly expanded Clean Air Act later that year. The act gave the federal government the authority to set and regulate clean air safety standards for pollution from factories and automobiles.[xv] Over the years, the act has been further amended—each time strengthening the ability of the federal government to protect our air quality. In addition to the Clean Air Act, Earth Day led to the creation of the U.S. Environmental Protection Agency (EPA), and the passage of both the Clean Water and Endangered Species acts.

We all can breathe easier because of the work of many nonprofit environmental organizations that not only pushed for the establishment of the Clean Air Act but work to ensure it remains strong. The Environmental Defense Fund, the Sierra Club, and other organizations have been actively promoting and protecting the act. Unfortunately, it's a continuing battle: Since its inception, the Clean Air Act has been aggressively challenged as being expensive and unnecessary by some members of the business community. As recently as September 2010, there were battles in Congress to weaken the EPA's ability to regulate carbon emissions and other greenhouse gases.

These stories are simple reminders of how great it is to take a deep breath of clean air and to have the opportunity to study with different types of students. They're about things you might have taken for granted or not given much thought to like being able to buy a house anywhere you want (assuming you have sufficient funds and good credit). Here's something else to add to that list: Every time you or someone you know roams around campus in a wheelchair, you can thank Justin Dart and the American Association of People with Disabilities—the organization he founded. Dart and his colleagues were the driving force behind the Americans with Disabilities Act of 1990 (ADA).

Similar to and modeled on the Civil Rights Act, the ADA provides broad protections and prohibits many types of discrimination against people with disabilities with regard to "employment, State and local government, public accommodations, commercial facilities, transportation, and telecommunications."[xvi] For example, prior to the act being signed into law, it was impossible for people in wheelchairs to do things that many others take for granted like go to college, get to the bank, ride a bus, go to a movie, walk into a town hall, or even cross a street because ramps, lifts, and handicapped bathrooms weren't part of the landscape. The ADA changed thousands of lives across the country—liberating people who otherwise wouldn't have access to education, jobs, and basic services. Before the law was passed, the main argument against it was that it was impractical because it would be too costly to implement.

All of these things are so vitally important to having a civil society that it's easy to forget that these laws didn't always exist in our country. You may be thinking, "That's cool, but it's more like *ancient* history than modern history" since all of those things happened way before the iPhone was invented. Let's look at some more current examples.

One of the most well-known modern-day grassroots advocacy efforts is the work of MADD—Mothers Against Drunk Driving—an organization that was founded in 1980 by Candy Lightner, a mother who was heartbroken and angry about her teen daughter's untimely death by a drunk driver. Not only was the man who killed her daughter drunk; he had repeatedly been arrested for drunk driving. In fact, he had been released from jail on another hit-and-run drunk driving charge just days before his car hit her daughter. Enraged by these facts, Lightner resolved to do something to prevent tragedies like this from happening to other families. She was joined early on in her crusade by Cindy Lamb, a mother whose infant daughter became a quadriplegic after being hit by a drunk driver. The car crash that injured her baby was that driver's fifth drunk driving offense.

MADD first coined and popularized the notion of a "designated driver," developed a slew of public awareness and education programs, and in 2000 managed to get the federal government to adopt a blood alcohol level of 0.08 as the federal standard for drunk driving. That federal standard was then tied to the distribution of national highway funds to states. As a result, by 2004 all 50 states and the District of Columbia had passed 0.08 as the legal drunk driving limit. Not too shabby. Lobbying isn't the only thing that MADD does to save lives—and it has truly saved tens of thousands of lives through its education work both in this country and in Canada. Lobbying is, however, a major thrust of MADD's work as a 501(c)(3) corporation. We're not saying that you have to aspire to become like MADD in terms of your own advocacy efforts, but it does give you a good sense of what can be accomplished (and—let's face it—it's awesome).

Many other great nonprofit organizations have racked up impressive legislative accomplishments as well. The Sierra Club in collaboration with other environmental organizations succeeded in getting legislation passed in 2001 that required the U.S. Environmental Protection Agency to reduce the amount of allowable levels of arsenic in drinking water. What's so bad about arsenic? According to the EPA, "Arsenic is a semi-metal element in the periodic table. It is odorless and tasteless. It enters drinking water supplies from natural deposits in the earth or from agricultural and industrial practices. Non-cancer effects can include thickening and discoloration of the skin, stomach pain, nausea, vomiting; diarrhea; numbness in hands and feet; partial paralysis; and blindness. Arsenic has been linked to cancer of the bladder, lungs, skin, kidney, nasal passages, liver, and prostate." [xvii] Seems like a good thing to monitor, don't you think?

The American Cancer Society also does a great job lobbying. In 2009 it was responsible for spearheading and getting passed sweeping legislation that gave power to the federal Food and Drug Administration to regulate how tobacco is marketed to adults and minors with new warning label requirements and packaging constraints. The law includes a whole slew of important provisions including some things that may seem simple such as banning candy and fruit-flavored cigarettes that were designed principally to attract young people to smoking (and get them addicted to tobacco). It also includes the following:

- A ban on the use of misleading descriptions such as "light," "mild," and "low-tar" in the marketing and packaging of cigarettes
- Larger, stronger warning labels on smokeless tobacco products
- A first-ever federal prohibition on cigarette and smokeless tobacco sales to minors
- A ban on all tobacco-brand sponsorships of sports and cultural events
- A ban on virtually all free tobacco samples and giveaways of non-tobacco items, such as hats and T-shirts, with the purchase of tobacco
- A prohibition on the sale of cigarettes in packs of fewer than 20—so-called "kiddie packs" that make cigarettes more affordable and appealing to kids.[xviii]

The American Cancer Society has also been responsible for leading several successful state campaigns to increase the tax on tobacco products in order to pay for public health programs.

If you stop to think about the major advocacy efforts that are going on in your state and local community, you'll realize that many of them are being led by nonprofit organizations. It isn't that nonprofits aren't out there lobbying to great success; it's that there aren't *enough* nonprofits engaged in the lobbying process. To borrow a line from Charles Dickens, it's really a tale of two types of nonprofits—those whose work focuses on advocacy and those who do all types of other things and lobby very little or not at all. It's the second group that needs to read this book and get going!

At this point you may be feeling inspired, overwhelmed, or maybe even intimidated by these massive accomplishments. Just remember that all of these leaders had to start at the beginning. Nobody was born knowing how to be a lobbyist or an advocate—these activists learned how over time. What they all had in common was a heartfelt commitment to addressing an injustice. If you have that type of commitment, you'll be likely to succeed as well. This book is going to show you how to make change on the state and local level by explaining the legal dos and don'ts of lobbying, demystifying the challenges and realities of government budgeting, walking you through the legislative process, introducing you to a step-by-step framework that you can use to launch a legislative campaign, demonstrating how three separate groups of students have used that framework to successfully lobby, describing effective Internet lobbying strategies, and, finally, telling you what to do once your legislation passes. In the end, it won't seem all that difficult or mysterious. The focus of this book is on lobbying at the local level as that's a good place for you to develop advocacy skills. Later on you can apply what you've learned to lobbying at the federal level to make even greater change.

Let's get going by becoming familiar with some of the terms that are used to describe and define the work of lobbying and advocacy.

First, what do we mean by the term *advocacy*? Advocacy can be defined in two distinct ways. Social workers often use the term to refer to case management work that is done to represent and advance the interests and needs of an individual client or multiple clients within a particular system or a variety of systems that are reluctant (or resistant) to provide needed services. For example, a client who is homeless may need a social worker to help her find a placement in an emergency shelter, a drug rehabilitation or detox program, or a job training program; child care; or all of the above. The social worker helps the client connect to and navigate through those systems.

Public advocacy, the second term to keep in mind and the one that pertains to the type of work that is discussed in this book, means influencing both public opinion and public policy. For example, when MADD promoted the concept of a "designated driver" (remember—it was a completely new idea to the general public at the time), the organization did a terrific job influencing public opinion about driving drunk. The mere act of making people aware that they should appoint someone in their group to be a designated driver raised the public's consciousness about the dangers of drinking and driving. When Gaylord Nelson launched Earth Day, he did so to raise awareness of the fragility of the environment. The "I Have a Dream" speech delivered so eloquently by Martin Luther King Jr. inspired millions of Americans to think about their personal relationship to the struggle for civil rights. In all of these cases, making the public aware of these issues and the need to act led eventually to important changes in the laws of this country. However, lobbying was required to make those changes occur.

Public advocacy is a broad umbrella encompassing many different types of activities that promote public awareness and policy change. It includes a wide range of actions such as organizing rallies, educating people about a particular issue, litigating for change, and submitting comments that influence the shape of government rules and regulation. It also includes informal "getting to know you" meetings with public officials to introduce them to the organization you represent and to the issues that are important to people in your community.

What do we mean by *lobbying*? According to the Center for Lobbying in the Public Interest (fondly known as CLPI), lobbying is "a specific, legally defined activity that involves stating your position on specific legislation to legislators and/or asking them to support your position."[xix] It is the act of directly expressing your views to elected officials (or their proxy—for instance, someone who works in the office of that official) in order to influence the action of that person or persons with the goal of affecting the law. Lobbying can also mean rallying others to carry a specific message to elected officials for the purpose of affecting the law. This is referred to as grassroots lobbying and will be discussed in greater detail in the next chapter. It does not matter if you or your allies are advocating in favor of or against a particular piece of legislation; you are lobbying when you make a direct appeal to an elected official to do something specific about a law or a proposed law. When the American Cancer Society lobbied to pass the Family Smoking Prevention and Tobacco Control Act in 2009, it lobbied members of Congress with a very specific package of proposals for new laws.

What is *legislation*? Legislation is a proposed law that is under consideration by a governing body that is capable of making laws. According to the IRS, it also includes "action . . . with respect to acts, bills, resolutions, or similar items (such as legislative confirmation of appointive office)."[xx] That governing body might be the Congress of the United States, a state legislature, a county government, or a city council. Occasionally, the general public performs the function of a legislature when it determines law as part of a ballot question such as an initiative petition, a referendum, or a proposed constitutional amendment. Legislation starts with a certain set of ideas and changes as it goes through the policy-making process where other legislators and the public have an opportunity to express their views on what is being proposed. Once legislation becomes law, it is called an "act" or a "statute." Many people are surprised to learn that school boards and zoning boards aren't legislative bodies. Therefore, when nonprofits approach those groups to express their views, they are not engaging in the lobbying process. Similarly, contact with the executive branch, independent administrative agencies, or the judicial branch is not considered lobbying.

What is *public policy*? Similar to how advocacy is broader than lobbying, public policy is broader than legislation. While legislation has to do with making laws, public policy is defined by CLPI as "decision-making that affects the public realm—laws, regulations, executive orders, judicial rulings, rules issued by elected and other government officials." For example, a city council may have a policy on which types of items residents can put in their curbside recycle bins; however, that policy isn't a law.

Finally, you may have heard the term *social welfare policy*. Social welfare policy refers to those government programs that are part of our social safety net, which is also known more broadly as the social welfare state. These programs might include, for example, Social Security, Medicare, Medicaid, housing subsidies, food stamps, and so on and will be discussed in greater detail in Chapter 3.

Having a basic understanding of these definitions is a good start. That said, if you read through them carefully, you'll notice that many of the definitions are intertwined—one thing leads to another and back again. What you really need to know is twofold:

1. *The rules concerning what is legal and illegal for nonprofits to do.* We'll discuss those in detail in the next chapter. The real surprise here is how much you *can* do (in a nutshell, pretty much everything except endorse a candidate for office. Still, don't skip that chapter).

2. *The facts about the issue you care about.* That's right. When you are lobbying at the city, county, state, or federal level, no one is going to give you a pop quiz about whether or not you know what the next

steps are in the process. More often, the policy makers with whom you'll work, and their aides (especially those aides—bless them!), will help you navigate your way through the process. What they will insist you know is everything possible about the idea or cause you are championing. That is the single most important thing you need to do in order to be an effective lobbyist. Know your stuff, and know how to present it effectively.

Chapter Questions

1. Have you ever been involved in a lobbying campaign led by a nonprofit organization? If so, what was your involvement?

2. Have you ever been in a situation where you thought a nonprofit organization should get involved with a public policy issue but it didn't?

3. Do you believe that human service nonprofits are hesitant to lobby because they are overly dependent on government grants?

4. Do you know anyone who was involved in any of the lobbying campaigns mentioned in this chapter (Civil Rights Act, Voting Rights Act, ADA, etc.)?

5. The Voting Rights Act was challenged in 2010. Why? What were the arguments put forth?

6. Name two nonprofit organizations in your state that are active advocates for legislative change. What kinds of campaigns are those organizations working on right now?

Endnotes

i   Bass, G., Arons, D., Guinane, K., & Carter, M. (2007). *Seen but not heard.* Washington, DC: The Aspen Institute.

ii   Ibid.

iii   Salamon, L., Geller, S., & Lorentz, S. (2009). *Nonprofit America: A force for democracy?* Paper delivered at the 2009 Conference of the Association for Research on Nonprofit Organizations and Voluntary Action, Cleveland, Ohio, November 19–21.

iv   Berry, J. (2003, November 27). Nonprofit groups shouldn't be afraid to lobby. *The Chronicle of Philanthropy.* Retrieved March 8, 2011, from http://philanthropy.com/article/Nonprofit-Groups-Shouldnt-Be/61998/

v   Hasenfeld, Y., & Garrow, E. (2007). *The welfare state, the non-profit sector and the politics of care.* A paper presented at the Dead Sea Conference for Third Sector Research, Israel, March 14–15.

vi   Wing, K., Roeger, K., & Pollak, T. (2009). *The nonprofit sector in brief: Public charities, giving and volunteering.* Washington, DC: The Urban Institute.

vii   Hasenfeld, Y., & Garrow, E. (2007). *The welfare state, the non-profit sector and the politics of care.* A paper presented at the Dead Sea Conference for Third Sector Research, Israel, March 14–15, p. 8.

viii   Lin, J. (2010, October 9). State budget fix seen as short-lived. *San Diego Union Tribune*, p. A3.

ix   National Association of Social Workers. (2011). *Code of Ethics of the National Association of Social Workers: Approved by the 1996 Delegate Assembly and Revised by the 2008 NASW Delegate Assembly.* Retrieved March 5, 2011, from http://www.naswdc.org/pubs/code/code.asp

x   Agency for Healthcare Research and Quality, Center for Financing, Access, and Cost Trends. 2008 Medical Expenditure Panel, Survey-Insurance Component. Available from http://www.meps.ahrq.gov/mepsweb/survey_comp/survey_ic.jsp

xi   Alabama Department of Archives and History. (2010). *Governor George C. Wallace's School House Door Speech.* Retrieved March 6, 2011, from http://www.archives.state.al.us/govs_list/schooldoor.html

xii   Alabama Department of Archives and History. (2002). *The 1963 Inaugural Address of Governor George C. Wallace.* Retrieved March 6, 2011, from http://www.archives.alabama.gov/govs_list/inauguralspeech.html

xiii   U.S. Department of Justice Civil Rights Division. (n.d.) *The Voting Rights Act of 1965.* Retrieved March 8, 2011, from www.justice.gov/crt/about/vot/intro/intro_b.php

xiv   National People's Action. (2009). *Report illustrates need for disclosure and transparency in lending.* Retrieved March 6, 2011, from http://www.npa-us.org/index.php?option=com_content&task=view&id=256&Itemid=5

xv   Rogers, P. (1990). *The Clean Air Act of 1970.* Retrieved March 6, 2011, from http://www.epa.gov/history/topics/caa70/11.htm

xvi   U.S. Department of Justice, Civil Rights Division. (2005). *A guide to disability rights laws: Americans with Disabilities Act.* Retrieved March 6, 2011, from http://www.ada.gov/cguide.htm#anchor62335

xvii   U.S. Environmental Protection Agency. (2010). *Arsenic in drinking water.* Retrieved March 6, 2011, from http://water.epa.gov/lawsregs/rulesregs/sdwa/arsenic/index.cfm

xviii   American Cancer Society Action Cancer Network. (2010, June 18). *First anniversary of federal tobacco regulation law brings new restrictions on tobacco industry.* Retrieved March 6, 2011, from http://acscan.org/mediacenter/view/id/315/

xix   Center for Lobbying in the Public Interest. (2008). *Make a difference for your cause: Strategies for nonprofit engagement in legislative advocacy.* Retrieved March 6, 2011, from http://www.clpi.org/press-publications/50-make-a-difference-for-your-cause-strategies-for-nonprofit-engagement-in-legislative-advocacy

xx   Internal Revenue Service. (2010). *Lobbying.* Retrieved March 6, 2011, from http://www.irs.gov/charities/article/0,,id=163392,00.html

2

The Rules
of Engagement

Elizabeth Heagy

Elizabeth Heagy

Introduction and Definitions

There are basically two kinds of nonprofits when it comes to lobbying and the legal rules: those that are willing to jump into the fray and ask questions later about the legal parameters, and those, the majority of 501(c)(3) organizations, that have misinformation regarding the laws and avoid the fray altogether.

As you explore launching an advocacy campaign, you need just a few rules of engagement. To the uninitiated, they might seem mysterious and confusing. This chapter will make them easy to understand, explain to others, and use.

Let's start with the first and most important lesson of this chapter: Nonprofit[1] lobbying is 100% legal. Indeed, the right of nonprofits to make their voices heard in the policy-making process is rooted in the U.S. Constitution, specifically the First Amendment rights to free speech and to the redress of grievances. Congress is constitutionally able to restrict political activity and lobbying by nonprofits, despite their being First Amendment rights, due to the special advantages given to nonprofits through tax exemption and the tax deductibility of contributions.[i] The history of the nonprofit lobbying laws is outlined below, but, suffice it to say, while there have been ups and downs when it comes to legal clarity, the U.S. Congress has always supported these rights.

---

[1] The term *nonprofit* as used throughout this chapter refers to 501(c)(3) public charities, unless otherwise noted.

The Regs _____

Tax law governs nonprofit activities including those geared toward influencing the public policy process. Accordingly, the Internal Revenue Service is the federal agency that issues regulations governing what nonprofits can and cannot do to influence legislation on the federal, state, and local levels. Nonprofit lobbying laws have been on the books since 1934 and remained constant until Congress passed new laws in 1976. Regulations for the 1976 lobby laws were issued (finally) in 1990.

From 1934 to 1976, one set of rules governed: the *substantial part* test. Under this test, lobbying cannot be a substantial part of a nonprofit's activities. It is hard to believe, but the rules did not (and still do not) define "substantial" or "lobbying." This lack of clarity caused decades of confusion, culminating in the Sierra Club "incident" of 1966. In that year the organization took out full-page ads in *The New York Times* and *The Washington Post* at the cost of $10,000, encouraging the public to contact a subcommittee chair to ask that he "kill" a bill to build two dams on the Colorado River that would have cut through parts of the Grand Canyon. This ad expenditure resulted in the Sierra Club's loss of tax-exempt status and sent panic through the nonprofit sector. Unfortunately the result was an overcorrection by many nonprofit organizations whose attorneys and CPAs advised them to avoid any work that smacked of influencing public policy.

It took 10 years to get there (as it often does in the process to make new laws), but eventually a new law was passed in 1976 to provide much-needed clarity and ease the panic. The new law—the *expenditure* test, otherwise known as the 501(h) election—set forth specific definitions of lobbying and expenditure limits. Instead of replacing the substantial part test, however, the expenditure test was passed as an alternative option that nonprofits could choose. All nonprofits are subject to the unclear substantial part test unless they proactively elect to come under the expenditure test rules. To choose this set of rules, an organization simply files a form with the IRS—Form 5768—that effectively notifies the IRS that it has chosen this option. Every year from that point on, the nonprofit must record its lobbying expenses on its Form 990 (which is otherwise known as "Return of Organization Exempt From Income Tax." It is a nonprofit organization's annual report to the IRS). See below for more information on making the election. The remainder of this chapter discusses the reporting of lobbying expenditures and, unless otherwise noted, only applies to nonprofits that have proactively elected to come under these rules.

Advocacy Versus Lobbying

While we laid out various definitions in Chapter 1, a few bear repeating before we lay out (or down) the law. *Advocacy* is the broad, umbrella term for any activities that promote a cause. These activities could be focused on public policy and also on public opinion or individual "case advocacy"—advocating an individual's case before an agency, for example. Advocacy activities focused specifically on influencing public policy are often referred to as "legislative advocacy."[ii] Legislative advocacy includes lobbying, and also includes other activities critical to influencing public policy that are not as specific (and regulated) as lobbying. Examples include media advocacy and grassroots organizing. Both are important and effective tools. Working with the media can target your message to the general public and policy makers. Grassroots organizing is the tool through which you organize the general public (or some logical subset for your issue) to push policy makers to do the right thing.

Expenditure Test (or the 501(h) Election)

The expenditure test can be summed up in one way—an organization is lobbying only when it expends money on a set of activities specifically defined as lobbying. That would be when it (1) states its position on specific legislation to legislators (and/or their staff)—this is *direct lobbying*—or (2) communicates its position on specific legislation to the general public and issues a "call to action" asking members of the general public to contact their elected representatives and ask them to support the position—this is grassroots lobbying. If there is no expenditure of money on these specific activities, there is no lobbying. Period. Note, though, that staff time spent on these activities does qualify as an expenditure of money.

> **Direct Lobbying Elements**
>
> - Position on specific legislation
> - Communicated to legislators (or their staff)
>
> **Grassroots Lobbying Elements**
>
> - Position on specific legislation
> - Communicated to general public
> - Call to action

Under the expenditure test, what an organization can spend on lobbying depends on its "exempt purpose expenditures." Exempt purpose expenditures are generally defined as amounts paid or incurred by an organization to accomplish its mission, including administrative overhead and excluding amounts paid for fund-raising operations or consultants, amounts paid for capital accounts, and amounts paid for the production of income.[iii] An organization's exempt purpose expenditures can generally be found on its Form 990. Figure 2.1 outlines what an organization can spend, depending on its annual expenditures. The amount is determined on a sliding scale—as an organization's annual expenditures increase, the overall percentage it can spend on lobbying decreases. To make things a bit more complicated, the amount an organization can spend on *grassroots lobbying* is further limited—it cannot be more than 25% of an organization's total lobbying expenditures.

Ballot Initiatives

Initiatives and referenda have become increasingly popular as a means of achieving legislative changes at the state and local levels. From minimum or

Figure 2.1

www.clpi.org

HOW TO ESTIMATE WHETHER YOUR ORGANIZATION MIGHT BE CLOSE TO THE MAXIMUM IT MAY SPEND ON LOBBYING UNDER THE 1976 LOBBY LAW

Nonprofits that lobby sometimes wonder whether they are coming close to the permissible limits of lobbying activity that they may conduct. If your group has elected to come under the 1976 lobby law (*see* "The 1976 Law Governing Nonprofit Lobbying"), it's relatively easy to make an educated estimate about whether your organization is approaching the maximum it may spend on lobbying.* The estimate is not difficult because the 1976 lobby law is strictly an expenditure test. That is, under that law, the only time lobbying takes place is when your organization is spending money on a lobbying activity. It's also important to note that under the 1976 law, the lobbying expenditure limits are quite liberal (see below). Our research shows that the vast majority of electing organizations do not come close to the limits.

> Under [the 1976 lobby] law, the only time lobbying takes place is when your organization is spending money on a lobbying activity.

Organizations that have not made the election are under the "no substantial part" test. This is a vague term that has never been definitively defined in the law. If your group is subject to this rule it's impossible to be certain how much lobbying you may conduct, so making an estimate is more difficult.

> Our research shows that the vast majority of electing organizations do not come close to the limits.

For organizations that have elected, the following information should be helpful to you in making an estimate of your lobbying expenditures to determine whether you might be coming close to the expenditure limits.

Make a rough calculation of the maximum amount you may spend on lobbying for the year, using the information in the chart below. Generally, organizations that elect the 1976 law may spend 20% of the first $500,000 of their annual expenditures on lobbying ($100,000), 15% of the next $500,000 and so on up to $1 million a year. Equally important, there are eight critically important legislation related activities, which nonprofits may conduct, that are not considered lobbying by the IRS.

Understanding what constitutes lobbying under the 1976 law is not difficult. In general, you are lobbying when you state your position on specific legislation to legislators or other government employees who participate in the formulation of legislation, or urge your members to do so (direct lobbying). In addition, you are lobbying when you state your position to the general public and ask the general public to contact legislators or other government employees who participate in the formulation of legislation (grassroots lobbying).

The chart that follows shows how much you may spend on lobbying, depending on the size of your organization's annual exempt purpose expenditures.** The amount that may be spent on grassroots lobbying is limited to one-quarter of the amount you are permitted to spend on direct lobbying. So, if your organization's total direct lobbying expenditures limit is $100,000, then it may spend the full $100,000 on direct lobbying or it may spend up to $25,000 on grassroots lobbying and the rest on direct lobbying. *(over)*

---

* More information is available on the 1976 lobby law from the Center for Lobbying in the Public Interest's Web site at *www.clpi.org*.
** Strictly speaking, the base of a nonprofit's exempt purpose expenditures excludes investment management, unrelated businesses, and certain fundraising costs.

CENTER FOR LOBBYING IN THE PUBLIC INTEREST

2040 S Street, NW, Washington, DC 20009 | *phone* 202-387-5048 | *fax* 202-387-5149 | www.clpi.org

After calculating the amount your organization can spend on lobbying using the Lobbying Expenditure Chart, it may become immediately obvious to you that your expenditures are well under the permissible limits. For example, if your permissible lobbying limits are $200,000 and your rough estimate of *total* costs for your government relations office including staff and related expenses are, say $170,000, then you need not be overly concerned about the lobbying expenditure limits.

Lobbying Ceilings Under the 1976 Lobby Law

Annual Exempt-Purpose Expenditures	Total Direct Lobbying Expenditures Ceiling	Total Grassroots Lobbying Expenditures Ceiling
Up to $500,000	20% of exempt-purpose expenditures up to $100,000	One-quarter of the total direct lobbying expenditures ceiling
$500,000–$1 million	$100,000 + 15% of excess over $500,000	$25,000 + 3.75% of excess over $500,000
$1 million–$1.5 million	$175,000 + 10% of excess over $1 million	$43,750 + 2.5% of excess over $1 million
$1.5 million–$17 million	$225,000 + 5% of excess over $1.5 million	$56,250 + 1.25% of excess over $1.5 million
Over $17 million	$1 million	$250,000

Source: clpi.org. Reprinted with permission.

living wages to affirmative action to smoking ordinances, ballot initiatives are sweeping the country. You have a ballot initiative when a specified number of voters propose a statute, a constitutional amendment, or an ordinance and compel a popular vote on its adoption.[iv] A referendum is a procedure for referring measures already passed by a legislative body to the electorate for approval or rejection.[v] As far as the regs go, any work done by a nonprofit to pass or defeat initiatives or referenda counts toward its direct lobbying limits, not its grassroots limits (as you might assume). With initiatives and referenda, the public is considered the legislature, and, accordingly, lobbying the public to vote a certain way is counted as *direct* lobbying. This is important because such campaigns can be costly, and an organization can spend much more on direct lobbying than grassroots lobbying.

Critical Exceptions

Not only do the expenditure test rules outline clear definitions of lobbying and set definite expenditure limits, but they also lay out multiple, critical exceptions to what constitutes lobbying. Engagement in the activities listed below *is not* lobbying, and, accordingly, expenditures on them do not need to be tracked and reported. Put another way, do these activities to your heart's content, and don't worry about a lot of pesky paperwork.[2]

Exceptions to lobbying under 501(h) include the following:

- Influencing regulations
- Member communications
- Testimony
- Discussion of broad, social, economic issues
- Nonpartisan research
- Self-defense lobbying

Regulations

Once a law passes through the legislature and is signed into law by the executive (president, governor, mayor, etc.), it will typically go through a regulatory process to flesh out the details on how it will be implemented. It is important that advocates stay engaged in this part of the process. As they say, the devil is in the details! How a law is implemented can make or break its original intent. (Howard covers this in greater detail in Chapter 12.) Even better, nonprofit "lobbying" of agencies and their executives on regulations is not lobbying according to the 1976 laws. This means that any expenditures and time spent to influence regulations do not need to be tracked and reported on an organization's Form 990.

Member Communications

An organization does not need to keep track of time and money spent in communicating with its members about legislation—even if it takes a position on it—as long as it does not directly ask its members to lobby. This is similar to grassroots lobbying—there must be a call to action in order for these activities to count as lobbying.

Testifying

Another important strategy for effectively impacting the legislative process is to be seen as an expert in your issue area. If you can take advantage of any opportunities to testify before legislative bodies, you will go a long way toward developing that reputation. An added bonus—like all of these exceptions—is that time spent preparing to testify, and actually delivering the testimony, does not count as lobbying, even if your organization takes a

---

[2]Organizations should always check state and local lobbying laws, which may require tracking of some of these activities as lobbying.

position on specific legislation and urges the body to support that position. This is referred to as the *technical advice exception*. The only requirement is that there must be a written request for testimony from a committee (versus an individual legislator). Open calls for written or oral testimony—where the general public is given the opportunity to testify—also count.

Discussion of Broad Issues

An organization can discuss broad social and economic issues with no limitations, and not have to track such discussions as lobbying, as long as it does not take a position on specific legislation. Whether you host a forum on the importance of environmental protections, a speech on the need for more funding for after-school programs, or a conference dedicated to the need for health care reforms, discussing these issues is not lobbying, even if legislation happens to be pending on that issue. The only thing you need to be careful of is that you do not push specific legislation during your speech or conference.

Nonpartisan Research

Good research to back up a legislative position is critical. Many policy makers want to see hard data that support your position. For example, how many of their constituents are affected by your issue? How many will be impacted by your proposal? Pat goes into detail on the importance of good research and provides examples of how to get it done in Chapter 5. For purposes of the rules and regulations, you just need to know that you *don't* have to count the expenditures related to research (which can be high!) as long as it is nonpartisan and its primary purpose is nonlobbying, even if it takes a position on legislation and is sent to legislators. Research is nonpartisan as long as it gives a full and fair exposition of the facts that allow a reader to form an independent opinion. Research has a primary nonlobbying purpose if there is a substantial nonlobbying distribution of the materials before, or in conjunction with, the lobbying use. Such a distribution is substantial when it is done through the normal distribution pattern of similar research. Also, if research takes a position on legislation *and* includes a call to action, it counts as *grassroots* lobbying since generally the public will be the target audience for research.

Self-Defense

Time and money spent on lobbying legislators on issues that would impact the larger nonprofit sector do not need to be tracked and reported as lobbying. These are issues that affect an organization as a nonprofit—for example, lobbying to protect property tax exemptions for nonprofits in your state, or related to the ability of nonitemizers to take charitable deductions. What surprisingly does not qualify for the self-defense exception is lobbying to protect your organization from budget cuts. Technically, you are defending your "self" or organization, but this is not the intent of the exception. Sorry!

Why Elect?

Very few 501(c)(3) nonprofit organizations registered with the IRS have taken the 501(h) election. Many reasons exist for this low number. Some organizations don't feel that they lobby enough to be concerned about the unclear substantial part test. Others are concerned about calling special attention to their lobbying efforts. The IRS, however, has stated in writing that taking the election would never flag an organization for an audit.[vi] Overall, if an organization lobbies more than just once a year, it should give serious consideration to taking the 501(h) election. In other words, unless your organization only attends a Lobby Day once a year, and has (or plans to have) only limited engagement in the public policy process, the clear definitions and set expenditure limits provided by the 501(h) election make tracking and reporting easier. There are not many gray areas in contrast to the alternative substantial part test, which is all gray with no black and white. In addition, the critical exceptions outlined above only apply to organizations that take the election. Non-electing organizations—that is, those organizations that don't elect 501(h)—should report these activities as lobbying, further adding to the burden. Finally, if you think there would ever be a chance of going over your lobbying expenditure limits, you are better off under the expenditure test. An organization can only lose its tax-exempt status under the expenditure test if it exceeds 150% of its lobbying limits generally over four years. In contrast, a non-electing organization can lose its tax-exempt status for one violation in one year. How's them apples?

Tracking and Reporting Lobbying Expenditures

While tracking lobbying expenses might seem like a headache waiting to happen, if you set up a simple system up front, you can save yourself and your organization a lot of grief later on. And, like pretty much everything in this book, it's really not as much work as it seems. We swear! Using the appropriate definitions as a guide, staff should track expenditures and time according to what is and is not lobbying. Cost codes should be created to reflect lobbying versus broader advocacy or education efforts. Time and expenditures can be recorded using these codes, allowing for ease in running summary reports on a quarterly and/or annual basis and for reporting on the annual IRS Form 990. On which part of the Form 990 an organization reports its lobbying expenditures depends upon whether the organization has chosen the 501(h) election or not.

501(h) Electors (aka Expenditure Test Electors)

501(h) electors report lobbying expenditures on Schedule C, Part II-A of the Form 990. 501(h) electors report only their actual expenditures on lobbying, as clearly defined in the regulations (and above in this chapter). It is this amount for the year that is reported in Part II-A. This section is short because that is all there is to it.

Non-Electing Organizations

Non-electing organizations report their lobbying expenditures in Schedule C, Part II-B of the Form 990. In contrast to 501(h) electors, non-electing organizations—that follow the substantial part test—not only have to track actual expenditures for lobbying but also must include time spent by *volunteers* to influence public policy on behalf of the organization. In other words, non-electing organizations have to track more than electors. In addition, non-electing organizations must provide a description of their lobbying activities. This is not required of electors in Part II-A.

Funding Advocacy Campaigns

Limited financial resources are one of the persistent barriers to nonprofit engagement in the public policy process.[vii] One of the reasons for this barrier is that the source of an organization's funding often precludes lobbying with the funds it provides. The most flexible funding source for lobbying is always individual contributions, which can be used freely to directly support lobbying. Indeed, organizations that engage actively in the public policy process might see an uptick in individual contributions, or even in government and foundation funding, as an active organization develops its community leadership reputation by focusing on policy solutions to critical needs. Sources of funding, however, can present particular problems in supporting advocacy campaigns specifically when it comes to government and private foundation funding.

Government Funding

With very few exceptions, government funds cannot be used for lobbying. Since more than 50% of nonprofit organizations receive government funds through contracts or grants, that makes a large percentage of funds not usable for engaging in the public policy process. Many organizations erroneously believe that they cannot lobby at all if they receive any government funding. Au contraire, being a recipient of government funding does not preclude the use of *nongovernment* funding for advocacy and lobbying activities. Government-funded nonprofit organizations just need to be careful not to spend their government funds on lobbying. Attempts to influence legislation by direct contact with legislators and grassroots appeals using "publicity or propaganda" are disallowed costs under federal government regulations.[viii]

Private Foundation Funding

Private foundations are also 501(c)(3) nonprofit organizations but separately classified if they receive most of their funds from one or a small set of donors. Unlike 501(c)(3) public charities, private foundations are not allowed to lobby, with the exception of lobbying on "self-defense" issues (see above). Private foundations also cannot earmark grants to nonprofit organizations specifically for lobbying. A grant is not considered earmarked just because a foundation has knowledge that a grantee engages in lobbying. Earmarking is a clear understanding in writing or orally that the funds will be used to lobby.[ix] Nonprofits, however, can use foundation general operating support funds for lobbying. In making a general operating grant to a nonprofit, it is not required that the foundation inquire about the nonprofit's lobbying activities or budget.

Despite the allowance of the use of general operating support funds for lobbying, many private foundations include overly restrictive language in grant agreement letters that disallow use of funding for lobbying. If such language exists in a nonprofit's grant agreement for general operating support funds, the organization should try to negotiate less restrictive, yet 100% legal, language. In a letter to the Center for Lobbying in the Public Interest in 2004, the IRS states that the following language meets legal requirements without unnecessarily limiting a nonprofit's activities: "There is no agreement, oral or written, that directs the grant funds to be used for lobbying activities."[x]

Community Foundation Funding

Unlike private foundations, community foundations can earmark grants for lobbying. This is because community foundations are designated as public charities under the law—they receive their funding from more than just one or a few sources. In fact, community foundations typically receive funding from a wide swath of their home communities, including donor-advised funds, which are growing in popularity and size. However, despite being legally allowed to earmark grants to nonprofits for lobbying, many community foundations are reticent to do so as they often see such grants as taking legislative positions that might jeopardize their standing as neutral conveners within their communities. Despite these hesitations, though, it is never a bad idea to explore your community foundation for support of your advocacy campaign.

Registration Requirements and State Laws

Remember Jack Abramoff? He was the central character and federal lobbyist in a series of political scandals in 2004 centered on defrauding clients and bribing public officials. Although lobbyist registration requirements have always existed at the different levels of government, the Abramoff scandal, and similar ones at the state level, has resulted in increased reporting and restrictions for those seeking to lobby their elected representatives.

Any nonprofit that engages in the public policy process should be aware of registration requirements at the federal, state, and local levels to ensure it is registered, if required.

Federal Registration Requirements

The Lobbying Disclosure Act of 1995 (LDA) governs whether an organization needs to register with the House and Senate as an organization that employs a lobbyist. An organization must register under the LDA if expenditures for lobbying activities exceed or are expected to exceed $11,500 *and* if someone on staff is spending 20% or more of his or her time on lobbying in a quarterly period. Once it meets this threshold, the organization formally registers with the Clerk of the House and the Secretary of the Senate. It will need to list as a lobbyist any employee (1) who is either employed or retained by a client for financial or other compensation, (2) whose services include more than one lobbying contact, and (3) whose lobbying activities constitute 20% or more of his or her work during any three-month period. Once an organization registers, it then will be required to electronically file quarterly lobbying reports on its lobbying expenditures.

Finally, once an organization and individuals are registered as federal lobbyists, there are additional requirements for continued compliance with various rules covering the reporting of political contributions, as well as gifts to legislators including the payment of legislator travel expenses.

State Registration Requirements

Many states (not all) and some cities have registration requirements for lobbyists. Definitions of what constitutes lobbying at these levels of government often differ and are broader than what constitutes lobbying at the federal level. Since every state has its own laws, we aren't able to cover each here. Some of the best resources for nonprofits in this area are state associations of nonprofits—in existence in 41 states at this time. To find your state association, and more information on your state lobbying registration requirements, visit the National Council of Nonprofits at http://www.councilofnonprofits.org/.

Other Tax Structures

This chapter, as well as the entire book, applies to lobbying by 501(c)(3) public charities. An organization is found by the IRS to be a public charity if it passed the "public support test" illustrating that it is supported by many funders, donors, agencies, or the general public. A public charity's primary purpose must be charitable, religious, scientific, or educational. In addition, churches and schools are considered public charities, though they have the luxury of not having to pass the public support test.

One of the primary benefits of the 501(c)(3) designation is tax exemption and the tax deductibility of contributions. However, with this benefit comes a trade-off. As outlined above, a 501(c)(3) public charity can lobby but to a restricted degree. In addition, 501(c)(3) nonprofits are absolutely prohibited from supporting or opposing candidates for public office.

In contrast, there are other tax designations for nonprofit organizations that allow for unlimited lobbying and the active involvement in political campaigns. One way to think about these distinctions is this: The more generous an organization's tax benefits, the more limited its public policy/political activities. 501(c)(4) nonprofit organizations can lobby with no limitations and can also endorse or oppose candidates for public office, although this must be a secondary activity. The benefit of lobbying with *no* limitation comes with a trade-off; contributions to 501(c)(4) nonprofits are not tax deductible, and foundations cannot give grants to 501(c)(4)s without being very tightly controlled.

Many well-recognized organizations are 501(c)(4)s or are 501(c)(3)s with a 501(c)(4) arm: Planned Parenthood, the American Association for Retired Persons (AARP), the National Rifle Association (NRA), and the National Wildlife Federation are all organizations that have had tremendous impact on public policy. These organizations have found it effective to have two sides to their work—one primarily charitable and educational in purpose (the 501(c)(3) side) and one primarily focused on legislative work as well as some political activity (the 501(c)(4) side). In order to do this in compliance with the law, there must be a separate board of directors and financial record keeping for each organization, although space may be shared.

501(c)(6) nonprofit organizations are business leagues or chambers of commerce that, like 501(c)(4)s, can lobby to an unlimited degree and conduct secondary political activity, but to which charitable contributions are *not* deductible.

Finally, another type of nonprofit organization about which you have likely heard a bit is 527s. A 527 group is created primarily to influence the nomination, election, appointment, or defeat of candidates for public office. 527s are not regulated by the Federal Election Commission (yet) and are not subject to the same contribution limits as political action committees. They have avoided FEC regulation to date by focusing on issue advocacy work, although the differences between issue and candidate advocacy have been hotly debated. Do the names Swift Boat Veterans for Truth, MoveOn.org, and America Coming Together sound familiar?

Election-Related Activities

We don't want to end this chapter emphasizing what 501(c)(3) nonprofits can't do during an election season—namely, support or oppose candidates for public office. Instead it's important to know that a nonprofit does not need to suspend lobbying activities during an election season. Nonprofits can do multiple activities actually aimed at candidates for public office or voters as long as they are nonpartisan in nature. Permissible election-related activities for nonprofits include voter registration drives, candidate questionnaires, dissemination of voting records and voter guides, candidate visits and forums, and acquiring candidate policy statements. There are important steps required for each of these activities to ensure nonpartisanship—the critical element between permissible election-related activities and impermissible political activity. Check out *The Connection: Strategies for Creating and Operating 501(c)(3)s, 501(c)(4)s, and Political Organizations*, a good resource for further detail on those steps from the Alliance for Justice.[xi] We encourage you to explore these activities as complementary to an advocacy campaign. By ensuring its issues are discussed during an election campaign, and that it is associated as a leader on that issue, an organization elevates its standing and is better positioned to push its agenda through the legislative and regulatory processes.

Chapter Questions

1. Having read this chapter, do you think the law is supportive of, or an impediment to, nonprofit advocacy?

2. How would you describe the primary differences between the substantial part and expenditure tests? What are the top reasons for an organization to elect to come under the expenditure test rules?

3. What is the best source of funding for advocacy campaigns? What are the most restricted?

4. Why would an organization want to become a 501(c)(4) instead of a 501(c)(3)? What are the other options?

Endnotes_____

i *Regan v. Taxation without Representation*, 461 U.S. 540 (1983).

ii Center for Lobbying in the Public Interest. (2008). *Make a difference for your cause: Strategies for nonprofit engagement in legislative advocacy*. Retrieved March 8, 2011, from http://www.clpi.org/press-publications/50-make-a-difference-for-your-cause-strategies-for-nonprofit-engagement-in-legislative-advocacy

iii Tax Almanac. (2005). *Treasury regulations, Subchapter D, Sec. 56.4911-4: Exempt purpose expenditures*. Retrieved March 8, 2011, from http://www.taxalmanac.org/index.php/Treasury_Regulations,_Subchapter_D,_Sec._56.4911-4

iv Center for Lobbying in the Public Interest. (2008). *IRS rules*. Retrieved March 8, 2011, from http://www.clpi.org/the-law/irs-rules

v Ibid.

vi Ibid.

vii Bass, G., Arons, D., Guinane, K., & Carter, M. (2007). *Seen but not heard: Strengthening nonprofit advocacy*. Washington, DC: The Aspen Institute.

viii White House Office of Management and Budget. (2004, May 10). Circular No. A-122. Retrieved March 8, 2011, from http://www.whitehouse.gov/omb/circulars_a122_2004

ix Center for Lobbying in the Public Interest. (2008). *IRS rules*. Retrieved March 8, 2011, from http://www.clpi.org/the-law/irs-rules

x Ibid.

xi Schadler, B. (2006). *The connection: Strategies for creating and operating 501(c)(3)s, 501(c)(4)s, and political organizations*. Washington, DC: Alliance for Justice.

3 Pork: "The Other White Meat" or Quagmires of Government Budgeting

Pat Libby

In this chapter we'll take a whirlwind tour of how governments spend money and get money. We'll start by getting the big-picture view of how things work at the federal level and work our way down to state budgets. We'll also take a look at common perceptions Americans have about the role of government and taxes. Finally, we'll look at how government spending on social welfare, taxes, and poverty are interrelated. Having a basic understanding of fiscal quagmires, constraints, contradictions, and common complaints will help you understand how your advocacy proposal fits into the bigger picture. It will also give you some insight about the best way to pitch your ideas to public officials.

From the outside looking in, some of us think government has the wrong spending priorities. Others believe there's a lot of waste in government too—a concept that started to build quite a bit of traction when it was popularized in the 1980s by President Ronald Reagan (Barry Goldwater, George Wallace, and Richard Nixon made those claims too; however, Reagan made it a theme of his administration). That notion, of waste in government (otherwise known as bloated bureaucracies, lots of "pork," money going to people and causes that it shouldn't, etc.), has continued to be a widely accepted idea for all the years since Reagan's presidency began and ended. Before Reagan became the chief evangelist of this idea, most Americans felt it was the *duty* of government to perform vital services for society and that government was best equipped to carry out those functions. Today government is branded a bastion of "waste and inefficiency" or of "waste, fraud, and abuse," which must not make it a very cheerful place to work.

The notion of waste is amazingly popular—so much so that it is practically embraced as a universally held truth. That leads some advocates to think they can approach their elected officials with the idea that if those officials would only cut waste, then money could be allocated to the thing the advocates want funded. The problem is that nearly all government officials have a hard time figuring out where all that waste is that people talk about all the time. You'll find this to be true regardless of whether those officials are Republicans, are Democrats, or call themselves independent. Ironically, some of these folks make the centerpiece of their election campaigns about the need to do away with waste in government yet change their minds about the problem shortly after they've been sworn into office.

So where's the disconnect?

Let's start with an overview of federal spending. Even though this book is focused on lobbying at the state and local level, you'll need to first gain a basic understanding of how things work in Washington, DC, since many components of state budgets are linked to and intertwined with the federal budget.

The easiest way to grab hold of how the federal government spends its money is to look at it in broad categories. Simply put, the federal government spends its money in three ways: on mandatory spending, discretionary spending, and net interest.[i]

Mandatory spending is by far the biggest budget category. In 2009 mandatory spending accounted for 60% of all federal government expenditures.[ii] That's because the lion's share of that money is dedicated to "entitlement programs," the biggest three being Social Security, Medicare, and Medicaid. Those programs combined accounted for 40% of all federal spending in 2009.[iii] Other entitlement programs include, for example, the Food Stamp Program (now officially known as the Supplemental Nutrition Assistance Program, or SNAP), Supplemental Security Income (SSI), a portion of unemployment insurance, some veterans' benefits, and other assorted items. What an entitlement program means is that every citizen who is eligible for those benefits receives them; in other words, these citizens are "entitled" to those benefits. Since Social Security and Medicare—the two highest-cost items— serve our rapidly aging baby boomer population, it's easy to see how those costs can spin out of control pretty quickly.

Discretionary spending includes the big-ticket category of military spending, which alone comprises another 20% of the federal budget.[iv] On top of that, government spends money for environmental protection, education, energy, transportation and highways, oversight of food and drugs, disaster relief, international aid, business development, farm subsidies, consumer protection, and a whole host of other things that in and of themselves fill several budget books.

If tax dollars decrease because the economy is sluggish or costs grow out of control, or both things happen at once and the federal government can't pay its bills, it borrows money to meet its obligations. That's what's known as government debt. As interest on that debt grows, the cost of paying it back gets pushed forward to future taxpayers. In fiscal 2010, more than one third of the federal budget was projected to be financed by debt.[v] The interest on that debt equaled 6% of the federal budget.[vi]

The Center on Budget and Policy Priorities (CBPP) is a national policy organization that does a nice job synthesizing and summarizing the federal budget so that everyday people can understand how things work. The focus of its work is on doing research and analysis of federal and state policies and programs that have an impact on the lives of low- and moderate-income families. These economists and policy analysts use baseline figures from an impartial source to conduct their work, information provided by the Congressional Budget Office (commonly referred to as the CBO). The CBO is a federal agency that is charged with giving Congress "objective, nonpartisan, and timely analyses to aid in economic and budgetary decisions on the wide array of programs covered by the federal budget." It provides Congress with "the information and estimates required for the Congressional budget process."[vii]

Figure 3.1 shows how the CBPP depicts federal spending using information provided to it by the CBO.

Figure 3.1

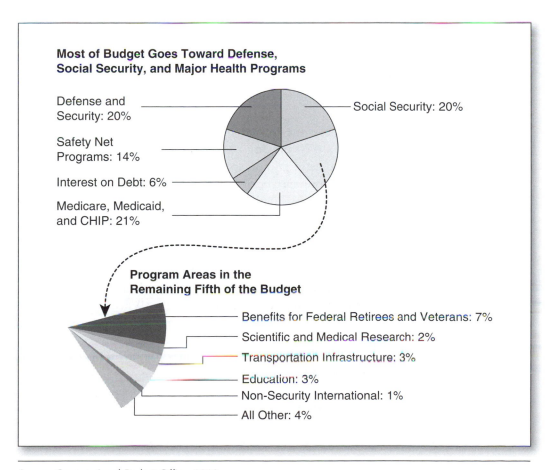

Source: Congressional Budget Office, 2010.

Note: Percentages may not total 100 due to rounding.

How State Budgets Operate

On the state level, many federal programs have matching requirements including the Food Stamp, Medicaid, and unemployment insurance programs. States put dollars into those programs and are able to access federal funds to support them as well. Let's take Medicaid, for example; the federal government provides a fixed amount of money for the program that is matched by each state (although in different ways since states have varying versions of how the program operates). If states decided not to put in that matching money, their citizens wouldn't get those benefits. For Food Stamps, the federal government provides funding for that benefit as well as half of the cost to administer the program; states match those administrative costs. In the case of unemployment insurance, the states pay the bulk of those benefits (through contributions that employers pay them), and the federal government provides administrative costs (with funds that are also raised from employers and states). When states run out of money to pay unemployment benefits, the federal government steps in to give them a loan so that benefits can continue for people who are still out of work. In recessions, the federal government often pays the full cost of additional unemployment benefits beyond the basic six months to which people are entitled. This money isn't given to the states for free—it is loaned to them by the federal government. Right off the bat when we think about things that state budgets need to fund, entitlement programs are at the top.

State budgets, unlike the federal budget, are required to be balanced although this wasn't always the case.[1] About 20 years ago, there was a movement among states to get a grip on spending in response to wide swings in the economy (and, more specifically, the economic decline of that time). Legislators grew seasick watching their revenues go from one extreme to the other, so they built in ways of forcing themselves to cover their core costs—commonly referred to as the state's *operating budget*—often by capping expenses and indexing them to inflation.

To use another analogy, the economy is like a bucking bronco, and state legislators are cowboys (and cowgirls) who are trying their best to hold on to the horse without falling off. What happens is this: When the economy is healthy, people pay more taxes because they're employed and earning more, and, at the same time, they buy more stuff, which translates into greater sales tax revenues.[2] At the same time, bigger corporate profits mean that companies pay more in taxes. When that's the case, the government has more money to spend. Like most of us, when government has extra dough, it usually uses some of it to pay down debt, spends some of it doing things it has been

---

[1] The state of Vermont, which is not required to have a balanced budget, is an exception.

[2] This assumes that a given state has sales tax and income tax—not all have both, but each state has at least one type of those taxes.

neglecting, and spends part of it on things that it wants to do because legislators believe those things will contribute to a better society.

In better economic times a state might establish a program that would monitor coastal water pollution, purchase land for new parks or nature preserves, start new child care or after school programs, or put extra money into community policing. It might also decide to reduce income tax rates for individuals or businesses, or lower other types of taxes like vehicle registration fees. When the economy experiences a downturn (and most downturns seem to come from out of the blue), many of the programs that have been created or expanded in those good times have to be cut, or the legislature needs to find other ways of funding them. In plain English that means restoring tax cuts or raising taxes (sometimes sneakily in the form of fees)—neither of which is particularly popular.

Where do states get their money? Let's take a look at the state of California and the revenue that was projected there for the 2010–2011 fiscal year as an example. Wait: Why is the year split in half between 2010 and 2011? The reason for the split is because the California state budget year begins on July 1 rather than with the calendar year. This isn't because people are free thinkers in California (although many are); many state budgets begin during the spring or summer months (the federal budget begins on October 1). There is logic to state budget calendars. Since their big payday comes on April 15, states are able to move into the new fiscal year knowing how much money they have in the bank. For this particular year, the Governor's office anticipated that state revenues would look like this:

Personal Income Tax:	40.9%
Sales Tax:	25.2%
Corporation Tax:	8.6%
Motor Vehicle Tax:	5.9%
Highway Tax:	4.3%
Insurance Tax:	1.8%
Liquor Tax:	3.0%
Tobacco Tax:	8.0%
Other:	12.2%

As you can see from looking at those numbers, if your paycheck shrinks—or disappears altogether because you've lost your job—government feels the pinch and tightens its belt because you're paying less in taxes. Ironically that belt tightening gets passed down to all citizens including those of us who need more help because our paycheck shrunk or disappeared. If you take a look at the revenue projections for your state, you'll find a breakdown that is very similar—it will vary, though, according to whether your state has personal income tax, sales tax, or both and the rate at which other categories of items are taxed. In the nonprofit social services sector when times are tough, it can become a vicious cycle because government has less to spend on community-based social welfare programs just when more people are knocking at the door for help.

State-balanced budget rules, like the folks who created them, come in all shapes and sizes. At the end of the day, though, having a balanced budget provision means that in tough economic times, states find themselves having to dig out of a big hole to make ends meet because so much of their dollars are committed to ongoing operating costs that keep rising with inflation.

It's not all that different from your own household budget. You have to pay rent; eat; pay for heat, electricity, your phone, and cable; maybe make a car payment; and replace things that wear out like clothes and shoes and broken appliances, and before you know it you're looking under the sofa cushions for loose change to do your laundry. If your salary stays flat—or, worse, if you lose your job and take a new one that pays even less—you still have the same pile of bills on your kitchen table every month. You might say to yourself, "I can live without HBO, my telephone landline, and my daily latte," and all will be good in the world for a while until the costs of your remaining expenses increase (as they inevitably do), and you find yourself in a bind again. As a result, you'll cut more and more from your budget until you find yourself with holes in your jeans that aren't a fashion statement. The long and the short of it is, once you take a good look at the federal budget, state budgets, county budgets, or city budgets, you'll see that it's not easy to find the fat.

To illustrate this point further, let's take a quick look at the budget the state of California proposed for the 2010–2011 fiscal year.[viii] In January, at the beginning of the budgeting process for the particular year we're talking about, the Governor's office projected general fund expenditures would be as follows[ix]:

K–12 Education   = 43.4% of the budget

Health and Human Services = 25.3% of the budget

Higher Education   = 14.3% of the budget

Corrections   = 9.6% of the budget

If you total it up, you'll find that 92.6% of the budget is consumed by those four categories, leaving all other costs such as environmental protection, business, transportation, housing, labor, workforce development, consumer affairs, and the judiciary (among other items) to squeeze into that last 7.4%. And, in case you were wondering, those health and human service programs are targeted to "essential medical, dental, mental health and social service needs" for the poorest and most at-risk citizens of California.[x]

Digging deeper into the Governor's proposal, we find that the human services budget, if approved at the proposed level, would take an 8% hit ($2.4 billion) from what it was allocated the previous year. That would translate into draconian cuts in in-home services for low-income people with disabilities and in health care for children and prisoners. That's not all; it would also entail the *elimination* of public assistance benefits (commonly referred to as "welfare") to poor families, which would affect 1.4 million Californians— two thirds of them children.[xi] All of those cuts would be *on top* of cuts the Governor made the previous year to other human service programs including steep slashes in funding for domestic violence shelters that forced many to shut their doors. And as Mr. T would say, "I pity the poor fool" who was trying to work in housing, transportation, or business; for 2010–2011 the Governor proposed a 72% reduction in those programs; natural resources were slated for an almost 30% cut. Ouch. Again, if you take a look at the proposed budget for your state, you are likely to find a similar scenario.

Regardless of where you reside, the Governor doesn't get the entire say in how states spend their money. The Governor's office has the job of writing the first draft of the budget. Then the legislature works on the budget a lot more before sending it back to the Governor for his or her signature. That process will be explained in much greater detail in Chapter 4. Right now, let's get back to the main principles of how states put their budgets together.

The other component that adds to state budget stress is debt. Again, it's just like you if you have a credit card that you don't pay off fully every month. Government has debt too—mainly in the form of bonds that the state sells to investors (and pays interest on) for specific items like building new public schools and prisons and purchasing parkland. The reason the state issues bonds rather than pays for these things outright is the same reason that you take out a car loan or get a mortgage on a home—it's just easier to amortize these costs over time rather than to absorb them all at once. Therefore, when it comes time for states to calculate their budgets, they have to factor in their bond obligations as well. All of that adds up to too many expenses and not enough income to pay the bills.

California, like most states in America (and countries around the world), has been in deep budget doo-doo for several years, and the situation is not getting any better. The Center on Budget and Policy Priorities reported that for the 2012 fiscal year, 44 of our 50 states were estimating budget shortfalls with 10 states estimating revenue gaps that were equal to 20% or more of the total state budget.[xii]

The panic and big cuts in California—and in states across the nation— started in 2008 when, faced with a mammoth shortage in revenue, the Governor proposed a 10% across-the-board cut in almost every major budget category. That left many nonprofit professionals and their clients worried about how people in need of basic services would get what they needed.[xiii] The initial cuts totaled $14 billion (you read that right; *billion* with a *b*); today the Governor and the state legislature are grappling with an even bigger

$25 billion gap.[xiv] It makes my head hurt just to think about those numbers. Then as now, almost every day newspapers across the state featured stories about how, for instance, public school districts throughout California sent layoff notices to approximately *ten thousand* teachers, nurses, librarians, maintenance people, music instructors, and all sorts of other key personnel in order to squeeze their operations into an education budget that had been cut in aggregate by $4.4 billion statewide.[xv] Lest you think this is all attributable to our then "Governator" dropping a heavy weight on his head, the fact is during that spring 2010, more than half of all state governments across the country were reporting serious budget shortfalls (obviously the problem has gotten worse since then).[xvi] Jennifer Steinhauer writing in *The New York Times* included this tidbit in a story about states struggling to make ends meet:

> In Maine the state is facing a $190 million shortfall for its current budget. It is starting with about $65 million in proposed cuts to social services.
>
> There has already been a reduction in money for home-based services for elderly, a lowered Medicaid reimbursement rate for hospital-affiliated physicians, a freeze in enrollment to the state's Medicaid program for some low-income adults, and a cut in reimbursement rates for foster parents.[xvii]

Not to belabor the point, but you'd think that if there was any fat in the budget it would be cut before the elderly were denied home-based services in the largely inhospitable Maine climate (in other words, it's darn cold in Maine, and those folks need some help).

From coast to coast and many places in between, state budgets look like victims of Freddy Krueger on a rampage. In Missouri, the revenue figures during spring 2010 hadn't been that low since the Great Depression of the 1920s and 30s, forcing the Governor to make substantial cuts midway through the fiscal year.[xviii] Terry Ganey, writing in the *Columbia Daily Tribune*, reported, "So far, more than $700 million in state spending has been sliced from the $23.7 billion budget lawmakers approved last year. Looking into the future, things might be worse." He was right: Missouri is projecting a $1.1 billion shortfall for 2012.[xix]

The situation was much bleaker in Illinois where the state budget deficit was a record $12 billion in spring 2010—equal to nearly half the state's $26 billion budget.[xx] The deficit was projected to rise to nearly 45% of the state's budget by fiscal 2012.[xxi]

Lest you think all these cuts have been directed at the poor, states have starved their higher education budgets to the point of anorexia. During April 2010 students in more than 30 states across the nation organized protests from Maryland to Massachusetts, Colorado to California, Georgia to Wisconsin, and lots of places in between to demonstrate against rising tuition and fees, larger classes, and cuts in classes.[xxii]

Many other things we take for granted as part of the social fabric of our nation have fallen victim to budget cuts as well. State funds for parks, campgrounds, and swimming pools are going the way of the dinosaur in Idaho, Georgia, Washington State, Arizona, New York, and many other states. William Yardley reported that during May 2010 the Bonny Lake State Park in Idalia, Colorado, had closed almost half of its campgrounds' sites, increased camping fees by 20%, and left the 5,000-acre park in the care of a single ranger.[xxiii]

Why the Tea Party Is a Brew

The Boston Tea Party—the one that took place in 1773—was all about taxation without representation. The colonists were upset that people on the other side of the ocean could decide willy-nilly what tax could be imposed on any given commodity without their input. In other words, they didn't have elected representatives who could make policy on their behalf.

Today's Tea Partiers feel similarly. They believe, among other things, that taxes are out of control, that government is too big, that the federal deficit is too large, and that the current cadre of elected officials isn't representing their interests. They're also really into costumes, but that's another story.

Fundamentally, the Tea Partiers hate Adolf Wagner. Adolf Wagner was a 19th-century economist who developed a theory that has since been known as Wagner's law. Wagner's law says the wealthier a society is, the more services its citizens want from government. It stands to reason that if you want more, you pay more. If you want good schools, responsive police and firefighters, a strong military, a good retirement system, nice parks, and so on—pretty much a lot of what government provides that we mostly take for granted—it's going to cost you.[xxiv]

In the United States people were pretty happy with that model for many years. Government expanded what it did, and people paid taxes to support additional services. Way back in 1913 when federal income tax was first established, taxes comprised 2% of the nation's gross domestic product (GDP is defined as "the value of all goods and services produced by a nation in a given year"[xxv]). By the year 2000, taxes had risen to 21% of the GDP.[xxvi] Presumably, most citizens were OK with that because they liked what they got from government in exchange for their tax contributions.

In fact, for most of the time since we've had taxes in America, people have asked government to do more on their behalf. During the 1930s in response to the Great Depression, Franklin Roosevelt shaped the New Deal, which was centered on a philosophy that government would care for and protect the poor through initiatives such as Social Security and public works projects (as employment generators) and through tax reforms that were designed to distribute wealth from the richest Americans to the rest of society. Incidentally, this taxation system included the first large-scale incentives for charitable giving, which in subsequent years fueled the growth of the nonprofit sector in this country. The New Deal was also responsible for regulating the stock market, insuring banks, and putting into place a whole bundle of rules to protect workers. It was an amazing amalgamation of laws that were enacted between 1933 and 1935 (many more than can be mentioned in this small space) that the American people rallied behind for the good of the country. Laws passed during the New Deal are some of the most important we have in place today.

Thirty years later during the 1960s, the Johnson administration declared a "War on Poverty" and worked with Congress to create a breathtaking array of social programs like Medicare, Medicaid, the National Endowment for the Arts, Head Start, Legal Services, Food Stamps, and HUD (the federal office of Housing and Urban Development). The idea was that America would dedicate itself to eliminating poverty in our country by providing essential support to its neediest citizens while also improving the quality of life for everyone else through programs that would set clean air standards, preserve the environment, and take care of our health in old age. Known as the "Great Society," this period set the stage for much of what the American people have come to expect from our government today.

Many people across the country were energized by this vision of America and were, for the most part, happy to pay for it, because much of the Great Society agenda would benefit them. In an instant, retired people were guaranteed government health insurance. That meant that you didn't have to worry about how you were going to deal with your dad's high blood pressure after he clocked out of his last shift because now, thanks to Uncle Sam, he would get both Social Security *and* Medicare.

This was also the beginning of new partnerships between government and nonprofit organizations. Before this time, government saw itself as a service provider. The Great Society looked at nonprofits as vehicles for delivering all types of services to people in communities. For instance, Medicaid and Medicare led to the creation of community health clinics; HUD led to the creation of neighborhood-based community development corporations. It was thought that nonprofits could be more effective at reaching people at the local level than government could through its efforts. While this might sound obvious, the idea that nonprofits could be trusted to act on behalf of the government was actually a fairly radical concept. Things just hadn't been done that way before, and although it may be hard to imagine now, back then having nonprofits deliver so many government services was a huge social experiment.

The Civil Rights Movement was an important part of the Great Society vision. As discussed in the first chapter of this book, the movement helped create many significant new laws, including several of those mentioned above. Citizen activists were critically important in this period of our history, and citizen activists still shape the backbone of laws that government creates for us. But you already know that, or you wouldn't be reading this book.

Let's get back to figuring out what all of this has to do with taxes. If we fast-forward to more recent years, all of a sudden through a combination of tax cuts and hard times, federal tax revenues fell in 2009 to a 60-year low of 15.1% of the GDP (remember, it had been 21% nine years earlier).[xxvii] What did that tell us? That Wagner's law went to hell in a handbasket quicker than Sarah Palin could say, "You betcha." It simply became impossible to give people everything they had come to expect without significantly raising taxes or making severe cuts in government services. People wanted their health insurance, social security, nice parks, safe streets, smooth roads, good schools, strong military, and everything else they were used to, but there just wasn't enough money to pay for all those things. As my friend Jackie would say, they wanted to have their cake, eat it, and not get fat.[xxviii]

At the same time tax revenues fell, there was a raucous discourse about the fundamental role of government. This is where the Tea Party folks are front and center. As mentioned before, the Tea Partiers believe that there's too much government, that it's inefficient, that it's wasting money, and that it's involved in things that it shouldn't be involved in. They also feel strongly that Americans are being taxed to death. To be fair, this is not just a view that the Tea Partiers hold; many Republicans have similar views (as do Libertarians), which is why conservatives by any name choose to align themselves with the Tea Party. They want smaller government, less regulation, and more opportunity for the free market to be free.

So What About Those Tax Rates?

There is a common misperception that tax rates in the United States are higher than anywhere else in the world. The fact is we are nowhere near the top. For starters Denmark's top individual tax rate is 59%, whereas ours is 35%. In fact, Australia, Austria, Belgium, Cyprus, France, Germany, Ireland, Israel, New Zealand, Norway, Portugal, South Africa, Spain, Sweden, and the United Kingdom (along with others) all have individual tax rates that are higher than ours. Argentina, Turkey, Vietnam, and Zambia are a few that have the same tax rate as the United States.[xxix]

In part because many prominent policy makers in the United States still believe strongly in the waste and inefficiency story line, the federal government has actually lowered individual and corporate tax rates during the past several decades. That makes it difficult for our government to pay its bills.

If we take a walk through time and look at top rates in the United States for individuals, we'll find the following highlights:

Year	Top tax rate	President
1964	**91**%	Johnson
1976	**70**%	Carter
1981	**50**%	Reagan lowered the rate with bipartisan support
1986	**28**%	Reagan Tax Reform Act
1993	**39.6**%	Clinton
1997	Introduction of Earned Income Tax Credit	
2001	Bush cuts rates down to 35%, and they are scheduled to drop to 33% over time	Bush
2010	**35**%[xxx]	Obama

It's a lot easier to imagine paying for all those great things in Johnson's Great Society package of programs when you have an individual tax rate of 91%! Of course there were all kinds of groovy tax deductions people could take then (because things really were groovy in those days), which meant that no one was actually paying 91% of his or her income toward taxes. Still, the overall individual tax contribution (or, as some would put it, tax "burden") was much higher than the 35% we have today.

The U.S. tax system, in fact, as you can see from Figure 3.2 (on the following page), favors the wealthy. While the wealthy do pay more money in income tax because they have more money to begin with, the percentage most get to keep is higher than the percentage that a working-class person gets to keep. It's important to note that these statistics for the year 2006 were compiled by the Congressional Budget Office, which again, by design, is an impartial source of information.

One of the consequences of having a smaller tax base is there is less money to spend on social welfare programs. Social welfare programs are designed to level the playing field among all members of society. In Europe, many countries have what is referred to as a large social welfare state, which provides, among other things, strong pensions for retirees, subsidized day care for working families, heavily subsidized unemployment insurance, national health care, and so on. Europeans are more predisposed to Wagner's law—they *like* government benefits and see those benefits as *rights* they have as citizens. They pay taxes because they want government to take care of them. Europeans view social welfare as benefits to which everyone is entitled, which is why there is widespread support for those benefits. However, as European economies have shrunk in the worldwide recession, many countries have moved to reduce social welfare. That's why we have been seeing protests and

Figure 3.2

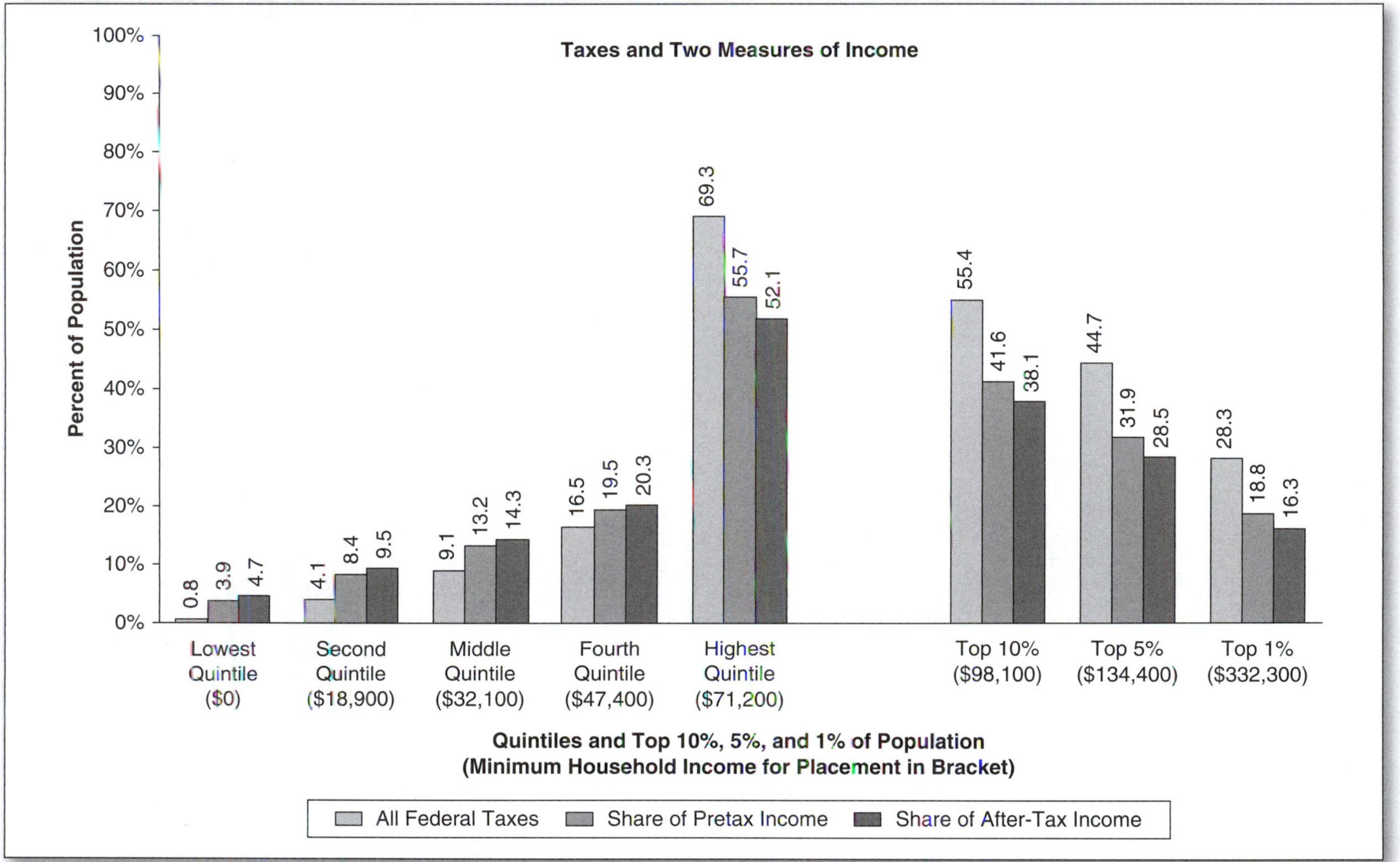

Taxes and Two Measures of Income

Quintiles and Top 10%, 5%, and 1% of Population
(Minimum Household Income for Placement in Bracket)

Lowest Quintile ($0): 0.8, 3.9, 4.7
Second Quintile ($18,900): 4.1, 8.4, 9.5
Middle Quintile ($32,100): 9.1, 13.2, 14.3
Fourth Quintile ($47,400): 16.5, 19.5, 20.3
Highest Quintile ($71,200): 69.3, 55.7, 52.1
Top 10% ($98,100): 55.4, 41.6, 38.1
Top 5% ($134,400): 44.7, 31.9, 28.5
Top 1% ($332,300): 28.3, 18.8, 16.3

Percent of Population: 0%, 10%, 20%, 30%, 40%, 50%, 60%, 70%, 80%, 90%, 100%

Legend: All Federal Taxes | Share of Pretax Income | Share of After-Tax Income

Source: Congressional Budget Office, Data on the Distribution of Federal Taxes and Household Income, April 2009 for 2006 Fiscal Year, http://www.cbo.gov/publications/collections/taxdistribution.cfm

45

riots in France, Spain, England, and Greece (among other places) by bus drivers, postal workers, teachers, and other government employees over proposals for smaller paychecks and rising retirement ages.

For example, in October 2010, tens of thousands of people across France participated in multiple-day demonstrations—many of which turned riotous. The protesters included everyone from truck drivers to high school and college students who were incensed at a proposal in the France legislature to increase the retirement age from 60 to 62. While you may scoff at that as being ridiculous, the French see early retirement as a critical element of their social contract with government. They see early retirement as being essential to having a good quality of life.[xxxi]

At the same time in England, Prime Minister David Cameron began delivering on his promise to limit government spending by passing a law to end child care subsidies for the middle and upper class. A few months later, in December, British students held massive and sometimes violent riots in London to protest the passage of an enormous hike in college tuition rates that will take effect in 2012.[xxxii] Even Denmark, which has historically been viewed as one of the most generous welfare state nations, has cut back on unemployment benefits.[xxxiii] Europeans are angry at all of these changes because they feel their basic rights are being taken away.[xxxiv]

In the United States the very word *welfare* has negative connotations. In fact, President Reagan popularized the phrase *welfare queen* during his 1976 presidential campaign. What he was trying to do (and accomplished to some success) was to implant an idea into our collective consciousness that people on public assistance have an easy life. That kind of rhetoric eventually led to the erosion of welfare benefits 20 years later when President Clinton promised and succeeded in his pledge to "end welfare as we know it." Today the welfare program in the United States has been renamed (it is now called Temporary Assistance for Needy Families), features a work requirement, and has a lifetime benefit limit of five years. There are many fascinating books that have been written on the subject of welfare and welfare reform in the United States. If you have the interest and opportunity, you should take a course on the subject. What is important for you to know here is that the types of social benefits we provide in the United States aren't nearly as robust as similar kinds of benefits people receive in other countries. For instance, our Social Security system provides pensions to retirees; however, the program is intended to *supplement* the savings of individuals, not support them in their older years. People who live only on Social Security in this country live in poverty.

The Connection Between Social Welfare, Poverty, and Taxes

All of that brings us to take a look at how tax rates and poverty are connected. Tim Smeeding, who directs the Institute for Research on Poverty at the La Follette School of Public Affairs at the University of Wisconsin–Madison, has done in-depth research on how the United States stacks up compared to other countries. He's found that the United States, by far, has the largest percentage of people living in poverty of any developed nation in the world. What he documents, specifically, is that poor people in the United States have a much more difficult time working themselves out of poverty because they don't have strong social benefits—like long-term subsidized day care, for example—that can help them become middle class (he also documents poverty among the elderly).[xxxv] Smeeding tells us that a person needs three things to avoid poverty—earned income, family support, and government support—and that if government support isn't around to make up for poor wages or other kinds of family support, you don't have much of a chance. He shows us that the United States ranks first compared to 11 other "rich" countries (and this is not a place where we want to chant, "We're number one!"), even when he factors in the array of social benefit programs (Food Stamps, Earned Income Tax Credit, housing vouchers, etc.) that are available to poor people. Table 3.1 summarizes this research.[xxxvi] Other researchers, including several at the Urban Institute, back him up.[xxxvii]

Internationally, the Organisation for Economic Co-operation and Development (OECD)—arguably the world's leading hub of comparative international economic statistics and social data, and probably the organization most used by governments around the world for information like this—also confirms Smeeding's findings. A 2008 OECD report titled "Growing Unequal? New Evidence on Changes in Poverty and Incomes Over the Past 20 Years" found that between 1985 and 2005, the United States had "the highest rate of income inequality and poverty after Mexico and Turkey and the gap has increased rapidly since 2000."[xxxviii]

Incidentally, here in the United States we measure poverty differently than people do in other countries. While there is no universal way for a country to measure how many of its citizens are poor, many developed countries refer to those people who have incomes that are less than 50% of the median income as being "poor." The United States uses a standard that equates to approximately 27% of the median income as our way of defining poverty.[xxxix] That leads one to wonder: If the official statistics from the U.S. Census Bureau tell us that in 2007, 37.3 million Americans were living in poverty (about 12.5% of the population), how many of us were really poor? A quick look at government poverty standards tells us, for instance, that poverty means an annual income of $21,203 or less for a family of *four*. You can go online to look up the whole range of poverty guidelines for the United States—it's fascinating (and depressing) reading.

The United States didn't even have a way of calculating poverty in our country until 1963 (a lot of stuff happened during the Great Society), when an economist named Mollie Orshansky who worked at Social Security came up with this formula. She estimated that families spent one third of their income on the U.S. Department of Agriculture Economy Food Plan,

Table 3.1   Relative Poverty Rates: Percent Below 50% Median Adjusted Income, by Type of Household, in 11 Rich Countries

		Households With Children (by number of parents)[3, 6]				
Nation (year)	Overall[2] (Rank)	All Children (Rank)	(1 Parent) (Rank)	(2 Parents) (Rank)	Elders[4] (Rank)	Childless[5] (Rank)
United States (2000)	17.0 (1)	18.8 (1)	(41.4) (2)	(13.2) (2)	28.4 (2)	11.2 (3)
Ireland (2000)	16.5 (2)	15.0 (3)	(45.8) (1)	(10.8) (3)	48.3 (1)	13.1 (1)
Italy (2000)	12.7 (3)	15.4 (2)	(20.1) (8)	(15.1) (1)	14.4 (6)	8.4 (6)
United Kingdom (1999)	12.4 (4)	13.2 (4)	(30.5) (6)	(9.1) (5)	23.9 (3)	8.4 (6)
Canada (2000)	11.4 (5)	13.2 (5)	(32.0) (4)	(10.1) (4)	6.3 (10)	11.9 (2)
Germany (2000)	8.3 (6)	7.6 (7)	(33.2) (3)	(4.4) (8)	11.2 (7)	8.7 (5)
Belgium (2000)	8.0 (7)	6.0 (9)	(21.8) (7)	(4.3) (9)	17.2 (5)	5.9 (11)
Austria (2000)	7.7 (8)	6.4 (8)	(17.9) (9)	(5.1) (7)	17.4 (4)	7.0 (9)
Netherlands (1999)	7.3 (9)	9.0 (6)	(30.7) (5)	(7.6) (6)	2.0 (11)	6.4 (10)
Sweden (2000)	6.5 (10)	3.8 (10)	(11.3) (10)	(2.2) (10)	8.3 (9)	9.8 (4)
Finland (2000)	5.4 (11)	2.9 (11)	(7.3) (11)	(2.2) (10)	10.1 (8)	7.6 (8)
Overall Average	10.3	10.1	(26.6)	(7.6)	17.0	8.9

The header above the data rows spans: *Poverty Rate (percent of population poor[1] and rank)*

Source: Author's calculations of LIS files.

Notes:

[1]Poverty is measured at 50% median adjusted disposable income (ADPI) for individuals. Incomes are adjusted by e = 0.5 where ADPI = unadjusted DPI divided by household size (s) to the power e: $ADPI = DPI/s^e$.

[2]All types of persons regardless of living situation.

[3]Households with children (under age 18, excluding ever married persons and heads and spouses) and no elderly (above 64). Children, and the non-elderly adults living with them in the same household, are further split into one- and two-parent columns.

[4]Adults aged 65 and over living in units with only elderly persons.

[5]Childless are couples or singles where there are no elderly or children.

[6]Other households include elderly and non-elderly persons living in the same households (often multiple generation families with children) and are omitted from this table.

multiplied that amount by three, and determined that as the rate of poverty. That same measurement is used today, updated only by using the consumer price index! It boggles the mind. While other economists have suggested new and different ways of calculating the poverty rate in the United States, Mollie Orshansky's standard rules to this day.

So what does all of this have to do with lobbying and state budgets? A lot. The shape that government takes and the services it provides are always at the center of political debate—and not just in the United States. England had one of the largest welfare states in the world; however, a shrinking tax base and soaring deficits pushed the country to elect David Cameron of the Conservative Party Prime Minister of Britain in May 2010. One of the first things he did upon coming to office was propose a 25% across-the-board cut in all government agencies. When world economies are increasingly intertwined as they are today, the issues become not just issues for Missouri, Nebraska, or the United States as a nation, but issues that affect people across the globe.

Back at home, as noted economist Robert Samuelson says, the issues Americans need to be debating are all about "the desirable role of government. How big should it be? Should it favor the old or the young? Will social spending crowd out defense spending? Will larger government dampen economic growth through higher deficits or taxes?"[xl]

How does all of this translate into your advocacy proposal? Simply put, if it costs money, it's going to be a hard sell unless you can identify a source of funding to pay for your idea. Now, if your idea is to propose a tax increase, then that's something altogether different (and given the prevailing views about waste and inefficiency, you're likely to have a long row to hoe on that front, but please don't let that discourage you from giving it a go). These days it is becoming fashionable for government to propose "fees" rather than taxes, which is pretty much like calling a "nor'easter" a blizzard (it's the same thing said differently). The point is, think carefully about what you'd like to propose. Does it cost money, or is it more of a policy shift? The lower the cost of your idea, the easier it will be to persuade people to get behind it. That is not to say that you shouldn't advocate for things that cost money; just be aware that it will be a much more difficult effort. Sometimes, if you think through your issue carefully, you may surprise yourself by coming up with some possible solutions that are more policy-focused than money-oriented. In any case, after having read this chapter, when you do lobby your officials, you'll have a much greater understanding of the types of problems they are grappling with as they make policy and budget decisions.

Chapter Questions

1. Should nonprofit organizations lobby to change the way the poverty rate is calculated in the United States?

2. Do you think student protests against budget cuts are an effective means of getting revenue restored?

3. Where do you stand in the argument for greater taxes or smaller government?

4. What is the total budget for your state, and what are its five biggest budget items?

5. Where does the money come from to support your state's budget?

6. What kind of balanced budget provision does your state have, and how does it work?

7. How did your state budget change from the previous year to this year?

Endnotes

i Austin, A., & Levit, M. (2010, February 16). *Mandatory spending since 1962*. Congressional Research Service Report 7-5700. Retrieved March 10, 2011, from http://assets.opencrs.com/rpts/RL33074_20100216.pdf

ii Ibid.

iii Ibid.

iv Center on Budget and Policy Priorities. (2010, April 14). *Policy basics: Where do our tax dollars go?* Retrieved June 11, 2010, from http://www.cbpp.org/cms/index.cfm?fa=view&id=1258

v Ibid.

vi Ibid.

vii Congressional Budget Office. (n.d.). *About CBO*. Retrieved March 10, 2011, from http://www.cbo.gov/aboutcbo/

viii California Department of Finance. (2010). *California Budget 2010–11*. Retrieved March 10, 2011, from http://2010-11.archives.ebudget.ca.gov/

ix Ibid.

x Ibid.

xi Magee, M. (2010, May 15). Big cuts in revised state budget. *The San Diego Union Tribune*, p. 1.

xii Marsh, B. (2011, January 22). Where budget gaps, and people, are few. *The New York Times*. Retrieved March 10, 2011, from http://www.nytimes.com/2011/01/23/weekinreview/23marsh.html

xiii Ibid.

xiv Ibid.

xv Calbreath, D. (2008, March 16). Education budget cuts barge into S.D. forums. *The San Diego Union Tribune*. Retrieved March 11, 2011, from http://www.signonsandiego.com/uniontrib/20080316/news_1b16dean.html

xvi Center on Budget and Policy Priorities. (2010, April 14). *Policy basics: Where do our tax dollars go?* Retrieved June 11, 2010, from http://www.cbpp.org/cms/index.cfm?fa=view&id=1258

xvii Steinhauer, J. (2008, March 17). As economy falters, so do state budgets. *The New York Times*. Retrieved March 11, 2011, from http://query.nytimes.com/gst/fullpage.html?res=9F0CE1D9173EF934A25750C0A96E9C8B63&pagewanted=1

xviii Ganey, T. (2010, February 26). Outlook for state budget continues decline. *Columbia Daily Tribune*. Retrieved March 11, 2011, from http://www.columbiatribune.com/news/2010/feb/25/outlook-worsens-state-budget/

xix Marsh, B. (2010, January 22). Where budget gaps, and people, are few. *The New York Times*. Retrieved March 10, 2011, from http://www.nytimes.com/2011/01/23/weekinreview/23marsh.html

xx Powell, M. (2010, July 2). Illinois stops paying its bills, but can't stop digging hole. *The New York Times*. Retrieved March 10, 2011, from http://www.nytimes.com/2010/07/03/business/economy/03illinois.html

xxi Marsh, B. (2010, January 23). Where budget gaps, and people, are few. *The New York Times*. Retrieved March 10, 2011, from http://www.nytimes.com/2011/01/23/weekinreview/23marsh.html

xxii CNN. (2010, March 4). *Protests over education cutbacks snarl traffic, lead to arrests*. Retrieved April 27, 2010, from http://www.cnn.com/2010/US/03/04/us.day.of.action/index.html

xxiii Yardley, W. (2010, May 31). Padlocking the gates to the great outdoors. *The New York Times*. Retrieved March 10, 2011, from http://www.nytimes.com/2010/05/31/us/31parkintro.html

xxiv Leonhardt, D. (2010, March 16). The perils of pay less, get more. *The New York Times*. Retrieved March 10, 2011, from http://www.nytimes.com/2010/03/17/business/economy/17leonhardt.html

xxv Central Intelligence Agency. (n.d.). *The world fact book*. Retrieved June 10, 2010, from https://www.cia.gov/library/publications/the-world-factbook/fields/2195.html

xxvi Leonhardt, D. (2010, March 16). The perils of pay less, get more. *The New York Times*. Retrieved March 10, 2011, from http://www.nytimes.com/2010/03/17/business/economy/17leonhardt.html

xxvii Ibid.

xxviii Jackie Borck, Brookline, MA.

xxix Worldwide-Tax.com. (n.d.). *Key data on world taxes, income tax rates, tax rates comparison table, business & finance worldwide*. Retrieved June 10, 2010, from http://www.worldwide-tax.com/

xxx Tax Foundation. (2011, January 1). *Tax data: U.S. federal individual income tax rates history, 1913–2011*. Retrieved June 24, 2010, from http://www.taxfoundation.org/publications/show/151.html

xxxi Doland, A., & Keller, G. (2010, October 19). Protests wreak havoc in France. *The San Diego Union Tribune*, p. 4.

xxxii Burns, John F. (2010, December 9). Protesters attack car carrying Prince Charles. *The New York Times*. Retrieved March 10, 2011, from http://www.nytimes.com/2010/12/10/world/europe/10britain.html

xxxiii Alderman, L. (2010, August 16). Denmark starts to trim its admired safety net. *The New York Times*. Retrieved March 10, 2011, from http://www.nytimes.com/2010/08/17/business/global/17denmark.html

xxxiv "Sarkozy, don't touch our pensions!" [Photo and caption]. (2010, June 25). *San Diego Union Tribune*, p. A3.

xxxv Smeeding, T. (2006). Poor people in rich nations: The United States in comparative perspective. *Journal of Economic Perspectives*, *20*(1), 69–90.

xxxvi Ibid.

xxxvii Urban Institute. (2010). *A new safety net for low-income families*. Retrieved March 10, 2011, from http://www.urban.org/projects/newsafetynet/

xxxviii Organisation for Economic Co-operation and Development. (2008, October). *Growing unequal? Income distribution and poverty in OECD countries*. Retrieved March 10, 2011, from http://www.oecd.org/document/53/0,3343,en_2649_33933_41460917_1_1_1_1,00.html

xxxix Smeeding, 2006, p. 74.

xl Time to wake up, America [Editorial]. (2010, May 17). *San Diego Union Tribune*, p. B5.

4 Making Law

Confessions of an Erstwhile Legislator

Howard Wayne

For six years I had the privilege of representing a portion of San Diego County in the California Legislature. I had majored in political science and practiced law for 24 years before I was elected. So this was a fascinating opportunity not only to serve the public good, but also to see how the legislative branch functions from the inside.

While the following is based on my experience with the California Legislature, it is not meant to be limited to a discussion of the California processes. Rather, it is meant as a way to guide you through diagrams like Figure 4.1 so that it makes more sense. Most legislative bodies in the United States will use a process similar to what California uses, although the specifics will vary.[1]

According to the National Conference of State Legislatures (NCSL), legislative organization and procedure represent the structural backbone of any state legislature. There is, however, no "off the shelf" formula for creating a

---

[1] There is one big difference between California's legislature and the legislatures of most of the rest of the country. We have a full-time legislature, we pay our legislators more than any other state, and the legislature has a professional staff. Many legislatures meet only a few months each year and, in a handful of cases, only every other year (see the Addendum to this book). The professionalization of the legislature is largely due to one person, Jesse Unruh, who was Speaker of the Assembly from 1961 to 1968 and became pejoratively known as "Big Daddy." One of two commemorative desks in the Assembly chamber is dedicated to him.

Figure 4.1

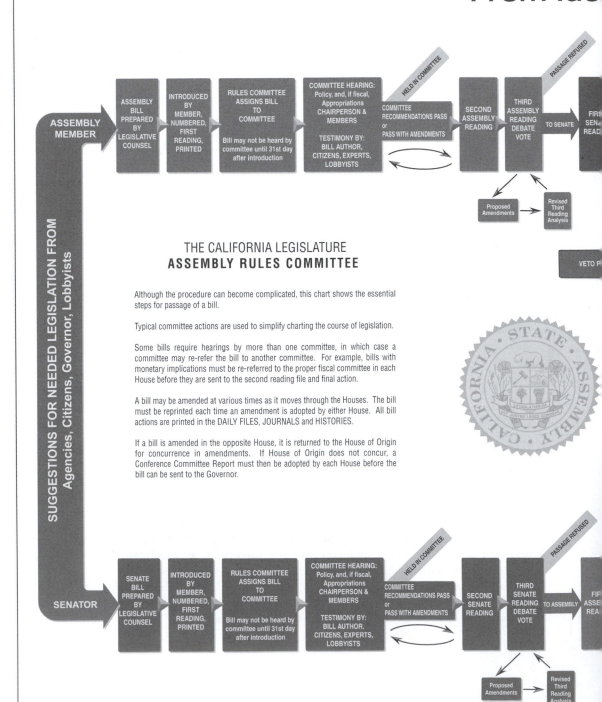

THE LIFE CYCLE

From Ide

ASSEMBLY MEMBER

ASSEMBLY BILL PREPARED BY LEGISLATIVE COUNSEL

INTRODUCED BY MEMBER, NUMBERED, FIRST READING, PRINTED

RULES COMMITTEE ASSIGNS BILL TO COMMITTEE

Bill may not be heard by committee until 31st day after introduction

COMMITTEE HEARING: Policy, and, if fiscal, Appropriations CHAIRPERSON & MEMBERS

TESTIMONY BY: BILL AUTHOR, CITIZENS, EXPERTS, LOBBYISTS

COMMITTEE RECOMMENDATIONS PASS or PASS WITH AMENDMENTS

HELD IN COMMITTEE

SECOND ASSEMBLY READING

THIRD ASSEMBLY READING DEBATE VOTE

PASSAGE REFUSED

TO SENATE

FIRST SENATE READING

Proposed Amendments → Revised Third Reading Analysis

VETO P

THE CALIFORNIA LEGISLATURE
ASSEMBLY RULES COMMITTEE

Although the procedure can become complicated, this chart shows the essential steps for passage of a bill.

Typical committee actions are used to simplify charting the course of legislation.

Some bills require hearings by more than one committee, in which case a committee may re-refer the bill to another committee. For example, bills with monetary implications must be re-referred to the proper fiscal committee in each House before they are sent to the second reading file and final action.

A bill may be amended at various times as it moves through the Houses. The bill must be reprinted each time an amendment is adopted by either House. All bill actions are printed in the DAILY FILES, JOURNALS and HISTORIES.

If a bill is amended in the opposite House, it is returned to the House of Origin for concurrence in amendments. If House of Origin does not concur, a Conference Committee Report must then be adopted by each House before the bill can be sent to the Governor.

SUGGESTIONS FOR NEEDED LEGISLATION FROM Agencies, Citizens, Governor, Lobbyists

SENATOR

SENATE BILL PREPARED BY LEGISLATIVE COUNSEL

INTRODUCED BY MEMBER, NUMBERED, FIRST READING, PRINTED

RULES COMMITTEE ASSIGNS BILL TO COMMITTEE

Bill may not be heard by committee until 31st day after introduction

COMMITTEE HEARING: Policy, and, if fiscal, Appropriations CHAIRPERSON & MEMBERS

TESTIMONY BY: BILL AUTHOR, CITIZENS, EXPERTS, LOBBYISTS

COMMITTEE RECOMMENDATIONS PASS or PASS WITH AMENDMENTS

HELD IN COMMITTEE

SECOND SENATE READING

THIRD SENATE READING DEBATE VOTE

PASSAGE REFUSED

TO ASSEMBLY

FIF ASSE REA

Proposed Amendments → Revised Third Reading Analysis

OF LEGISLATION
nto Law

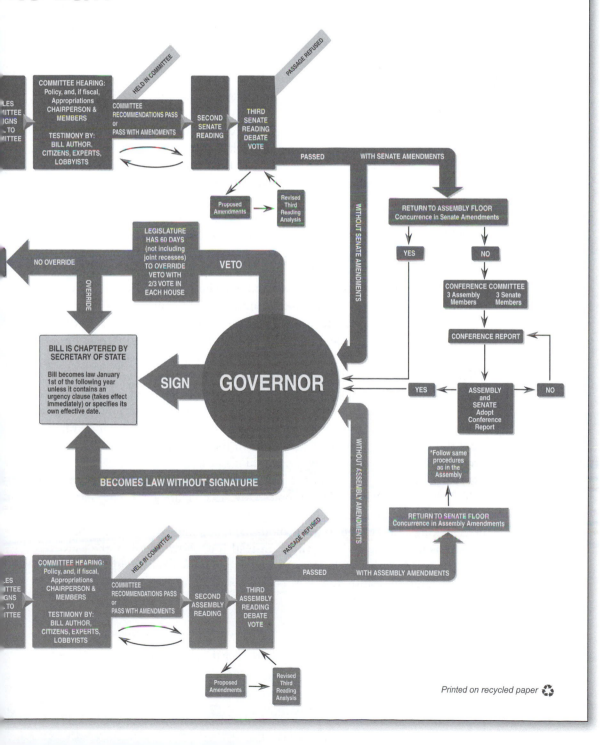

state legislature, and legislative assemblies in the United States illustrate the wide variety of organizational patterns. For example:

- They vary in size from 49 to 424.
- They may have one or two chambers.
- Session length may be extremely short or virtually unlimited.
- Each legislative chamber may determine its own rules of procedure. Parliamentary procedure provides a foundation for effective conduct of legislative business. Clearly articulated parliamentary procedure and effective operation of committees contribute to overall legislative efficiency.
- Every occupation has its special jargon, and legislatures are no exceptions. NCSL offers a glossary of many terms used in legislative circles.[i]

An oft-repeated quip about the legislature is that those who like sausages or laws should avoid seeing how they are made. While I can't speak about sausage making, the latter half of the observation is both naive and condescending.[2] The legislative process is about settling differences between groups of people to arrive at enforceable rulings. In earlier times there were "cleaner" ways of doing this. Some caveman named Ug had a big club and used it to settle differences he had with his fellow cavemen—and did so until a larger brute with a bigger club came along. Later, groups of armed thugs showed up, killed anyone who got in their way, and said their will was the law. Their leaders became kings or emperors, they declared themselves and their descendants to be royalty, and they called their form of government aristocracy rule by "the best." Then dictators came along and skipped the royalty nonsense, but their methods were pretty much the same if not more ruthless.

The legislative process is a lot messier, but far preferable. Decisions with the force of law still need to be made. Because you just can't hit your adversary over the head with a club, consultation, compromises, and ultimately voting are required. If you are not at the table, you may find yourself on the menu (I prefer that quip). It's better to learn the legislative process than to turn away from it because you've been told it's unseemly.

Typically people learn about the legislative process by examining a chart with a title such as "How a Bill Becomes Law" (see Figure 4.1).[3] The chart is useful, but examining it to understand the legislative process is about as helpful as looking at a skeleton to learn about the functioning of the body, and it is about as interesting. What I will do instead is to show you how the legislature really works by walking you through the steps I took with a major environmental bill I authored. But, before that, I need to provide you with some background.

---

[2]Besides, if you believed it, why would you be reading this chapter or taking this class?

[3]A more humorous approach is provided by Figure 4.2.

Figure 4.2

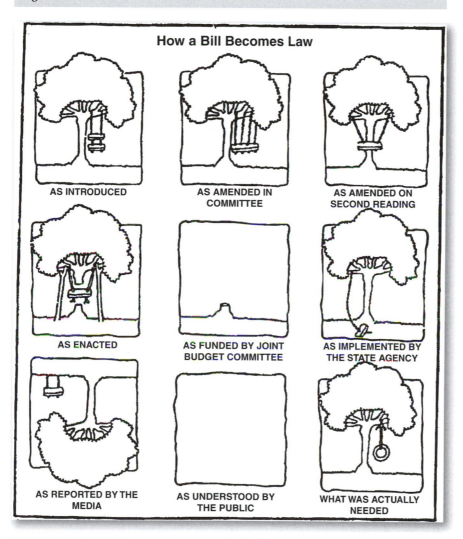

How a Bill Becomes Law

AS INTRODUCED · AS AMENDED IN COMMITTEE · AS AMENDED ON SECOND READING · AS ENACTED · AS FUNDED BY JOINT BUDGET COMMITTEE · AS IMPLEMENTED BY THE STATE AGENCY · AS REPORTED BY THE MEDIA · AS UNDERSTOOD BY THE PUBLIC · WHAT WAS ACTUALLY NEEDED

Source: Adapted from *Trial Talk,* June 1984.

Legislative Power

The California Constitution, just like the U.S. Constitution, vests legislative power in the legislative branch of government.[4] That means that the primary job of legislators is to make law, or to prevent laws from being made. Of course legislators engage in the casework of assisting constituents through the red tape of the bureaucracy, seek appropriations to benefit their con-

[4]Unlike the federal Constitution, not *all* legislative power is vested in the legislative branch. The California Constitution provides the people with the powers of initiative and referendum, which are discussed later in this chapter (California Constitution, Article IV, Section 1).

stituents, and appear at public functions, but their raison d'etre is the law-making process. I include the oversight function in the lawmaking process, and discuss that in a later chapter.

The California Legislature, like all other state legislatures (with the exception of Nebraska), is divided into two houses, a Senate of 40 members and an Assembly of 80 members. In some states the Assembly is referred to as the House of Representatives or House of Delegates, and the members are called "representatives" or "delegates." For the sake of consistency, in this chapter we will refer to the body as the Assembly and its members as Assembly Members. Following the 2010 census each Senate district will encompass approximately 950,000 people, and each Assembly district will have half that many residents. When that redistricting occurs, two Assembly districts will be "nested" in one Senate district.[5] That is, a Senate district will be composed of exactly two Assembly districts in their entirety. In every state where there are two houses, the Senate district will be larger than the Assembly district. People registered to vote in those districts are eligible to vote for a Senator and an Assembly Member to represent them.

How district lines are drawn has tremendous consequences because the line drawing will determine not only the composition of the legislature but, ultimately, the laws that are enacted. As the result of a 2008 initiative measure, district lines in California will be drawn for the first time by an independent redistricting commission. Prior to that, and still the rule in most states, districts were drawn by the legislature. Historically districts were drawn for partisan advantage, but even absent that intent it would be difficult, for example, to draw a Republican legislative district in San Francisco, which is politically liberal, or a Democratic district in southern Orange County, where the residents are largely conservative. People with similar party registrations tend to cluster together.

This is a good time to discuss the initiative process, which is part of lawmaking in California, 23 other states, the District of Columbia, and many local governments. The term *initiative* is frequently misused to mean any ballot measure. An initiative is simply a proposed law initiated by the public through petitions signed by the required number of registered voters and that appears on the ballot for a vote of the electorate. An initiative may be designed to enact a statute (including a bond measure) or to amend the state constitution, with a greater number of signatures required for the latter. If you refer to Liz's chapter, you'll remember that time you spend lobbying the public in support of or opposition to an initiative counts toward your legal limit as a nonprofit.

Initiatives may be either direct or indirect. Under the former, which is the only type used in California, a measure is put directly to the voters after a

---

[5]I use the word *redistricting* rather than *reapportionment*. Reapportionment refers to changing the allocation of legislative seats due to population changes. Thus, following each census, the number of seats in the U.S. House of Representatives is reallocated to the states depending on their change of population relative to other states. In contrast, decade after decade, California retains the same number of seats in its legislature, and the district lines are redrawn—redistricted—based on population changes.

sufficient number of signatures are gathered. With an indirect initiative a measure that obtains the necessary number of signatures is first referred to the legislature. The legislature may then enact the measure, but if it does not, then it goes to a popular vote.[6]

The chief weakness of initiative-created legislation is the lack of oversight in the drafting. A legislative bill must run a gauntlet of reviews in which poor drafting or unintended consequences of drafting can be discovered and mini- mized. At worst, a poorly drafted law can be amended in the next legislative session. In contrast, an initiative is drafted by a handful of people, and once it goes into circulation the language cannot be changed. It often leads to courts guessing what the measure means. In a worst-case situation a poorly drafted initiative that is passed can only be altered by a vote of the public. California's tax cutting initiative of 1978, Proposition 13, is a classic exam- ple. The measure was intended to limit taxes on real estate to one percent (1%) of the property's value, based on its acquisition price.

When the California Supreme Court first considered Proposition 13, it said that it had to acknowledge "that [Proposition 13] in a number of par- ticulars is imprecise and ambiguous."[ii] Did the measure prohibit special assessments for improvements, such as for streets that benefited only specific parcels of property? A court decided that it probably did not.[iii] The measure appeared to prevent the passage of any subsequent local bond measures because paying for them would require a tax rate of more than 1%. So a fix- it measure was required, and Proposition 46 passed in 1986 to allow prop- erty tax rates to increase to cover bonds passed by the public.

A second weakness of the initiative has been the inversion of its use. It was created by the Progressives as a means for citizens to make an end-run around the legislature, which was then dominated by the railroads. Today, due to the large number of signatures required to qualify a measure, there is an initiative industry that employs lawyers, both to guide the measure to the ballot and to defend attacks on it; paid signature gatherers to get voters to sign the petitions; and campaign consultants. A proponent first has to answer "the million-dollar question," which is "Do you have a million dollars to pay for qualifying the measure?" The average citizen does not, but moneyed interests do. The initia- tive, rather than being a tool for citizens to overcome the institutional advan- tages of special interest, has instead become a tool of those interests.[7]

---

[6]For more information on initiatives, check out the Initiative & Referendum Institute at the University of Southern California School of Law (http://www.iandrinstitute .org/California.htm).

[7]Another aspect has been the so-called "dueling initiatives" whereby an initia- tive appears on the ballot to impair another initiative that is also on the ballot or, at the minimum, to confuse voters. An example of the former was the cam- paign reform initiatives of 1988. One measure provided for public financing of political campaigns, and the other prohibited public financing. The electorate passed both measures! Because the initiative prohibiting public financing received more votes, it repealed the authorization for public financing contained in the other measure. (Continues on p. 60.)

The term *referendum* is frequently improperly applied to an initiative, but it is a very different animal. A referendum seeks to challenge a law passed by the legislature and signed by the Governor. After a bill has been enacted, opponents have a limited number of days to obtain the required number of signatures to qualify a public vote on that measure. If the petition drive is successful, the law is suspended until the public at the next statewide election can vote on it.[8] At that election supporters of the law would vote yes and need a majority to sustain the law.[9] In recent years the referendum has been successfully used by the insurance industry to overturn a law that reestablished third-party bad-faith liability against insurers and by business interests to defeat mandatory medical insurance coverage for employees of medium- to large-size businesses.

The Election Process

Members of the legislature are chosen in partisan elections held every two years. Assembly Members serve two-year terms, and Senators have four-year terms. In California, Senate terms are staggered so that the odd-numbered districts are elected in presidential election years and the even-numbered districts are elected at the same time as the Governor.[10] In most states candidates are nominated in partisan primaries, and the nominees of the parties square off the following November.

Most districts are "safe" for one party or the other. In those districts the fall campaign is so much going through the motions because the winner was already determined in the primary of the party holding the dominant registration advantage in that district. The real battle was for the nomination of that party. Even those only tend to be competitive when there is not an incumbent running for reelection. Since the advent of term limits in 1990 in California, one could chart with a great deal of perspicacity when there will be a real primary election.

---

[7](Continued) An example of confusing dueling initiatives occurred in the 2005 special election. That year one initiative proposed controlling drug prices by employing California's market leverage of purchasing drugs for Medi-Cal. The pharmaceutical industry qualified a competing initiative to establish voluntary reduced prices for drugs, although any company could have voluntarily reduced its prices without any measure. Both initiatives failed passage, which satisfied the needs of the pharmaceutical industry.

[8]In California, laws passed in a regular session of the legislature typically go into effect January 1 of the following year, so the suspension of the law means that it does not go into effect until it is approved in the referendum election. The way to immunize a law from being subject to referendum is to enact it as an "urgency" measure, which requires a two-thirds approval of each house of the legislature. An urgency measure becomes effective upon the Governor's signature.

[9]People frequently express confusion about the effect of a yes or no vote. A ballot measure proposes a change in the law, so a yes vote is a vote to enact that change and a no vote is one to reject it.

[10]Special elections to fill vacancies in the legislature can be held anytime, but the Governor will usually try to consolidate these elections with regular or primary elections to save money and voter fatigue.

In 2010 California voters passed a measure for a "top two" primary. Under that system all candidates of all parties will appear on the same primary ballot. The top two finishers will run off in November, regardless of their party. Hence, it is possible that the general election in some districts could have two Democrats running against each other, or two Republicans doing the same. In those instances a competitive election could be held in the general election even in a "safe" district, and proponents theorize it will tend to result in the election of more moderate candidates.

This system has recently been used in the state of Washington. The first two times it was used for congressional races, each November contest had a Democrat running against a Republican. However, all but one of those contests involved incumbents, so the outcomes could be different in open seats. There is a likelihood the new California systems will be challenged in the courts.

Regardless of what state you reside in, some districts are "competitive," as neither major party has a significant registration advantage. Those districts have real competition in almost every election, and particularly so when there is no incumbent running for reelection. Because winning these districts is usually the key to a party winning control of the legislative body, these races attract money from throughout the state. Of course much of this might change when districts are drawn by a commission rather than by the legislature.

There are contribution limits for legislative seats. Unlike federal campaign laws,[11] in California corporate contributions are permitted, and the maximum contribution is adjusted by the cost of living. There are higher contribution limits for broad-based political action committees. Candidates are required to report contributions, as are large contributors.

Just six states place no limits on contributions at all. Another seven states have weak contribution limits. Seven states, including California, use the Consumer Price Index to adjust their contribution limits. Campaign finance law is a complex area that has spawned a specialized field of law.

Both Assembly Members and Senators in California are subject to term limits that impose a lifetime ban. Members of the Assembly are limited to serving three terms and Senators to two terms, after which they may never seek election to those offices.[12] Since I have served three terms in the Assembly, I am constitutionally prohibited from ever running for the Assembly, but I could run for the Senate.

The term limits movement, which peaked in the early 1990s, was designed to end domination by career politicians and instead create "citizen lawmakers" who, after reaching term limits, would return to civilian life and live under the laws they created. What has happened instead is that the legislature has become

---

[11]Of course that may change too, based on further expansion of the rules set out in the *Citizens United* case decided by the U.S. Supreme Court. Campaign financing is a dynamic area of the law.

[12]Term limits were only enacted in states that had the initiative—and for obvious reasons only by the initiative. Fifteen states have term limits, of which six impose a California-like lifetime ban. Six states have repealed their term limit laws—in four of those states it was by the courts.

part of a career path whereby individuals get elected to city councils and boards of supervisors, and then go to the legislature and on reaching term limits seek to run for Congress or to return to positions in local government. "Termed-out" Senators who have not exhausted their number of terms in the Assembly frequently run for that house, although incumbent Senators almost never ran for the Assembly prior to term limits.

Moreover, term limits have created an imbalance between the legislative and executive branches of government. Experienced legislators with institutional knowledge are forced out of office even though their constituents may desire to reelect them. In contrast, those entrenched in the executive branch can impede the implementation of laws and then "outwait" the legislators advocating such laws. The professional legislative staff also suffers. Staff members have no tenure rights and serve at the pleasure of the legislators who hire them. Good staffers establish a rapport with their legislators, but the relationship is no better than how long the legislator serves. As legislators depart with the expiration of their terms, their staff often leave for jobs outside the Capitol. It is difficult to overstate how much money is wasted by this enforced turnover.

Governing magazine has said the following of the term limits experiment:

> There are questions about how effective term limits have been in states that have a long track record with them. A 2004 study by the Public Policy Institute of California, for example, found that instead of revolutionizing the state Legislature with innovation, new members often emulated their precursors, and the policy-making process suffered. "Legislative committees screen out fewer bills, the legislative process does not encourage fiscal discipline nor link requests to spending limits," the report noted, "and committee membership and leadership continuity impacts experience and expertise crucial to effective policymaking."
>
> In Michigan, a 12-year study by Wayne State University found that term limits have dissolved important checks and balances and increased lobbyists' influence. Marjorie Sarbaugh-Thompson, a political science professor at the university and the study's lead author, says there is no question that the problem stems from the limited time new legislators have to understand their jobs and a lack of veteran leadership to guide them. "It is very difficult to bring new legislators up to speed," she says. "They're just barely getting a grasp of what the job consists of when they're on their way out the door."[iv]

New classes of Assembly Members are elected every two years, and every two years one third of the Assembly faces a steep learning curve. This is particularly true for incoming members of the majority party because they have a good chance of becoming chairs of standing committees in their first year and may not have a background in the policy area for which they have been designated to be the driving force.[13]

---

[13]I was appointed the chair of a standing committee nine days after being sworn in for my first term.

Opening Day—The Legislature Organizes

All state legislatures operate according to a calendar. In California, the legislature convenes on the first Monday in December of each even-numbered year so that each house can organize itself. This is the beginning of the "Session," which will last until August 31 of the next even-numbered year, although it is possible for the Governor to call the legislature back for a special session until November of the next even-numbered year. An Assembly Member's term expires on November 30 of the next even-numbered year after his or her election (for example, the term of a legislator elected November 2, 2010, would end November 30, 2012). The first part of the Regular Session is from the first Monday in December until mid-September of the following year, and the second part is from the first working day of the following even-numbered year to August 31 of that year.

After taking the oath of office, each legislator will cast his or her single most important vote of the session—the vote on Speaker for the Assembly or President Pro Tempore for the Senate.[14]

These are party line votes, and the winners have been predetermined by the November election and in the party caucus votes of the majority party in each house.[15] It is a crucial election because the party controlling the body will appoint the chairs and members of all the committees—with each committee dominated by the majority party—which will control the Rules Committee of each house, and will determine the flow of business.

The second most important activity on this day is the adoption of the rules of the house. The rules include a series of deadlines for bills. The legislature is a deadline-driven operation. There are deadlines by which a bill must be introduced, when it must pass committee or die, when it must pass its house of origin, and so on (see Figure 4.3). The effect of the deadlines is not only to keep bills moving, but to create a logjam at each critical date. Perhaps it is just human nature to wait for the last minute, but the adrenaline level of the last night of a session is something to behold.

Following some ministerial activities such as election of the Chaplain of the house and the introduction of bills (no more than one per member), the legislature adjourns for the rest of the year. Between Christmas and New Year's one could shoot a cannon off in the Capitol building and not hit anyone. Everything waits for the first workday of the New Year.

---

[14]In most states the Lieutenant Governor is the nominal president of the Senate, which is why the Senate's elected president is deemed "Pro Tempore."

[15]Of course this is not always the case. In 1994 Republicans won a 41–39 nominal control of the Assembly. However, one Republican was excluded because he had also been elected to the Senate on the same day he was reelected to the Assembly, and another Republican voted for the Democratic Speaker candidate Willie Brown. The Republicans quickly put together a successful recall against that apostate member. It took a special election and another recall election for the Republicans to finally gain the speakership, which they then held for less than a year.

Figure 4.3

2011 Tentative Legislative Calendar

COMPILED BY THE OFFICE OF THE ASSEMBLY CHIEF CLERK

Deadlines based on custom and usage, pending adoption of the Joint Rules.

11-17-10

- January
- February
- March
- April
- May
- June
- July
- August
- September

JANUARY	S	M	T	W	Th	F	S
							1
Wk.1	2	3	4	5	6	7	8
Wk.2	9	10	11	12	13	14	15
Wk.3	16	17	18	19	20	21	22
Wk.4	23	24	25	26	27	28	29
Wk.1	30	31					

Deadlines

Jan. 1 Statutes take effect (Art. IV, Sec. 8(c)).

Jan. 3 Legislature reconvenes (J.R. 51(a)(1)).

Jan. 10 Budget must be submitted by Governor on or before this date (Art. IV, Sec. 12 (a)).

Jan. 17 Martin Luther King, Jr. Day

Jan. 21 Last day to submit bill requests to the Office of the Legislative Counsel.

FEBRUARY	S	M	T	W	Th	F	S
Wk.1			1	2	3	4	5
Wk.2	6	7	8	9	10	11	12
Wk.3	13	14	15	16	17	18	19
Wk.4	20	21	22	23	24	25	26
Wk.1	27	28					

Feb. 18 Last day for bills to be introduced (J.R. 61(a)(1)) (J.R. 54(a)).

Feb. 21 President's Day

MARCH							
	S	M	T	W	Th	F	S
Wk.1			1	2	3	4	5
Wk.2	6	7	8	9	10	11	12
Wk.3	13	14	15	16	17	18	19
Wk.4	20	21	22	23	24	25	26
Wk.1	27	28	29	30	31		

Mar. 28 Cesar Chavez Day observed.

APRIL							
	S	M	T	W	Th	F	S
Wk.1						1	2
Wk.2	3	4	5	6	7	8	9
Wk.3	10	11	12	13	14	15	16
Spring Recess	17	18	19	20	21	22	23
Wk.4	24	25	26	27	28	29	30

Apr. 14 Spring Recess begins upon adjournment (J.R. 51(a)(2)).

Apr. 25 Legislature reconvenes (J.R. 51(a)(2)).

MAY							
	S	M	T	W	Th	F	S
Wk.1	1	2	3	4	5	6	7
Wk.2	8	9	10	11	12	13	14
Wk.3	15	16	17	18	19	20	21
Wk.4	22	23	24	25	26	27	28
No Hrgs	29	30	31				

May 6 Last day for **policy committees** to hear and report to **fiscal bills** introduced in their house (J.R. 61(a)(2)).

May 13 Last day for **policy committees** to hear and report to the floor nonfiscal bills introduced in their house (J.R. 61(a)(3)).

May 20 Last day for **policy committees** to meet prior to June 6 (J.R. 61(a)(4)).

May 27 Last day for **fiscal committees** to hear and report to the floor bills introduced in their house (J.R. 61 (a)(5)). Last day for fiscal committees to meet prior to June 6 (J.R. 61 (a)(6)).

May 30 Memorial Day.

May 31 – June 3 Floor session only. No committee may meet for any purpose (J.R. 61(a)(7)).

(Continued)

Figure 4.3 (Continued)

JUNE	S	M	T	W	Th	F	S
No Hrgs.				1	2	3	4
Wk.1	5	6	7	8	9	10	11
Wk.2	12	13	14	15	16	17	18
Wk.3	19	20	21	22	23	24	25
Wk.4	26	27	28	29	30		

June 3 Last day for each house to pass bills introduced in that house (J.R. 61(a)(8)).

June 6 Committee meetings may resume (J.R. 61(a)(9)).

June 15 Budget Bill shall be passed by midnight (Art. IV, Sec. 12(c)(3)).

JULY	S	M	T	W	Th	F	S
Wk.4						1	2
Wk.1	3	4	5	6	7	8	9
Wk.2	10	11	12	13	14	15	16
Summer Recess	17	18	19	20	21	22	23
Summer Recess	24	25	26	27	28	29	30
Summer Recess	31						

July 4 Independence Day observed

July 8 Last day for **policy committees** to meet and report bills (J.R. 61(a)(10)).

July 15 Summer Recess begins on adjournment, provided Budget Bill has been enacted (J.R. 51(a)(3)).

AUGUST	S	M	T	W	Th	F	S
Summer Recess		1	2	3	4	5	6
Summer Recess	7	8	9	10	11	12	13
Wk.3	14	15	16	17	18	19	20
Wk.4	21	22	23	24	25	26	27
No Hrgs.	28	29	30	31			

Aug. 15 Legislature reconvenes (J.R. 51(a)(3)).

Aug. 26 Last day for **fiscal committees** to meet and report bills (J.R. 61(a)(11)).

Aug. 29 Floor session only. No committee may meet for any purpose (J.R. 61(a)(12)).

SEPTEMBER							
	S	M	T	W	Th	F	S
No Hgrs.					1	2	3
No Hgrs.	4	5	6	7	8	9	10
Interim Recess	11	12	13	14	15	16	17
Interim Recess	18	19	20	21	22	23	24
Interim Recess	25	26	27	28	29	30	

Sept. 2 Last day to amend on the floor (J.R. 61(a)(13)).

Sept. 5 Labor Day

Sept. 9 Last day for any bill to be passed (J.R. 61(a)(14)). Interim recess begins on adjournment (J.R. 51(a)(4)).

IMPORTANT DATES OCCURRING AFTER ADJOURNMENT FOR INTERIM RECESS

2011
Oct. 9 Last day for Governor to sign or veto bills passed by the Legislature before Sept. 9 and in the Governor's possession on or after Sept. 9 (Art. IV, Sec.10(b)(1)).

2012
Jan. 1 Statutes take effect (Art. IV, Sec. 8(c)).
Jan. 4 Legislature reconvenes (J.R. 51(a)(4)).

January—The Work Begins, Sort Of

Whether it is an odd or even year the legislature reconvenes in January. After the welcoming hugs and greetings, the legislature waits for the State of the State address by the Governor. Both houses convene in the Assembly chamber. After introductions by the Speaker and the Lieutenant Governor, the Governor has center stage. It is his (so far we have had only male governors in California) opportunity to set the tone of the session. In my first year, when the state was faced with enacting changes in the welfare law to comply with federal welfare reform law, Governor Pete Wilson used the State of the State address to lambaste Democrats for creating "welfare dependency." Republicans applauded, and the Democratic side of the aisle sat on its hands. I knew we were in for two years of nasty infighting, which is exactly what happened. In 2005, intent on calling a special election to enact his initiatives, Governor Arnold Schwarzenegger used the State of the State to declare war on the legislature. What followed was one of the least productive legislative sessions in memory, and all of the Governor's initiatives were defeated. Governor Gray Davis's addresses were so bland that at one of them he had to ask the legislators for applause.

A few days later the Governor issues his proposed budget. The executive branch has been working on this since no later than shortly after the last budget was passed, and it has been a major focus for the preceding two months. It will be the working draft on which budget subcommittee hearings will be based. The budget goes to the nonpartisan Legislative Analyst's Office (LAO) for review. About 80% of the states utilize a professional body—by whatever name—to assist in the preparation of the budget. The LAO employs a professional staff of analysts who specialize in one area of the budget or another. In a little over a month's time the LAO prepares two blue-covered books that are the bible of the budget. The analysts then testify at the budget subcommittee hearings, are available for individual consultations, and, when not so engaged, prepare reports on financial matters that are issued periodically. Unlike the Congressional Budget Office, which does not offer its opinions on matters of policy, the LAO is required to make recommendations. For example, in 2007 the LAO's pessimistic budget analysis was considered a major factor in killing a proposal for universal health coverage for all Californians.[v]

The principal difference between even- and odd-year sessions in January is the pace of work. In odd years (i.e., the January after the election) the membership of committees has not been established, and few bills have been introduced.[16] January meetings in odd-numbered years tend to be ceremonial and pro forma events.

In the Assembly, the determination of which committees exist, including their jurisdictions, sizes, and membership, and the designation of the chairs are all in the hands of the Speaker. Usually the minority party will designate the vice chair of each committee. In the Senate the same function is exercised by a five-member Rules Committee, which is substantially in the control of the President Pro Tempore. Once committees are appointed and their chairs established, some hearings of the committee may be held pending the referral of bills.[17]

In the even-numbered, second year of a session, the activity level in January is far more frantic. Bills introduced in the prior year ("two-year

---

[16]In this respect the legislature has failed the promise of being a full-time operation. It was envisioned that following the organizational meeting in December, committees would be appointed before the end of the year, and the legislature would hit the ground running. Sadly, it has rarely worked out that way.

[17]In my first year I convened a hearing of the Environmental Safety and Toxic Materials Committee to discuss regulatory efforts of the Department of Toxic Substances Control. It was a chance to put the staff through their paces and an opportunity for committee members to begin to work together. It set the tone for the bipartisan cooperation we were to have that year that was assisted by having a very good vice chair from the minority party.

bills") that have not passed their house of origin (e.g., bills introduced by Assembly Members the previous year that have not passed the Assembly) must pass the Assembly by the end of the month or they are dead. In many cases these bills have not passed out of committee, so committees meet to hear them. If passed by the committee, the bills go to the floor of their respective body for a vote before the deadline.

Assembly Bill 411 Is Introduced

With the above construct in mind, we are in a position to see how an idea becomes a bill and then a law.

I represented a coastal area, and when I was running for election I was approached about beach water pollution. I was told that people who use the beaches were becoming sick because contaminants were getting into the surf, but there was no testing of the beach waters and no notice of pollution, so people did not know there was a problem before they got into the water. I promised to do something about it if I was elected.[18]

When I won I called these concerned citizens together and asked them to develop a proposal. What emerged was the concept of establishing standards for when waters would be considered unsafe for human contact, regularly testing beach waters, and then posting adverse results at the beach. This may happen to you when you approach your legislator with an idea, assuming he or she likes what you are proposing. I submitted this concept to the Legislative Counsel to draft a bill.

Legislators, in general, do not draft their own bills. This job is done by the Legislative Counsel, which employs well over 100 attorneys, each of whom specializes in certain areas of California statutory law. Each bill proposal is sent to a designated Deputy Legislative Counsel who attempts to find the correct code (e.g., the Health and Safety Code) and where in that code to place the proposal, and who then drafts the language of the bill. The product is then returned to the legislative office from which the proposal originated.[19] The deadline to get proposals to the Legislative Counsel is one of the earliest in the schedule, and it is common practice for legislators to submit far more ideas than they intend to offer as bills. This defers the legislator's decision of which bills will be introduced. The legislature operates under a "bill limit"

---

[18]Where do ideas for bills originate? The first place to look is the promises winning candidates have made.

[19]Some members have authorized designated lobbyists to submit bill proposals to the Legislative Counsel in their name. This is not a commitment by the legislator to introduce a bill, but permits a lobbyist to get a concept past the early deadline for getting a proposal into bill form. Often the lobbyist will "shop" these bills in search of an author. Selection of an author is an art, but as the deadline for bill introduction approaches, a lobbyist may require a set of knee pads to obtain an author.

rule.[20] Each member of the Assembly is entitled to introduce 30 bills in each two-year session, and each Senator 45 bills in that period, although there are numerous ways of getting around this limitation. Your job as an advocate, as you will come to understand in the chapters that follow, will be to find a legislator who is willing to "carry" or "author" a bill that will enable your proposal to become law.

Bills, except for budget bills, are limited to a "single subject." While a bill may cover hundreds of pages and amend numerous codes, the contents of the bill must be related.

My practice was to determine which bills were a priority—those bills I knew I was going to introduce. I would then decide how many more bills I would carry that year based on the bill limitation and the expected workload. As the bill introduction deadline approached, I would convene the staff. We would prioritize bills I had received from the Legislative Counsel and discuss which of them I would author. Again, your role will be to convince the legislator and the staff to make your bill a priority.

While a bill may be introduced at any time prior to the bill introduction deadline, the deferral of the decisions on which bills will be "carried" creates a crunch as the deadline approaches. Introduction is accomplished by an Assembly Member or a Senator signing the backing of the bill and then (more often by their staff person) putting the bill "across the desk."[21] That means handing the bill to the clerk of the house, who then stamps it with a sequentially issued number. My coastal water-testing bill was the 411th bill introduced in the Assembly that session, and thus became Assembly Bill 411—AB 411.

Senate bills are designated with the prefix SB, and their numbering follows the same procedure. There may be other types of legislation introduced, such as constitutional amendments (ACA and SCA) and joint resolutions (AJR and SJR).

One way of avoiding the bill introduction deadline is by the means of a "spot" bill. That involves introducing a bill that makes only an immaterial change in the law, such as the substitution of a semicolon for a comma. A spot bill is thus a vehicle for any legislation the author desires, subject to the rule that it must relate to the general area of law that the "spot" indicates, such as, for example, education. While I was in the Assembly the practice was not to refer a spot bill to a policy committee until content was added to it.

I introduced AB 411 on February 20, which was right up against the bill introduction deadline.[22] I had a staff member put the bill across the desk while I held a press conference at La Jolla Shores near the lifeguard station.

---

[20]About a quarter of the states use some form of bill limit.

[21]Members often seek coauthors for bills to show there is support for them. A coauthor would also sign the back of a bill, but which member is "carrying" the bill would be clearly indicated.

[22]Hundreds of bills were introduced in the Assembly that day. The clerk was very busy.

I gave a short talk about the need to protect our coastal waters—the "crown jewels" of California—and introduced coastal water advocates who added their comments. Reporters and television cameras were present, and the event received good coverage. It was one of the efforts to build support.

After it was introduced, AB 411 was printed, as appears in Figure 4.4. The top line of the bill indicates each time it has been amended (none in Figure 4.4, but once in Figure 4.5), with the most recent amendment date appearing first. Next will be the number of the bill. The next line will list the authors and coauthors (again, see Figure 4.5). Below that will be the date the bill was introduced.

Following that will be two portions from the Legislative Counsel. The first specifies the sections of law affected, and the second is the digest, which summarizes the bill and sets forth its vote threshold (e.g., majority, two-thirds), whether the bill requires an appropriation, whether the bill must be referred to a fiscal committee, and whether the bill creates a state-mandated program.

From that point on the language of the bill will be set forth in numbered lines. When introduced, existing law will appear in roman type, proposed deletions from existing law will be indicated by strikeouts, and language to be added will appear in italics. However, once a bill has been amended, the rules change, and the bill is printed as though the prior version of the bill was law, as can be seen in Figure 4.5. Thus the language sought to be repealed by the bill will simply disappear from the text, the language added by the bill in its prior versions will be in the same type form as the existing law, and only the changes made by the last amendment to the bill will be clearly set forth by strikeouts and italics. Consequently, it may be impossible to determine from the face of a subsequent version of a bill how it affects existing law.[23] Rather, one needs to compare the bill to the statutes in effect to see how the bill would change the law.[24]

In California, before a bill can be heard by a committee, it must be "in print" for 30 days. This requirement in the state constitution was designed to afford a comment period to the public in the preelectronic communications era and is one of the longest periods of bill dormancy in the country. The effect of this delay combined with the late appointment of committees, the

[23]Artie Samish, a famed lobbyist from the 1930s to the early 1950s, in his classic book *The Secret Boss of California* (1971), told how he had a massive bill introduced that changed only one word of the law, and then immediately had the bill amended to hide that change. This bill printing protocol has a tremendous potential for abuse. Reform is needed, but this was a change I sought and was unable to achieve. Indeed, it was related to me that one legislative leader thought this confusion was a tool to give experienced legislators an advantage!

[24]When I arrived in the Assembly, it was virtually impossible to do this on the Assembly floor because there was no set of California codes there. The space previously occupied by the codes had been commandeered for the new computer equipment. Before I left I had a set of the codes placed just outside the Assembly chamber where the members could easily access them.

Figure 4.4

CALIFORNIA LEGISLATURE—1997–98 REGULAR SESSION

ASSEMBLY BILL   No. 411

Introduced by Assembly Member Wayne

February 20, 1997

An act to amend Sections 115880, 115885, and 115915 of the Health and Safety Code, relating to public beaches.

LEGISLATIVE COUNSEL'S DIGEST

AB 411, as introduced, Wayne.   Beach sanitation: posting.

Existing law requires the State Department of Health Services to adopt regulations establishing minimum standards for the sanitation of public beaches. Violation of these regulations adopted by the department is a crime.

This bill would require these regulations to require the testing of all beaches for total coliform, fecal coliform, enterococci, and streptococci bacteria, establish protective minimum standards for the location of monitoring sites and monitoring frequency, to require posting in clearly visible points along affected beaches whenever state standards are violated, and to require that beaches be tested for total coliform, fecal coliform, enterococci, and streptococci bacteria and chemical pollutants including, but not limited to, PCBs, PAHs, and mercury on a weekly basis from April 1 to October 31, inclusive, of each year if certain conditions are met. By changing the definition of a crime, this bill would impose a state-mandated local program.

This bill would require local health officers to be responsible for testing beaches within this jurisdiction except state beaches which the bill would require the department to test.

AB 411

By increasing the duties of local health officers, this bill would impose a state-mandated local program.

Existing law requires the local health officer to post a beach with conspicuous warning signs whenever the beach fails to meet certain bacteriological standards, and it is determined that the cause of the elevated levels constitutes a public health hazard.

This bill would, in addition, require the local health officer to post a beach with conspicuous warning signs whenever the beach fails to meet the standards developed by the department established pursuant to this bill.

Existing law requires each local health officer to notify the Director of Parks and Recreation when a beach is in violation of the sanitation standards.

This bill would, instead, require the local health officer to notify the Director of Parks and Recreation within 24 hours of any beach posting, closure, or restriction, and would require the Director of Parks and Recreation to establish a telephone hotline and update it daily to inform the public of beach postings, closures, and restrictions. By increasing the duties of the local health officer, this bill would impose a state-mandated local program.

The California Constitution requires the state to reimburse local agencies and school districts for certain costs mandated by the state. Statutory provisions establish procedures for making that reimbursement, including the creation of a State Mandates Claims Fund to pay the costs of mandates that do not exceed $1,000,000 statewide and other procedures for claims whose statewide costs exceed $1,000,000.

This bill would provide that with regard to certain mandates no reimbursement is required by this act for a specified reason.

With regard to any other mandates, this bill would provide that, if the Commission on State Mandates determines that the bill contains costs so mandated by the state, reimbursement for those costs shall be made pursuant to the statutory provisions noted above.

Vote: majority. Appropriation: no. Fiscal committee: yes. State-mandated local program: yes.

(Continued)

Figure 4.4 (Continued)

AB 411

The people of the State of California do enact as follows:

1   SECTION 1.   Section 115880 of the Health and Safety
2 Code is amended to read:
3   115880. *(a)* The   department   shall   by   regulation
4 *establish minimum standards for the sanitation of public*
5 *beaches, including, but not limited to, the removal of*
6 *refuse, as it determines are reasonably necessary for the*
7 protection of the public health and safety.
8   *(b) The regulations shall, at a minimum, do all of the*
9 *following:*
10   *(1) Require the testing of all beaches for total coliform,*
11 *fecal coliform, enterococci, and streptococci bacteria.*
12   *(2) Establish   protective   minimum   standards   for   the*
13 *location of monitoring sites and monitoring frequency.*
14   *(3) Require   posting   in   clearly   visible   points   along*
15 *affected beaches whenever state standards are violated.*
16   *(4) Require that beaches be tested for total coliform,*
17 *fecal coliform, enterococci, and streptococci bacteria and*
18 *chemical   pollutants   including,   but   not   limited   to,*
19 *polychlorinated   biphenyls   (PCBs),   polyaromatic*
20 *hydrocarbons (PAHs), and mercury on a weekly basis*
21 *from April 1 to October 31, inclusive, of each year if all of*
22 *the following apply:*
23   *(a) The beach is visited by more than 50,000 people*
24 *annually.*
25   *(b) The beach is located on an area adjacent to a storm*
26 *drain that flows in the summer.*
27   *(c) The local health officer shall be responsible for*
28 *testing all beaches within his or her jurisdiction, except*
29 *state beaches which shall be tested by the department.*
30   *(d)* Any city or county may adopt standards for the
31 sanitation of public beaches within its jurisdiction that are
32 stricter   than   the   standards   adopted   by   the   state
33 department pursuant to this section.
34   SEC. 2.   Section 115885 of the Health and Safety Code
35 is amended to read:
36   115885.   The health officer having jurisdiction over
37 the area in which a public beach is created shall:

AB 411

1   (a) Inspect the public beach to determine whether the
2 standards established pursuant to Section 115880 are
3 being complied with. If the health officer finds any
4 violation of the standards, he or she shall restrict the use
5 of, or close, the public beach or portion thereof in which
6 the violation occurs until such time as the standard
7 violated is complied with.
8   (b) Investigate any complaint of a person of a violation
9 of any standard established by the department pursuant
10 to Section 115880. If the health officer finds any violation
11 of the standards prescribed by the department, he or she
12 shall restrict the use of, or close, the public beach or
13 portion thereof until the time as the standard violated is
14 complied with. If the person who made the complaint is
15 not satisfied with the action taken by the health officer,
16 he or she may report the violation to the department. The
17 department shall investigate the reported violation, and,
18 if it finds that the violation exists, it shall restrict the use
19 of or close the public beach or portion thereof until the
20 standard violated is complied with.
21 ~~(c) Report any violation of the standards established~~
22 ~~pursuant to Section 115880 to the Director of Parks and~~
23 ~~Recreation.~~
24 *(c) (1) Whenever a beach is posted, closed, or*
25 *otherwise restricted, the health officer shall inform the*
26 *Director of Parks and Recreation within 24 hours of the*
27 *posting, closure, or restriction.*
28 *(2) The Director of Parks and Recreation shall*
29 *establish a telephone hotline to inform the public of all*
30 *beaches currently closed, posted, or otherwise restricted.*
31 *The hotline shall be updated daily.*
32 (d) Report any violation of the standards established
33 pursuant to Section 115880 to the district attorney, or if
34 the violation occurred in a city and, pursuant to Section
35 41803.5 of the Government Code, the city attorney is
36 authorized to prosecute misdemeanors, to the city
37 attorney.
38   SEC. 3. Section 115915 of the Health and Safety Code
39 is amended to read:

(Continued)

Figure 4.4 (Continued)

AB 411

1   115915. Whenever any beach fails to meet the
2 bacteriological standards of Section 7958 of Title 17 of the
3 California Code of Regulations, *or any of the standards*
4 *established pursuant to subdivision (b) of Section 115880,*
5 the health officer, ~~after determining that the cause of the~~
6 ~~elevated bacteriological levels constitutes a public health~~
7 ~~hazard,~~ shall, at a minimum, post the beach with
8 conspicuous warning signs to inform the public of the
9 nature of the problem and the possibility of risk to public
10 health.
11   SEC. 4. No reimbursement is required by this act
12 pursuant to Section 6 of Article XIII B of the California
13 Constitution for certain costs that may be incurred by a
14 local agency or school district because in that regard this
15 act creates a new crime or infraction, eliminates a crime
16 or infraction, or changes the penalty for a crime or
17 infraction, within the meaning of Section 17556 of the
18 Government Code, or changes the definition of a crime
19 within the meaning of Section 6 of Article XIII B of the
20 California Constitution.
21   However, notwithstanding Section 17610 of the
22 Government Code, if the Commission on State Mandates
23 determines that this act contains other costs mandated by
24 the state, reimbursement to local agencies and school
25 districts for those costs shall be made pursuant to Part 7
26 (commencing with Section 17500) of Division 4 of Title
27 2 of the Government Code. If the statewide cost of the
28 claim for reimbursement does not exceed one million
29 dollars ($1,000,000), reimbursement shall be made from
30 the State Mandates Claims Fund.
31   Notwithstanding Section 17580 of the Government
32 Code, unless otherwise specified, the provisions of this act
33 shall become operative on the same date that the act
34 takes effect pursuant to the California Constitution.

Figure 4.5

AMENDED IN ASSEMBLY APRIL 9, 1997

CALIFORNIA LEGISLATURE—1997–98 REGULAR SESSION

ASSEMBLY BILL   No. 411

Introduced by Assembly ~~Member Wayne~~ *Members Wayne*
and Shelley
(Coauthors: Assembly Members Bowen and Lempert)
(Coauthors: Senators Alpert, Craven, Karnette, and
Watson)

February 20, 1997

An act to amend Sections 115880, 115885, and 115915 of the Health and Safety Code, relating to public beaches.

LEGISLATIVE COUNSEL'S DIGEST

AB 411, as amended, Wayne.   Beach sanitation: posting.

Existing law requires the State Department of Health Services to adopt regulations establishing minimum standards for the sanitation of public beaches. Violation of these regulations adopted by the department is a crime.

This bill would require these regulations to require the testing of all *public* beaches*, as defined,* for total coliform, fecal coliform, enterococci, and streptococci bacteria, *to* establish protective minimum standards for the location of monitoring sites and monitoring frequency, to require posting in clearly visible points along affected *public* beaches whenever state standards are violated, and to require that *public* beaches be tested for total coliform, fecal coliform, enterococci, and streptococci bacteria ~~and chemical~~ ~~pollutants including, but not limited to, PCBs, PAHs, and~~

(Continued)

Figure 4.5 (Continued)

AB 411

~~mercury~~ on a weekly basis from April 1 to October 31, inclusive, of each year if certain conditions are met. By changing the definition of a crime, this bill would impose a state-mandated local program.

This bill would require local health officers to be responsible for testing *public* beaches within ~~this~~ *their* jurisdiction, except state beaches, which the bill would require the department to test. By increasing the duties of local health officers, this bill would impose a state-mandated local program.

Existing law requires the local health officer to post a beach with conspicuous warning signs whenever the beach fails to meet certain bacteriological standards, and it is determined that the cause of the elevated levels constitutes a public health hazard.

This bill would, in addition, require the local health officer to post a beach with conspicuous warning signs, *as described,* whenever the beach fails to meet the standards developed by the department established pursuant to this bill.

Existing law requires each local health officer to notify the Director of Parks and Recreation when a *public* beach is in violation of the sanitation standards.

This bill would, instead, require the local health officer to notify the Director of Parks and Recreation within 24 hours of any *public* beach posting, closure, or restriction, and would require the Director of Parks and Recreation to establish a telephone hotline and update it daily to inform the public of beach postings, closures, and restrictions. By increasing the duties of the local health officer, this bill would impose a state-mandated local program.

The California Constitution requires the state to reimburse local agencies and school districts for certain costs mandated by the state. Statutory provisions establish procedures for making that reimbursement, including the creation of a State Mandates Claims Fund to pay the costs of mandates that do not exceed $1,000,000 statewide and other procedures for claims whose statewide costs exceed $1,000,000.

This bill would provide that with regard to certain mandates no reimbursement is required by this act for a specified reason.

AB 411

With regard to any other mandates, this bill would provide that, if the Commission on State Mandates determines that the bill contains costs so mandated by the state, reimbursement for those costs shall be made pursuant to the statutory provisions noted above.

Vote: majority. Appropriation: no. Fiscal committee: yes. State-mandated local program: yes.

The people of the State of California do enact as follows:

1   SECTION 1.   Section 115880 of the Health and Safety
2 Code is amended to read:
3   115880. (a) The department shall by regulation
4 establish minimum standards for the sanitation of public
5 beaches, including, but not limited to, the removal of
6 refuse, as it determines are reasonably necessary for the
7 protection of the public health and safety.
8   (b) The regulations shall, at a minimum, do all of the
9 following:
10   (1) Require the testing of all *public* beaches for total
11 coliform, fecal coliform, enterococci, and streptococci
12 bacteria.
13   (2) Establish protective minimum standards for the
14 location of monitoring sites and monitoring frequency.
15   (3) Require posting in clearly visible points along
16 affected *public* beaches whenever state standards are
17 violated.
18   (4) Require that *public* beaches be tested for total
19 coliform, fecal coliform, enterococci, and streptococci
20 bacteria ~~and chemical pollutants including, but not~~
21 ~~limited to, polychlorinated biphenyls (PCBs),~~
22 ~~polyaromatic hydrocarbons (PAHs), and mercury on a~~
23 ~~weekly basis~~ *on a weekly basis* from April 1 to October 31,
24 inclusive, of each year if all of the following apply:
25   (a) The beach is visited by more than 50,000 people
26 annually.
27   (b) The beach is located on an area adjacent to a storm
28 drain that flows in the summer.
29   (c) The local health officer shall be responsible for
30 testing all *public* beaches within his or her jurisdiction,

(Continued)

Figure 4.5 (Continued)

AB 411

1   except state beaches which shall be tested by the
2   department.
3   (d) Any city or county may adopt standards for the
4   sanitation of public beaches within its jurisdiction that are
5   stricter than the standards adopted by the state
6   department pursuant to this section.
7   *(e) For purposes of this section, "public beach" means*
8   *any public beach located within the coastal zone, as*
9   *defined in Section 30103 of the Public Resources Code.*
10   SEC. 2.   Section 115885 of the Health and Safety Code
11 is amended to read:
12   115885.   The health officer having jurisdiction over
13 the area in which a public beach is created shall:
14   (a) Inspect the public beach to determine whether the
15 standards established pursuant to Section 115880 are
16 being complied with. If the health officer finds any
17 violation of the standards, he or she shall restrict the use
18 of, or close, the public beach or portion thereof in which
19 the violation occurs until such time as the standard
20 violated is complied with.
21   (b) Investigate any complaint of a person of a violation
22 of any standard established by the department pursuant
23 to Section 115880. If the health officer finds any violation
24 of the standards prescribed by the department, he or she
25 shall restrict the use of, or close, the public beach or
26 portion thereof until the time as the standard violated is
27 complied with. If the person who made the complaint is
28 not satisfied with the action taken by the health officer,
29 he or she may report the violation to the department. The
30 department shall investigate the reported violation, and,
31 if it finds that the violation exists, it shall restrict the use
32 of or close the public beach or portion thereof until the
33 standard violated is complied with.
34   (c) (1) Whenever a beach is posted, closed, or
35 otherwise restricted, the health officer shall inform the
36 Director of Parks and Recreation within 24 hours of the
37 posting, closure, or restriction.
38   (2) The Director of Parks and Recreation shall
39 establish a telephone hotline to inform the public of all

AB 411

1   beaches currently closed, posted, or otherwise restricted.
2   The hotline shall be updated daily.
3   (d) Report any violation of the standards established
4   pursuant to Section 115880 to the district attorney, or if
5   the violation occurred in a city and, pursuant to Section
6   41803.5 of the Government Code, the city attorney is
7   authorized to prosecute misdemeanors, to the city
8   attorney.
9   SEC. 3.   Section 115915 of the Health and Safety Code
10 is amended to read:
11   115915. *(a)* Whenever any beach fails to meet the
12 bacteriological standards of Section 7958 of Title 17 of the
13 California Code of Regulations, or any of the standards
14 established pursuant to subdivision (b) of Section 115880,
15 the health officer shall, at a minimum, post the beach with
16 conspicuous warning signs to inform the public of the
17 nature of the problem and the possibility of risk to public
18 health.
19   *(b) A warning sign shall be visible from each legal*
20 *primary beach access point, as identified in the coastal*
21 *access inventory prepared and updated pursuant to*
22 *Section 30531 of the Public Resources Code, and any*
23 *additional access points identified by the health officer.*
24   SEC. 4.   No reimbursement is required by this act
25 pursuant to Section 6 of Article XIII B of the California
26 Constitution for certain costs that may be incurred by a
27 local agency or school district because in that regard this
28 act creates a new crime or infraction, eliminates a crime
29 or infraction, or changes the penalty for a crime or
30 infraction, within the meaning of Section 17556 of the
31 Government Code, or changes the definition of a crime
32 within the meaning of Section 6 of Article XIII B of the
33 California Constitution.
34   However, notwithstanding Section 17610 of the
35 Government Code, if the Commission on State Mandates
36 determines that this act contains other costs mandated by
37 the state, reimbursement to local agencies and school
38 districts for those costs shall be made pursuant to Part 7
39 (commencing with Section 17500) of Division 4 of Title
40 2 of the Government Code. If the statewide cost of the

(Continued)

Figure 4.5 (Continued)

AB 411

1   claim for reimbursement does not exceed one million
2   dollars ($1,000,000), reimbursement shall be made from
3   the State Mandates Claims Fund.
4   Notwithstanding Section 17580 of the Government
5   Code, unless otherwise specified, the provisions of this act
6   shall become operative on the same date that the act
7   takes effect pursuant to the California Constitution.

---

bill limitation, the Easter holidays, and other deadlines means that policy committees hear most bills during April. Because of the glut of bills that must be considered within a constrained period, bills often do not receive the attention they deserve.[25]

The 30-day "in-print rule" can be suspended by a three-quarters vote of the house of origin. It can be flouted by the "gut and amend" process. In that process the language of an existing bill is amended out (i.e., the bill is "gutted"), and entirely new language is amended into it. Presto, a de facto new bill has been created without being subject to the bill introduction deadline or the 30-day in-print rule. This will most typically happen during the closing days of a session.

The Art of the Committee

After AB 411 was introduced, it was referred to the Assembly Rules Committee, which acts as the traffic cop of the Assembly by determining which policy committee (i.e., a committee with jurisdiction over a certain area of law) will hear a bill. In most cases the decision is cut-and-dried based on the assigned written jurisdictions of each policy committee, but sometimes competing jurisdictions may make bill assignment both problematic and critical to the success of a bill. I authored a bill dealing with the allocation of funds from the cigarette tax. The question was whether it should be assigned to the Revenue and Taxation Committee (with jurisdiction over taxes) or the tobacco-friendly Governmental Organization

---

[25]Bills with a fiscal impact such as AB 411 must clear their policy committee by an early date so they can go before the Appropriations Committee. The limited number of bills without fiscal impact have their hearings deferred by a few weeks to give fiscal bills a chance to be heard in the Appropriations Committee.

Committee (that hears tobacco legislation), which would have killed the bill. I successfully argued to get it assigned to the former committee and got the bill through its initial policy committee stage. No matter where you live, the process in your legislature will require that your bill be referred to a committee for hearing.

AB 411 was double referred, first to the Environmental Safety and Toxic Materials Committee and then to the Local Government Committee. The first referral could not have been better, since I was the chair of that committee and chairs have a good record of getting their own bills passed by their committees.

This starts with the staff. Every committee has a staff of consultants, with the number of consultants varying by the workload of the committee. The committee consultants are hired by the chair of the committee. Each bill sent to a committee will be assigned to a committee consultant, whose job is to prepare an analysis of the bill.[26] The analysis is a public document and is available prior to the hearing on the bill.

Figure 4.6 is the policy committee analysis of AB 411, as the bill was introduced. As can be seen, the analysis includes a summary of the bill and of existing law, the fiscal effect (which will be more extensively set forth in the analysis by the Appropriations Committee), staff comments on the bill, and a list of supporters and opponents. When a bill is assigned to a committee, advocates should get in contact with the consultant charged with writing the analysis to register their positions. That way their views on the bill can be reflected in the comments and their support or opposition clearly indicated. Some advocates will take a position of "support if amended" or "oppose unless by amended" based on their proposed changes to the bill. By working with the consultant, advocates who desire changes in the bill may succeed in having the author offer amendments at the committee hearing to resolve their concerns and remove their opposition.

Before a bill can be heard in committee, it must be noticed in the Daily File at least 72 hours before it is to be heard. A bill may be noticed for hearing this way, and then its hearing may be postponed at the request either of the author or of the committee. If you are planning to testify on a bill, it is best to confirm that the hearing will take place as scheduled before you go to the state capitol.

Committee hearings are an opportunity for anyone to speak, within reasonable limits. As an advocate, this is when you can formally tell decision makers why the bill should be passed or defeated. When I chaired a committee, my practice was to give the bill's author unlimited time to present the bill. Frequently authors would use part of this time to offer amendments, which

---

[26]The minority party will have a caucus consultant prepare an analysis of these bills for consideration by members of the minority party on the committee. That is not a public document, but frequently members of the minority party will share that analysis with members of the majority party.

Figure 4.6

```
BILL ANALYSIS
                                                          AB 411
                                                          Page 1


Date of Hearing: April 1, 1997

            ASSEMBLY COMMITTEE ON ENVIRONMENTAL SAFETY AND
                         TOXIC MATERIALS
                       Howard Wayne, Chair


          AB 411 (Wayne) - As Introduced: February 20, 1997


   SUBJECT   :   Beach safety and testing.


   SUMMARY   :   Establishes uniform requirements for regular state and
local monitoring of coastal waters and for informing the public when
the waters pose a health hazard.  Specifically,  this bill  :


1) Requires comprehensive statewide monitoring of beaches for total
coliform, fecal coliform, enterococci and streptococci bacteria.

2) Requires the Department of Health Services (DHS) to set minimum
standards for the location of monitoring sites and frequency of
monitoring.

3) At beaches visited by more than 50,000 people annually and located
adjacent to a storm drain that flows in the summer, requires weekly
testing from April 1st to October 31st for bacterial and chemical
pollutants.

4) Mandates posting of health warnings at visible points along the
beach whenever state health standards are exceeded.

5) Establishes a telephone hotline to inform the public of all
beaches posted or restricted.


   EXISTING LAW   :


1) Requires the posting and closing of beaches when standards set by
the Department of Health Services (DHS) are exceeded and requires the
reporting of closings and advisories to the state.
2) Contains only one regulatory standard set by DHS, for total
coliform bacteria. This standard was set in the 1940's and is based
on aesthetic considerations, not health data. According to the U.S.
Environmental Protection Agency, total coliform is an inadequate
indicator of swimming-associated gastrointestinal illness.
3) The California Ocean Plan, developed by the State Water Resources
Control Board (SWRCB) to comply with the state's water quality protec-
tion law (Porter-Cologne), sets water quality objectives for total
coliform, fecal coliform and enterococcus. These standards are enforced
```

```
                                                        AB  411
                                                        Page  2


in cases where point source dischargers are the source of bacterial
contaminants but not where non-point source surface runoff enters
beaches and ocean waters.
   4) Individual counties have established their own monitoring pro-
grams  and  standards  and  procedures  vary  widely  throughout  the
state. Eight coastal counties have no regular beach monitoring programs
(1995 data).


   FISCAL EFFECT  : Unknown costs to the Department of Health Services
to develop regulations; unknown costs to state and local entities for
monitoring and posting.
```

were accepted with the consent of the committee.[27] I would then allow the proponents to make two presentations of up to five minutes each, and all others in support of the bill to state their name and organization and to register support. The process would be repeated for the opponents. Then members of the committee would post questions as they sought fit. This process, with some variations, is used by most committees.

After testimony was completed, we would go to a vote. An affirmative vote of a majority of the members of the committee was required to pass a bill; with this committee that would mean five of the eight members would have to vote yes to pass a bill. If a bill lacked a majority after the first roll call, but some members were missing and unable to vote, the bill would be placed "on call." We would then go to the next bill, but as missing members appeared the "call" could be lifted, and those members were allowed to vote on that bill. Bills that failed to have the requisite five votes by the conclusion of the hearing would be defeated.[28]

When AB 411 came before the Environmental Safety Committee for consideration, I temporarily surrendered my gavel to the vice chair and took the lectern before the committee. After presenting the bill, I had representatives of groups in support of the bill testify. No one spoke in opposition to the bill, there were minimal questions from the members of the committee, and the

---

[27]Technically the amendments are only recommended and not adopted by the committee. Adoption of amendment is by the full house when the bill is returned following the committee action. The approval of amendments is a pro forma event on the floor.

[28]Defeated bills were routinely granted reconsideration to give them new life, but that was no assurance the bill would be passed. At times it just saved face for the author not to have a bill defeated in committee.

bill passed the committee without a negative vote. See Figure 4.7. If only
things could have remained so easy!

Because the bill required the water testing to be conducted by counties, the
bill also had to be heard by the Local Government Committee. Not only was
I not a member of this committee, but in the two weeks after the Environmental
Safety Committee hearing the Republicans had decided to oppose the bill.
Even though I made the same presentation as I had made to my committee,
and brought the original proponent from San Diego to testify, the bill did not
fare as well. While all Democrats voted for it, every Republican, except one
who did not vote, opposed it. This was not a good sign.

Because it would cost money to conduct the testing, the bill was referred
to the Appropriations Committee. The Appropriations Committee is a "fiscal" committee, and theoretically is supposed to consider only the fiscal
impact of a bill. In fact it is a superpolicy committee that can defeat legislation because of policy reasons. At times this veto is exercised by the leadership through the committee.

Figure 4.7

```
VOTES - ROLL CALL
MEASURE:       AB 411
AUTHOR: Wayne
TOPIC:  Beach sanitation:  posting.
DATE:   04/01/1997
LOCATION:   ASM. E.S. & T.M.
MOTION: Do pass and be re-referred to the Committee on
Local Government.
          (AYES    7. NOES    0.)   (PASS)



          AYES
          ****

Wayne    Cunneen  Bowen     Ducheny
Keeley   Knox     Richter



          NOES
          ****



          ABSENT, ABSTAINING, OR NOT VOTING
          * * * * * * * * * * * * * * * * * * * * * * * * * * * * * * *


Baldwin
```

The Appropriations Committee voted to put AB 411 on the "Suspense File" because the potential cost of the bill exceeded the dollar threshold limit established by the committee. Although the Appropriations Committee later voted to pass the bill—again by a split, partisan vote—the effect of placing AB 411 on suspense was to delay consideration of the bill by the full Assembly until the deadline week for bills to pass their house of origin or become two-year bills. In fact many bills are placed in that posture because the Appropriations Committee does not take up its Suspense File until very late.

Presenting the Bill to the Assembly

Once the Appropriations Committee approved AB 411, it was returned to the Assembly and placed on the "Third Reading" File for consideration by the house. The caucus of each party prepared a floor analysis of the bill, which briefly discussed the bill's provisions and merits, showed the votes in each committee, and made a recommendation to their partisans on how to vote. The text of the bill was in a binder provided to each member, and the analysis of each committee that heard AB 411 was available on a computer on each member's desk.

The first thing an Assembly Member should do, when the Assembly goes into session, is open the desk, remove the key inside it, and "key in" to activate the electronic voting device. The single most important thing the public gives a legislator by electing him or her is this vote. On the member's desk are two buttons, a green one to vote yes and a red one to vote no. When a vote is being taken, members push one of these buttons, and their votes are reflected on a pair of tabulator boards at the front of the chamber. The tabulator boards show the total votes cast each way, the vote of each member, and the number of the bill being voted upon. Most votes require a majority of the house—41 votes in favor.[29] Should a measure fall short, the author can place a "call" on the bill, but only if the presiding officer has not announced the results of the vote. While the bill is on call, the member tries to round up the necessary votes as other business continues, and when the member believes the necessary votes have been obtained, the member will ask that the "call be lifted." Voting on the measure will be reinstated. By practice a proponent can only place two calls on a bill. Opponents can also place a call on a bill to see if they can peel off enough votes to defeat the bill. Once a bill has been passed or defeated, members are free to add their votes for or against the bill if they had not voted, or even to change

---

[29]However, a constitutional amendment, bond measure, or tax increase requires a two-thirds vote of the house. Some procedural measures require only a majority of those voting. In about a third of the states, a bill can be passed by a majority of those "present and voting" rather than a vote threshold of a majority of the membership.

their votes, but only if the changes or additions do not alter the passage or defeat of the measure.[30]

When my bill came up on the Third Reading File, I was recognized by the presiding officer and raised the microphone at my desk. I had five minutes to make my presentation. Other members could then seek recognition and either speak for five minutes or use part of their time to pose questions to me. Once all members who desired to speak had the opportunity to do so, or once debate was closed by a majority vote, I had the right to speak last. The "roll" was opened, people pushed their green or red buttons, and at the final tally AB 411 passed the Assembly by a vote of 53 (all but one of the Democrats, plus 12 Republicans) to 26 (only Republicans).

The tabulator boards told me everything I needed to know. I could get this bill through the legislature, but I was looking at a veto from the Republican governor. The likelihood of a veto override, which takes a two-thirds vote, was nonexistent. There has not been a successful override of a governor's veto since the late 1970s.

Negotiations: A Key to Legislative Success

At this point I knew that if I was going to have anything more than a vetoed bill I was going to have to negotiate some amendments to my bill.[31] AB 411 is an example where good fortune and socializing assisted the legislative process by facilitating negotiations.

Early in the session the Natural Resources Committee, of which I was a member, heard a deficiency bill. Because of a greater number of forest fires than anticipated, the Department of Forestry had overspent its budget and needed a supplementary appropriation to pay its bills. This was not the first time this had happened, and I quizzed the department's representatives about its repeated lowballing of appropriation requests. The Governor's legislative aide for environmental issues was in the audience and heard the dialogue.

A few weeks later I was at a conference away from Sacramento where environmental issues were to be discussed, and as luck would have it I was seated across from that aide during dinner. She said she had been impressed with my questioning at the Natural Resources Committee, and we developed a rapport over the meal.

---

[30]In the Senate, in contrast, votes are cast by an oral roll call. Once a bill has been passed or defeated, members who failed to vote cannot "add on." Thus it frequently appears that Senators, more often than Assembly Members, fail to vote because only the latter can add on.

[31]The careful reader will have noted I had already amended my bill following the Environmental Safety Committee hearing to narrow the scope of the bill to protecting the public health, and also to add coauthors to the bill (see Figure 4.5). The substantive changes were based on comments about the bill and the cost of testing. The changes did not alleviate the Republican concerns at the Local Government Committee.

She turned out to be the member of the Governor's staff tasked to track AB 411. After I saw the partisan split, I talked with her and quickly ascertained the Governor was not simply determined to veto the bill, but could sign it with changes.

During the legislative break following the adoption of the budget,[32] we put together a conference call with the two of us, plus senior staff at the Department of Health Services and representatives of the environmental community supporting the bill. As we talked, the department representatives began to say they saw no reason for the bill, while some environmental representatives almost dared the Governor to veto it. I could see the bill's whole life flashing in front of it and quickly terminated the conference call.

When the Governor's aide and I got back on the telephone, it was just the two of us. She explained that the administration's concerns were (1) what contaminants would be included in the testing protocol and (2) how to pay for the testing. My goal was to establish a testing program. I'm not a scientist and could not definitely say what tests were required to accurately determine whether the water was unsafe for human contact. We agreed to have staffs of the Department of Health Services and of the Environmental Safety Committee hash out the language of how standards would be established. I offered to make the requirement for testing contingent on a legislative appropriation. Both of us supported the concept of testing and knew what we needed to achieve from the bill. The negotiation was a success.

Although the specifics I described above might seem like an unusual set of circumstances, negotiation is essential when a bill has some controversy. Figuring out what the stakeholders need, and what is vital to you, is critically important to resolving the conflict and moving forward.

The Path Through the Senate

In the days before one person/one vote, the Assembly and the Senate were natural rivals since they represented different constituencies. The Assembly represented population and was heavily weighted toward Southern California, while the Senate represented counties and was weighted toward the "cow counties" of the North. Since the 1967–1968 Session both houses have been based on population, and there is nearly an identical ratio of party membership in each house.[33] Still the rivalry remains. Senators usually have more

---

[32]The legislative schedule provides for a break following the adoption of the budget, but more often than not the budget is late. When that happens, the legislature keeps meeting until a budget is adopted. Consequently it is risky to schedule a vacation during the scheduled break because the break might not happen. One legislator planned a trip to Hawaii during what was to be the legislative break. The budget did not pass on time, and, unwilling to lose her deposit, she went anyway. She was defeated for reelection the following November.

[33]Following the 2004 election the Assembly was composed of 48 Democrats and 32 Republicans, while the Senate had 25 Democrats and 15 Republicans.

legislative experience than members of the Assembly and sometimes treat them as rank amateurs.[34]

This was particularly so in 1997 because term limits had not completely affected the Senate. Instead, it was composed of some Senators who had served for many years and had not reached term limits, and former Assembly Members, some of whom had extensive legislative experience and had recently been forced out of the Assembly by term limits. In contrast, few in the Assembly had served more than two terms, and most of us had served 30 months or less.[35]

The process in the Senate is similar to that in the Assembly. Bills passed by the Assembly are referred to the Senate Rules Committee, which assigns them to the appropriate policy committee. AB 411 was assigned to the Senate Health Committee. The hearing was prior to the legislative break, and the bill passed on a vote of 5 to 2, with both negative votes coming from Republicans.

Because AB 411 was a fiscal bill, it had to be heard by the Senate Appropriations Committee. Due to the need to negotiate acceptable language, I asked that the Appropriations Committee cancel its scheduled meeting on the bill. For the next two months seemingly nothing happened—at least in public—with the bill. The critical negotiations on substance and language took place during that time.

The language of the amendments was worked out by staff and submitted to the Legislative Counsel for formal drafting in its approved format. After the legislature reconvened, the Appropriations Committee placed AB 411 on the Suspense Calendar. On September 4, I submitted the amendments to the committee, and the hearing was pro forma. The bill passed unanimously and was on its way to the Senate floor.

As in the Assembly, a member of the body must formally present a bill for debate. Since this was an Assembly bill and I was not a member of the Senate, I had to find a Senate floor manager, colloquially called a "jockey," to act for me. I chose Bruce McPherson, a highly respected moderate Republican who, like me, represented a coastal district. The bill was approved 28-7, with the no votes primarily coming from Republicans who were significantly to the right of the administration.

The Final Steps

Even though AB 411 had passed both houses, it had passed the Senate with different language than it had passed the Assembly. That meant the bill had to be returned to the Assembly for concurrence.

---

[34]The Latin phrase at the front of the Senate Chamber is translated by old-school members as "It is the duty of the Senate to protect the public from the Assembly."

[35]There were a few members in the Assembly with greater experience who had served prior to the passage of term limits, since that prior service did not count against the limit.

A bill may not be amended when it is returned to the house of origin for concurrence.[36] It is a straight up or down vote on the bill as presented. If the house of origin does not concur in the bill, the bill is not necessarily dead. Instead, a conference committee can be appointed, composed of three members from each house: two members who voted on the prevailing side and one who voted on the losing side. If a conference committee reaches agreement on a bill, which requires an affirmative vote by two of the appointed members from each house (that is, two members of the Assembly and two Senators appointed to the conference committee), the conference report is returned to both houses for adoption.

AB 411 did not have to go the conference committee route. As with the initial presentation to the Assembly, the bill had to come up on file. Then I was recognized and had five minutes to speak, and then others could also speak or question me. However, the caucuses of the two parties recommended support for the bill, so there was little drama. With Republican buy-in the Assembly concurred by a vote of 75 to 2. And I had gotten the bill acted upon before that last frantic night of the session.[37]

The bill still had to go to the Governor. The best practice is to write a letter to the Governor requesting his signature. It is a chance to make the case for the bill. While I was pretty sure who would be creating the Governor's "packet" for AB 411, with other bills I was never sure whether the Governor's staff person putting together packets would be equally knowledgeable of the bills and was well disposed toward them. It always made sense to make one more pitch, and as an advocate you may also wish to ask the Governor to sign your bill once it has passed the legislature.

Because AB 411, like most bills, had passed late in the session, the Governor had a month to decide what to do with it. The Governor has three options: He can sign the bill; he can veto the bill, which requires him to deliver the veto message to the clerk of the house of origin by the deadline; or he can do nothing, and the bill will become law without his signature. One year Governor Wilson, going right up to the deadline to act, decided to veto a number of bills. He wrote his veto messages, and the staff made copies of the veto messages. However, they left several veto messages on the copying machine and did not get them to the clerk within the

---

[36]If a bill has been dramatically changed in the other house, such as when it has been gutted and amended, it is referred to the appropriate policy committee in the house of origin for a hearing. The bill cannot be amended in committee and faces an up or down vote there.

[37]It is a good idea to get your bill resolved before that night, and it is not only to avoid stress. If your bill fails, you will still have the opportunity to seek reconsideration or, if on concurrence, to seek to have a conference committee. At the end of the 1999–2000 Session we voted on bills until midnight of the last day, because bills passed after that hour were constitutionally suspect. Some bills died on the file because we ran out of time, including a controversial transportation measure that was on call when the clock struck 12.

required time. The bills were treated as becoming law without the Governor's signature.

After adjournment my wife and I went on vacation to Vermont. I made arrangements with my legislative chief to call my home number and leave messages on the voice mail as the Governor acted on my bills. This was before cell phones were common. I called regularly and was pleased with the progress of my bills, but had no word on AB 411.

Toward the end of our trip we were in Bennington. It's a wonderful place, but they roll up the sidewalks shortly after 5 at night. We had dinner in one of the best restaurants in town, but I just don't remember the name of that pizza parlor. When we got back to our room, I called the voice mail number. The message from my legislative chief told me to go celebrate because the Governor had signed AB 411.[38] There was nothing else to do in Bennington but to share a candy bar we bought from the hotel vending machine.

AB 411 went on to appear as part of the Health and Safety Code (see Figure 4.8), where it amended three sections of that code. The regulations required to implement it appear in the California Code of Regulations.

Some Thoughts on Helping Your Bill Become Law

While the purpose of this chapter is to walk you through the legislature to help you understand the process, I want to give you a few pointers on how you can help your bill become law. In a sense, this section is a prelude to much of the material that Pat will cover in the "10 steps" chapters that follow.

Assuming you have been successful in getting your bill introduced, you need to establish a working relationship with the legislator who is carrying your bill and, more particularly, with his or her staff member who will have responsibility for the bill. In 1997, in addition to AB 411, I had 14 other bills, served on five committees (including chairing one of them), and had the usual floor and community responsibilities of any other member. My staff made it possible to do all of these things, and my practice was to assign each of my bills to a particular staff member. This is fairly standard practice and means that as an advocate you will have far more interaction with staff than with the legislator.

You need to coordinate with that staff member. As matters occur that will affect the bill (e.g., did a lot of people suddenly get sick after swimming in coastal waters?), or if you are planning a media event, you need to advise the staff member. Don't make the author look bad by staging a rally on the Capitol steps and forgetting to invite the legislator carrying the bill. The staff

---

[38]Actually, this was not the end of it. I had to seek appropriations in the budget to pay for the scientific studies to establish standards for beach water testing and to pay for the testing. See Chapter 12 for the further adventures of AB 411.

Figure 4.8

Assembly Bill No. 411

CHAPTER 765

An act to amend Sections 115880, 115885, and 115915 of the Health and Safety Code, relating to public beaches.

[Approved by Governor October 7, 1997. Filed
with Secretary of State October 8, 1997.]

LEGISLATIVE COUNSEL'S DIGEST

AB 411, Wayne.   Beach sanitation: posting.

Existing law requires the State Department of Health Services to adopt regulations establishing minimum standards for the sanitation of public beaches. Violation of these regulations adopted by the department is a crime.

This bill would require these regulations to require the testing of the waters adjacent to all public beaches, as defined, for microbiological contaminations, including, but not limited to, total coliform, fecal coliform, and enterococci bacteria, to establish protocols for determining the location of monitoring sites and monitoring frequency based on risks to public health, and for public notification of health hazards, including, but not limited to, the posting, closing, and reopening of public beaches, and to require that public beaches, with certain exceptions, be tested for microbiological contaminations, including, but not limited to, total coliform, fecal coliform, and enterococci bacteria on a weekly basis from April 1 to October 31, inclusive, of each year if certain conditions are met. By changing the definition of a crime, this bill would impose a state-mandated local program.

This bill would, subject to appropriation of sufficient funds, require local health officers to be responsible for testing waters adjacent to public beaches within their jurisdiction. This bill would require the local health officer to immediately test the waters adjacent to a public beach and to take related action in the event of a known untreated sewage release, and in the event of an untreated sewage release that is known to have reached recreational waters adjacent to a public beach, would require the local health officer to immediately close those waters until it has been determined by the local health officer that the waters are in compliance with the standards. By increasing the duties of local health officers, this bill would impose a state-mandated local program.

Existing law requires the health officer having jurisdiction of the area in which a public beach is created to close, or restrict the use of, the public beach if he or she finds any violation of the standards.

(Continued)

Figure 4.8 (Continued)

Ch. 765

This bill would, instead, authorize the health officer to close, or restrict the use of, the public beach if he or she finds that a violation exists.

Existing law requires the department, upon investigation of a complaint, to close, or restrict the use of, any public beach if it finds that a violation exists.

This bill would, instead, authorize the department to close, or restrict the use of, a public beach if it finds that a violation exists.

Existing law requires the local health officer to post a beach with conspicuous warning signs whenever the beach fails to meet certain bacteriological standards, and it is determined that the cause of the elevated levels constitutes a public health hazard.

This bill would, in addition, require the local health officer to post a beach with conspicuous warning signs, as described, whenever the beach fails to meet the standards developed by the department established pursuant to this bill.

Existing law requires each local health officer to notify the Director of Parks and Recreation when a public beach is in violation of the sanitation standards.

This bill would, instead, require the local health officer to notify the agency responsible for the operation and maintenance of the public beach within 24 hours of any public beach posting, closure, or restriction, and would, subject to appropriation, require the agency responsible for the operation and maintenance of the public beach to establish a telephone hotline and update it as needed to convey changes in public health risks, to inform the public of beach postings, closures, and restrictions. By increasing the duties of the local health officer, this bill would impose a state-mandated local program.

This bill would make any duty imposed upon a local public officer or agency pursuant to these provisions mandatory only during a fiscal year in which the Legislature has appropriated sufficient funds, as determined by the State Director of Health Services, in the annual Budget Act or otherwise for local agencies to cover the costs to those agencies associated with the performance of those duties, and would require the director to annually, within 15 days after enactment of the Budget Act, file a written statement with the Secretary of the Senate and with the Chief Clerk of the Assembly memorializing whether sufficient funds have been appropriated.

The California Constitution requires the state to reimburse local agencies and school districts for certain costs mandated by the state. Statutory provisions establish procedures for making that reimbursement, including the creation of a State Mandates Claims Fund to pay the costs of mandates that do not exceed $1,000,000 statewide and other procedures for claims whose statewide costs exceed $1,000,000.

This bill would provide that for certain mandates, no reimbursement is required by this act for a specified reason. With

Ch. 765

regard to other mandates, this bill would provide that no reimbursement shall be made from the State Mandates Claims Fund for costs mandated by the state pursuant to this act, but would recognize that local agencies and school districts may pursue any available remedies to seek reimbursement for these costs.

The people of the State of California do enact as follows:

SECTION 1. Section 115880 of the Health and Safety Code is amended to read:

115880. (a) The department shall by regulation, in consultation with local health officers and the public, establish minimum standards for the sanitation of public beaches, including, but not limited to, the removal of refuse, as it determines are reasonably necessary for the protection of the public health and safety.

(b) Prior to final adoption by the department, the regulations and standards required by this section shall undergo an external comprehensive review process similar to the process set forth in Section 57004 of the Health and Safety Code.

(c) The regulations shall, at a minimum, do all of the following, by December 31, 1998:

(1) Require the testing of the waters adjacent to all public beaches for microbiological contaminants, including, but not limited to, total coliform, fecal coliform, and enterococci bacteria. The department may require the testing of waters adjacent to all public beaches for microbiological indicators other than those set forth in this paragraph, or a subset of those set forth in this paragraph, if the department affirmatively establishes, based on the best available scientific studies and the weight of the evidence, that the alternative indicators are as protective of the public health.

(2) Establish protective minimum standards for total coliform, fecal coliform, and enterococci bacteria, or for other microbiological indicators that the department determines are appropriate for testing pursuant to paragraph (1).

(3) Establish protocols for all of the following:

(A) Determining monitoring site locations and monitoring frequency based on risks to public health.

(B) Making decisions regarding public notification of health hazards, including, but not limited to, the posting, closing, and reopening of public beaches.

(4) Require that the waters adjacent to public beaches be tested for total coliform, fecal coliform, and enterococci bacteria, or for other microbiological indicators that the department determines are appropriate for testing pursuant to paragraph (1). Except as set forth in paragraph (5), testing shall be conducted on at least a weekly basis, from April 1 to October 31, inclusive, of each year, beginning in 1999, if all of the following apply:

(Continued)

Figure 4.8 (Continued)

Ch. 765

(A) The beach is visited by more than 50,000 people annually.

(B) The beach is located on an area adjacent to a storm drain that flows in the summer.

(5) The monitoring frequency and locations established pursuant to this subdivision and related regulations may only be reduced or altered after the testing required pursuant to paragraph (4) reveals levels of microbiological contaminants that do not exceed for a period of two years the minimum protective standards established pursuant to paragraph (2).

(d) The local health officer shall be responsible for testing the waters adjacent to, and coordinating the testing of, all public beaches within his or her jurisdiction.

(e) The local health officer may meet the testing requirements of this section by utilizing test results from other agencies conducting microbiological contamination testing of the waters under his or her jurisdiction.

(f) Any city or county may adopt standards for the sanitation of public beaches within its jurisdiction that are stricter than the standards adopted by the state department pursuant to this section.

(g) For purposes of this section, "public beach" means any public beach located within the coastal zone, as defined in Section 30103 of the Public Resources Code.

(h) Any duty imposed upon a local public officer or agency pursuant to this section shall be mandatory only during a fiscal year in which the Legislature has appropriated sufficient funds, as determined by the State Director of Health Services, in the annual Budget Act or otherwise for local agencies to cover the costs to those agencies associated with the performance of these duties. The State Director of Health Services shall annually, within 15 days after enactment of the Budget Act, file a written statement with the Secretary of the Senate and with the Chief Clerk of the Assembly memorializing whether sufficient funds have been appropriated.

SEC. 2. Section 115885 of the Health and Safety Code is amended to read:

115885. The health officer having jurisdiction over the area in which a public beach is created shall:

(a) Inspect the public beach to determine whether the standards established pursuant to Section 115880 are being complied with. If the health officer finds any violation of the standards, he or she may restrict the use of, or close, the public beach or portion thereof in which the violation occurs until the standard is complied with.

(b) Investigate any complaint of a person of a violation of any standard established by the department pursuant to Section 115880. If the health officer finds any violation of the standards prescribed by the department, he or she may restrict the use of, or close, the public beach or portion thereof until the standard is complied with. If the person who made the complaint is not satisfied with the action taken

Ch. 765

by the health officer, he or she may report the violation to the department. The department shall investigate the reported violation, and, if it finds that the violation exists, it may restrict the use of or close the public beach or portion thereof until the standard violated is complied with.

(c) (1) Whenever a beach is posted, closed, or otherwise restricted in accordance with Section 115915, the health officer shall inform the agency responsible for the operation and maintenance of the public beach within 24 hours of the posting, closure, or restriction.

(2) The health officer shall establish a telephone hotline to inform the public of all beaches currently closed, posted, or otherwise restricted. The hotline shall be updated as needed in order to convey changes in public health risks.

(d) Report any violation of the standards established pursuant to Section 115880 to the district attorney, or if the violation occurred in a city and, pursuant to Section 41803.5 of the Government Code, the city attorney is authorized to prosecute misdemeanors, to the city attorney.

(e) In the event of a known untreated sewage release, the local health officer shall immediately test the waters adjacent to the public beach and to take action pursuant to regulations established under Section 115880.

(f) Notwithstanding any other provision of law, in the event of an untreated sewage release that is known to have reached recreational waters adjacent to a public beach, the local health officer shall immediately close those waters until it has been determined by the local health officer that the waters are in compliance with the standards established pursuant to Section 115880.

(g) Any duty imposed upon a local public officer or agency pursuant to this section shall be mandatory only during a fiscal year in which the Legislature has appropriated sufficient funds, as determined by the State Director of Health Services, in the annual Budget Act or otherwise for local agencies to cover the costs to those agencies associated with the performance of these duties. The State Director of Health Services shall annually, within 15 days after enactment of the Budget Act, file a written statement with the Secretary of the Senate and with the Chief Clerk of the Assembly memorializing whether sufficient funds have been appropriated.

SEC. 3. Section 115915 of the Health and Safety Code is amended to read:

115915. (a) Whenever any beach fails to meet the bacteriological standards established pursuant to subdivision (b) of Section 115880, the health officer shall, at a minimum, post the beach with conspicuous warning signs to inform the public of the nature of the problem and the possibility of risk to public health.

(b) A warning sign shall be visible from each legal primary beach access point, as identified in the coastal access inventory prepared

Figure 4.8 (Continued)

Ch. 765

and updated pursuant to Section 30531 of the Public Resources Code, and any additional access points identified by the health officer.

(c) Any duty imposed upon a local public officer or agency pursuant to this section shall be mandatory only during a fiscal year in which the Legislature has appropriated sufficient funds, as determined by the State Director of Health Services, in the annual Budget Act or otherwise for local agencies to cover the costs to those agencies associated with the performance of these duties. The State Director of Health Services shall annually, within 15 days after enactment of the Budget Act, file a written statement with the Secretary of the Senate and with the Chief Clerk of the Assembly memorializing whether sufficient funds have been appropriated.

SEC. 4. No reimbursement is required by this act pursuant to Section 6 of Article XIII B of the California Constitution for certain costs that may be incurred by a local agency or school district because this act creates a new crime or infraction, eliminates a crime or infraction, or changes the penalty for a crime or infraction, within the meaning of Section 17556 of the Government Code, or changes the definition of a crime within the meaning of Section 6 of Article XIII B of the California Constitution.

Moreover, as to other costs, no reimbursement shall be made from the State Mandates Claims Fund pursuant to Part 7 (commencing with Section 17500) of Division 4 of Title 2 of the Government Code for costs mandated by the state pursuant to this act. It is recognized, however, that a local agency or school district may pursue any remedies to obtain reimbursement available to it under Part 7 (commencing with Section 17500) and any other provisions of law.

Also, notwithstanding Section 17580 of the Government Code, unless otherwise specified, the provisions of this act shall become operative on the same date that the act takes effect pursuant to the California Constitution.

person will let you know when hearings are planned and when amendments are being considered.

Sometimes an organization, or more likely an agency, will be designated as the "sponsor" of a bill. Sponsors are stakeholders and often negotiate language. However, the bill is under the control of the legislator carrying it. If you are unhappy with how your sponsored bill is amended, the most you can do is withdraw your sponsorship (or even go to a position of oppose, but that can be dangerous).

Let me add a few words about lobbyists. They have an undeservedly bad reputation. Their function in the legislature is similar to the function of an attorney in the legal system—to help their clients navigate the process.

Unlike lawyers, they are required to publicly disclose their clients and how much their clients pay them. The best lobbyists are those who have experience in the Capitol building—former staff members and legislators—because they know the system from the inside, usually have detailed substantive knowledge and institutional memory, and have relationships with legislators.

There is no requirement or right to have a lobbyist.[39] The advantage of employing a lobbyist is to have someone on the scene who knows the ropes and who can stay on top of bills. While some lobbyists are in-house for organizations, such as the California Medical Association, contract lobbyists represent multiple clients. If you retain a lobbyist, be sure to find out who in the lobbyist's office will have responsibility for your bill (it may not be the one who has the reputation) and whether the firm will provide you with enough of its time to do an adequate job. A number of nonprofits have lobbyists either in-house or under contract.

You need to track your bill when it is going through the legislature, particularly when it is a bill you are opposing and no legislator has taken a lead position of opposing it. This can be done over the Internet, and my favorite website for this purpose is one maintained by the Legislative Counsel, www.leginfo.ca.gov. The site will contain each of the iterations of the bill, each committee analysis, and the status and history of the bill.

Every day of session each house produces a Daily File. It will list committee agendas and lists the order that bills will be considered on the floor. A second legislative publication is the Daily Journal, which is the official diary of the legislature. Finally, each house produces a History, which lists the bills introduced in the session and summarizes all actions taken on each bill. All three publications are obtainable through the Bill Room at the Capitol, and usually can be found at your county law library.

In communicating with legislators whom you to hope to influence on the bill, you must consider the message, the means of communication, and the audience. If the message is substantive and particularly if it is technical, such as a biologist's specialized information about water pollution, that is a person who is helpful to bring to the attention of any legislator you want to influence. On the other hand, if the purpose of the message is to show community support, only a legislator's constituents will carry weight with that legislator. The fact that someone in Yuba City (located in rural Northern California) supports a bill doesn't mean much to a legislator from La Mesa (a city located in Southern California). However, a delegation of La Mesans will at least be listened to by that legislator (or a staff member). It is even better if one or more members of that delegation already have some type of personal relationship with that legislator.

---

[39]Similarly, the right to a lawyer is only the right to retain one, and parties (other than corporations) can always represent themselves. Only indigents in criminal cases have the right to have an attorney provided to them.

How to communicate with a legislator? A personal meeting can be arranged in the Capitol; however, a legislator's time there is extremely tight, and you may have to talk with a staff member instead. It is better, and less expensive, to try to meet with the legislator in the district. Typically legislators will be available on Fridays when the legislature is in session, and most working days during recess. Each legislator maintains an office in the district he or she represents.

At that meeting you should have a "fact sheet" of no more than two pages that starts off with the number and author of the bill (e.g., AB 411 [Wayne]), explains the problem, sets forth what the bill does (my personal preference is to include a copy of the bill), tells how the bill solves the problem, and has a list of supporters. If there are arguments against the bill, you should rebut them. There should be a contact person listed, with a phone number, physical address, and e-mail address. Leave a lot of white space on the fact sheet so the legislator can take notes in response to questions. Pat will discuss fact sheets in greater detail in the next chapter.

Start your presentation from the beginning, not in the middle. You may have been living this matter for the past five years, but the legislator may never have given it a thought before or have any familiarity with the field. An approach I find helpful is Need, Plan, and Advantage, which some readers may recognize from formal debate. In the Need step you explain the problem. Then, you set out your proposal, the Plan, to address the Need. Finally, in the Advantage step, you set out how the plan solves the problem and may even have other advantages such as saving money.

Be prepared to answer questions, or to state you will get back to the legislator (or a designated staff member) with the answers. The legislator knows you are there as an advocate and you are presenting the case for the bill, but don't ever misrepresent the facts. If I knew an advocate lied, that person might as well never try to influence me again; that person would have no credibility.

Don't expect the legislator to commit during this first visit. It is enough to get the legislator thinking along the lines of your bill, and the bill may change several times before the legislator sees it, particularly if that legislator is not on the policy committee that hears the bill or is not a member of the house where the bill originated. After the meeting you should send a thank-you note—consider it another chance to put in a plug for your message. If you have promised to provide more information, be sure to do so.

If a visit is not possible, a personal letter from a constituent is the next best thing. The letter should be in the writer's own words and not just the constituent affixing a signature to a prewritten letter.[40] The letter should clearly

---

[40]On one occasion an advocacy group sent preprinted postcards to voters in my district that asked them to sign the postcard and mail it to me. I had my office write a standard response to each sender, several of whom wrote back to say they had no recollection of signing the postcard. I remembered that when I received other generic communications.

identify the relevant bill and whether the letter is in support, opposition, or some other position such as "support if amended."

E-mails are more acceptable now, but only from the legislator's constituents. The least effective means are petitions and any type of scripted letter because they show the least individual commitment. Don't use threats such as "If you don't support this bill, I'll never vote for you!" Whenever I got such a letter, I knew that even if I supported the writer's position on this bill I'd alienate that person some other way.

Consider whom you are approaching. The first targets are legislators who serve on committees that will hear the bill. A meeting with a legislator who will not see the bill for many months may not be the best use of your time.

If you are advocating an environmental bill, it's all right to approach a legislator with a 100% pro-environment voting record since it will show support for a position that legislator is likely to take. That legislator may decide to coauthor the bill and speak in support of it on the floor or in committee. However, if you are pushing a gun control bill, you should shy away from a pro-NRA legislator. Not only won't that person support the bill, but you may be undercutting your ability to influence him or her on another bill where there is not such a strong predilection.

When a legislator you have lobbied votes in support of your position, another thank-you note is also advisable. It will reinforce the legislator's position on the issue, as you may have a related matter coming before the legislature. It will also build your relationship with the legislator because you may have many occasions to seek support for your positions.

Finally, don't get discouraged. Sometimes it takes a few efforts to get a bill passed.[41] Larry O'Brien, the Chair of the Democratic National Committee during the Watergate burglary, wrote that in politics there are no final victories. He added there are also no final defeats. Keep fighting for what you believe is right. You just might win and help a lot of people.

Chapter Questions

1. Is the legislature in your state part-time or full-time?

2. If your legislature is part-time, what does that mean for you as an advocate in terms of the timing for putting your idea forward?

3. How many members are there in each house of your state legislature?

4. Who has the authority for drawing districts in your state?

5. Does your state limit terms for the legislature? For statewide offices?

---

[41]At the end of my first term, Governor Wilson vetoed one of my health care bills. I reintroduced the bill on the opening day of the next session. It took me another year and a half to convince Governor Davis to support it.

6. Can you find a diagram of how your legislature works, similar to Figure 4.1?

7. Does your state have an initiative process? If so, what type?

Endnotes

i National Conference of State Legislatures. (2011). *Glossary of legislative terms*. Retrieved March 13, 2011, from http://www.ncsl.org/default.aspx?tabid=13539

ii *Amador Valley Joint Union High School District v. State Board of Equalization* (1978) 22 Cal., App. 3d 208, 245.

iii *County of Fresno v. Malmstrom* (1979) 94 Cal., App. 3d 974, 982.

iv Nichols, R. (2011). Dealing with term-limited legislators. *Governing*. Retrieved March 13, 2011, from http://www.governing.com/topics/politics/dealing-with-term-limited-legislators.html

v For California's budget examiner, an ease with diplomacy and dollar signs. (2011). *The New York Times*, January 16.

5 Ten Common Elements of Successful Advocacy Campaigns

Steps 1 to 3

Pat Libby

Ten is a great number. There are Ten Commandments, ten bowling pins, ten items on David Letterman's nightly lists, and who can forget those ten lords-a-leaping. In this chapter you will be introduced to ten common elements of successful advocacy campaigns. You'll read through the complete list, be presented with an explanation of how the first three work, and see how a group of students used each step to construct a successful advocacy campaign—their story will unfold in the ensuing chapters as the details of the ten steps are revealed to you.

Think of each element in the ten-point framework as being like a Lego. The object is to learn how every piece works and interrelates to the others so that you can snap them together to create a campaign. What follows is a quick overview of each of the ten elements.

1. **Identify an issue.** The issue or problem you'll want to address is usually something that many people in your profession or community recognize.

2. **Research the issue.** Research involves searching for facts and figures from expert sources that back up your position. Ultimately you'll distill that information into a "white paper" that explains in simple terms why this issue is important, why there is a need for the change you propose, and, ideally, how other places have adopted similar laws to address the issue.

3. **Create a fact sheet.** The fact sheet will be a boiled-down version of the white paper. You'll take those reams of research and condense them into a graphically pleasing, easy-to-read, double-sided single page.

4. **"Brand" the issue.** Think about "Got Milk?" or some other catchy slogan when you develop a way to name, frame, and package your issue to make it immediately recognizable and easy for others to remember.

5. Map out possible supporters and detractors. To plot your strategy, you'll create a map that shows who your possible allies and opponents are along with the arguments you anticipate they'll make for or against your cause. The map will be a working tool that can help you identify those people and organizations you should approach to help with your campaign. It will also help you think through the arguments your opponents are likely to make and how you can frame a response to their concerns.

6. Form a coalition. When forming a coalition, you'll enlist the broadest possible array of stakeholders to show that it is more than just the "usual suspects" that are affiliated with your cause.

7. Develop educational materials. These materials will be the "dummies' guide" to your cause. They'll include simple talking points and strategies that advocates of your issue can use to take action on your behalf—such as making a phone call to a city councilor or legislator—without having to do a lot of extra work.

8. Launch a media campaign. This is where you'll use your brand to tell the world why this issue is important and what action needs to take place to make it right.

9. Approach elected officials and/or other appropriate policy makers. This is the scariest-sounding part, yet for most people it's very gratifying and fun.

10. Monitor progress on the issue. Once you find a person to take up your cause, you will have to be vigilant about helping him or her move your ball down the field to make sure that it continues on the right path.

Now that you know the concepts, let's explore how each one works in greater detail. To help you see where we are as we move through the process, each element along the campaign trail will be highlighted.

One thing you'll notice as we go along is that the list is, well, not really a list. What that means is that you can't go through and check off each item when it's "done" (sorry). The reason for that is because you'll revisit some of these steps regularly during your campaign as you work through the process of refining your ideas and involving more people in your quest. As confusing as this may sound now, it should make a little more sense to you as each item unfolds (and even greater sense still when you actually use this model to create your own campaign).

So with that caveat, let's begin by taking a look at the first item on our list that's not a list: identifying an issue.

1. Identify an issue.

2. Research the issue.

3. Create a fact sheet.

4. "Brand" the issue.

5. Map out possible supporters and detractors.

6. Form a coalition.

7. Develop educational materials.

8. Launch a media campaign.

9. Approach elected officials.

10. Monitor progress on the issue.

Identify an Issue: How It's Done

Right now you may be thinking, "Jeez, I'm going to just skip over this section because it's a no-brainer." It's certainly easy when the issue you want to work on is literally staring at you in the face because people you work with every day, colleagues at other organizations, or other people affected by your work keep telling you about a problem they encounter time and again. The problem is so obvious it screams out for a solution that is also so obvious you end up saying to yourself and your colleagues, "Why in the world hasn't anyone done anything about this?"

The surprising answer may be that even though it's obvious to you and everyone around you, no one else thought to do something about it before you came along. It might be something that is relatively easy to fix, but no one in your circle understands how the policy-making process works (quick: buy each one a copy of this book!). It may also be because things are sometimes more complicated than they first appear; however, you won't know that until you try to bring about the change you believe is needed. The bottom line is, if you think something needs fixing and others think so too, it probably does.

There is one glaring exception to the "obvious problem/simple solution" issue, which is when the solution you're thinking of involves any amount of money. As you know from Chapter 3, government budgets are tighter than the swimsuits on Olympic athletes. If there is even the teeniest amount of money needed to make your idea happen, you'll need to take some time in the process of researching the issue to familiarize yourself *generally* with the budget of the entity that would be responsible for assuming those costs and administering the program. The reason the word *generally* is emphasized here is to let you know that you aren't expected to become a budget expert.

You'll find it's very helpful if you have a broad understanding of the budget as a whole —for instance, of your state, county, or city government and, then, of the particular department under which your initiative would fall. The greater your familiarity with what policy makers have to work with day in and day out, the more receptive they'll be to your ideas. Conversely, if you don't show an understanding of the constraints they face, they're probably not going to take your idea seriously. You might as well say, "I'd like you to make it rain marshmallows." The great thing about this type of budget information is that it's pretty easy to access on the Internet. In addition, there are many helpful people who work in support positions for key policy makers who would be happy to take some time to explain it to you.

Once you understand how the budget works, you'll need to figure out a way that government is going to pay for the cost of implementing your idea. In some cases, you might be able to prove that government will actually *save* money if your idea is implemented. That's, of course, ideal. Then there is that magical word *fee*, which, as we've discussed before, is beginning to sound a lot like that dreaded word *tax*. You can try offering your idea in the form of a pilot program so that the economic consequences of it will be short-lived if the measure doesn't prove to be successful. In rare instances, you might have to say, "This thing is so critical to the health and well-being of people that extraordinary means need to be found to pay for it." That is obviously the hardest argument to make and has the least chance of succeeding.

There is always an exception to every rule. New ideas that carry high price tags sometimes become law at lightning speed when there is a groundswell of community support. In situations when there is a public outcry for government officials to *do something and do something now*, legislators can jump to make changes that, to be honest, don't always make sense.

To give you an example of such a bill, in fall 2010, California legislators passed a law that was dubbed "Chelsea's law" in memory of a teenager who had been raped and murdered by a paroled sex offender. It was a horrible sad crime that became even sadder when the perpetrator confessed to murdering another teenage girl the year before. As you can imagine, hundreds of people—classmates, friends, neighbors, folks in surrounding communities who were angry and heartbroken by what had occurred—turned out for candlelight vigils and marches. Everyone asked how such a thing could have happened. Almost immediately a core group began to think about legislative solutions for making sure that nothing like that *would* ever happen again.

The local state legislator, who represented the district where Chelsea lived, was fired up with rage about the crime. He immediately proposed legislation that would lengthen the prison terms of sex offenders (some would now get "life"), put many of these criminals on lifetime parole with GPS tracking, lengthen parole for other offenders to 20 years with an option of indefinite extension, mandate new polygraph technology to test their likelihood of reoffending, and require new types of treatment.[i] You might have read that and thought, "That makes perfect sense to me; let's lock up those monsters and throw away the key!" But, before you let those words out of your mouth, let's take a step back for a minute. We need to remember that this legislation was passed during the same year that California was forced to cut $20 billion from its budget. The state's prison agency and California's impartial Legislative Analyst's Office estimated the bill would cost hundreds of millions of dollars in the ensuing years. Think about all of the extra prison costs, extra costs for treatment, extra parole officers, and so on, and ask yourself if those expenditures are more important than, say, funding domestic violence shelters and in-home services for low-income disabled adults, both of which the Governor's budget had practically wiped out.

In addition, the facts weren't on the side of Chelsea's law; study after study including research conducted by the U.S. Bureau of Justice Statistics showed that only 3.3%–5% of sex offenders were repeat offenders—figures that are far lower than those for other types of repeat crimes.[ii] Chelsea's law sailed through the legislature despite these facts because it rode on a wave of public outrage about the crime. The lesson here is that some laws get passed because of widespread public sentiment. If you can harness that type of energy to promote your cause, then you've got a good chance of creating a new law. In most cases, though, it's not that easy to pass new laws because legislators tend to spend lots of time weighing the pros and cons of ideas that are brought before them. As part of that process, they do a careful cost analysis to consider whether the cost of implementing a law is worth the benefit to be gained. We'll explore that idea in greater detail a little later on.

Sometimes as an advocate you'll identify an issue that a bunch of people will recognize as being a problem, but none of you can put your fingers on a way to fix it for all the money in the world. When that's the case, if you spend time researching legislation or policy that deals with a similar issue, it may spark your thinking about potential solutions. You can also read independent research reports on the topic that have been written by experts on the subject. Later on you can use what you've learned from that research to engage in an open-ended brainstorming session with a few friendly public officials about possible ways to approach the problem; however, we're getting ahead of ourselves.

Regardless of whether your problem is obvious or complicated, you'll need to do some research on it. The reason you need to do research is that your opinion alone, no matter how brilliant or articulate, will not be enough to convince policy makers that your idea needs to become law.

OK, so let's say you have an "in your face" problem; where do you begin? To show you how, we are going to tell you about an actual legislative campaign that was carried out by a group of students at the University of San Diego (USD). All were seasoned nonprofit professionals with zero prior experience doing legislative advocacy. It is safe to say too that each of them started the advocacy course with complete amnesia about basic civics.

The first day of class the students were told that during the course they were going to work in small groups of three to five people to identify an advocacy issue, create a campaign for that issue, and fly to our state capital (Sacramento) to meet with legislators in an effort to find someone to sponsor their concept as a bill. The first time the course was taught, the students broke out in convulsive laughter and practically fell off their chairs when we reviewed the syllabus—"You expect us to do *what*???!!!" Yet, somehow, at the end of the term, they managed to prove how smart they were (or we, for having faith in their ability to learn this stuff in a few short months) by ending up with terrific results. Time after time successive groups of students repeated that success, which has provided wonderful material to share with you in this book.

Identify an Issue: How They Did It _____

An actual student advocacy campaign will be used throughout these next few chapters to illustrate the 10-step framework. The project began when one student, Carolyn Smyth, talked about a recurring problem she was seeing at work: domestic violence victims who couldn't bring themselves to leave their abusers because they were afraid that if they did, the abusers would do something unspeakable to their pets. Another woman in the class, Darla Trapp, who worked at the same organization, instantly agreed.

The other students had wide-ranging reactions to this statement: Was it a pervasive problem, or was it something that had happened in only a few isolated cases? If it was a real problem, what could be done about it? Would people laugh at the idea of protecting these animals? The idea sparked a debate. Some students felt immediate sympathy toward the pets and saw it as an animal rights issue; others had a visceral understanding of why victims couldn't walk away from an abuser if there was any chance their pets would be tortured or killed; others squirmed in their seats feeling uncomfortable with the whole concept—they couldn't imagine it was true that someone wouldn't get out of a violent situation because a gerbil was standing in the way. Were Carolyn and Darla just pet fanatics whose love of animals skewed their perceptions about the extent of the problem? There were a few snide comments about "Fluffy's law" and a decision that some research had to be done to see if the issue was real. Two other students decided to join the team to explore the idea. The project was set in motion.

Which brings us to the second item on our list: researching an issue.

1. Identify an issue.
2. **Research the issue.**
3. Create a fact sheet.
4. "Brand" the issue.
5. Map out possible supporters and detractors.
6. Form a coalition.
7. Develop educational materials.
8. Launch a media campaign.
9. Approach elected officials.
10. Monitor progress on the issue.

Research the Issue: How It's Done

Doing research on an issue can take many different forms. The first and most obvious thing that needs to be done is a reality check with people outside your close circle of friends and colleagues to make sure that others perceive the problem the same way you do. The key to this part of the process is, ironically, *not* to be an advocate but to listen actively to what others are saying. Your job here isn't to convince your buddies that an issue is real; it is to figure out whether or not *they* feel the same way.

When students form working groups for their advocacy project, the strongest groups tend to be composed of people who don't think alike since the group is able to look at an issue from a variety of perspectives. That ultimately makes the case they lobby for that much stronger because it is well thought-out. There is a real danger in "groupthink," which is when all of your colleagues are so like-minded you can't imagine that there will be people who don't look at the issue the same way you do. The lesson here is to not be afraid of disagreements or differing views as long as there is general agreement that the issue you've identified is a concern to many people.

Let's use an imaginary example of a group of students who want to pass laws to strengthen gun safety. If all of those students are gun-control advocates and none are gun owners, they would probably have a much more narrow view of possible solutions than if some members of their group owned guns, hunted, or belonged to rifle associations. While it's not as easy to find common ground when you have differing opinions, a diverse group is generally more representative of society as a whole. Therefore, the ideas you generate as a result of that diversity are often quite good because they appeal to a broad spectrum of views.

At the same time, there's no need for you to arrive at consensus. If, for instance, most representatives of a diverse group agree to a particular solution but a few members keep arguing another viewpoint (driving everyone else insane), it's perfectly OK to decide to move in the direction of the majority. That assumes that the majority is also a diverse group. In other words, if 5 out of 7 members agree with one another because they *all* are gun-control advocates or, conversely, all members of the National Rifle Association, you haven't achieved your goal. The idea is not for everyone to hold hands and sing "Kumbaya"; it's to get sensible ideas passed into law that appeal to most citizens.

Once you've determined that the issue you've identified is something that others are also concerned about, then it's time to move on to the next phase of your research. This phase will be focused on assembling the facts of your case and is best accomplished with a team of people who are willing to dig in on the project. As you read through this next section, think of how you might divide up the various research tasks among a group of classmates, colleagues, or like-minded citizen activists. Ideally you've come across these folks during the first stage of identifying the problem or issue to be addressed. Sometimes you can stumble on existing advocacy groups or organizations that are dedicated to policy analysis that have done terrific research on your issue. As a bonus, these folks might eventually agree to become part of your coalition. In other words, even though coalition building isn't on our radar until we get to Step 6, you need to be thinking about the steps as interrelated activities.

For reasons that are hopefully obvious to you, you can't wage any legislative or policy campaign simply by talking about a feeling you have that something isn't right and needs to be changed. You have to present cold hard facts that demonstrate to the people whose support you want that others have taken an objective look at the problem and documented its existence. It's ideal if you can cite independent reports, studies, and statistics that illustrate the magnitude of the problem in a way that is easy for the average person to grasp. What's tricky is sorting through the mountains of material that are out there supporting your case and boiling them down to something that is easy to digest. Start by gathering all of the information you can find on the topic and then winnowing it down later as your campaign takes shape.

The next phase of your research involves finding out whether anyone has tackled this problem previously. You need to begin by doing a search of legislation that was filed in your state on that topic. Most states have online search engines that can help you do this research fairly easily. If you have trouble figuring out how to use those search engines, volunteers at organizations like the League of Women Voters will teach you how to navigate the system.

Through the process of searching for previous bills, it's possible to discover that a similar piece of legislation was attempted and failed. If someone tried to pass a similar piece of legislation before, who sponsored the bill? How long ago? What did it look like? As you move along in the process, you'll want to find out why it failed. Who opposed this idea, and what were their reasons for doing so?

The analysis of what happened, which will be available through the policy analyst of the committee to which the bill was assigned, will provide you with a treasure trove of information. For example, if it is a bill pertaining to health, the health committee analyst may be able to provide you with a complete summary—including letters of opposition and support—that are contained in the bill file. Studying the opposition arguments will provide you with invaluable clues about how to shape the idea for which you are advocating.

You also want to take a look at what's been done in other states. You'll be surprised at how often similar efforts have been attempted elsewhere (it's been said that "great minds think alike"), and at the innovative ways people in other parts of the country have dreamed up to address the issue through policy or legislative means.

Specifically, you should get ahold of the actual legislation that passed. If the language is dense and somewhat confusing to you, search for news articles that describe the bill, which will help you decipher what was in the legislation. You may find a handful of states have passed similar legislation, and if so, you'll likely see slight variations on a theme. These will help you think through what's possible in your area. The Internet makes this kind of work easy to do. The added bonus is that your research will often lead you to key people in other states who were successful in getting that legislation or policy passed. Many of them will be passionate advocates for the cause who will be eager to help you pass similar measures in your state. The advocates can also let you know how the implementation of the legislation is working, which may or may not lead to information about things that they would have included or done differently had they known about them originally. If you're working on an issue at the local level, or a policy issue, use the same strategy—get your hands on what has been done in other places.

Legislation that has been enacted and implemented in other states (again, just substitute the word *county* or *city* if that's your focus) will also provide you with invaluable data on costs. You'll be able to use that information to approximate the cost of deploying your idea. For instance, if New Mexico has 200,000 people that are affected by *that* problem and your state has 400,000 people that are affected by *that* problem, then you might calculate that it would cost your state twice as much to address *that* problem. You need to dig a bit deeper, though, to understand exactly how New Mexico is addressing the problem. Perhaps New Mexico has a sophisticated computer database in place or some other mechanism like a network of offices in every county of the state that are open on late evenings and Saturdays to provide eligibility screening for *that* service—or whatever it is that makes it relatively easy for New Mexico to provide *that*. If your state is not set up that way, you'll need to determine if additional and, therefore, more costly measures would have to be put into place to make a similar idea work in your area. The bottom line is that you need to determine as best you can what it would cost your state, county, or city to provide *that*. This is commonly referred to as a cost-benefit analysis. You need to be honest with your calculations because if you're not, the legislators to whom you're proposing the idea will see through your flimsy math in no time flat. You may have the most fabulous idea in the world, but if it costs too much money, no one will buy it.

Sometimes you have to go out and collect the data you need—in other words, do your own research—in order to calculate the cost benefit of your idea because otherwise the information you want doesn't exist. A great example of this involves an advocacy campaign that was conducted in 2003 by the New York Public Interest Research Group, which was centered on the importance of having the city invest in planting and maintaining street trees. To make their case, the advocates organized a group of volunteers to carry out a unique survey of neighborhood trees. According to an article on the effort that appeared in *The New York Times*,

> Unlike many tree tallies, this one compiled extensive information with an ambitious goal some tree-huggers might consider crudely capitalistic: to break down each tree, its parts and its labor, into dollars and cents.

Money has yet to grow on trees, but trees can provide crucial de-pollution services quantifiable in cold, hard cash.

Most broadly, the survey concluded that the 322 trees had an average value of $3,225 per tree and a total value of $1,038,458. The value was said to be the amount the city would have to pay to replace the tree. The most expensive one, a 214-year-old tulip tree on Fillmore Street on Staten Island, came in at $23,069, while a scrawny 6-year-old ginkgo on Hunts Point Avenue in the South Bronx brought up the rear, at $54.

The advocates were so successful with their campaign that the Parks Department's chief of forestry and horticulture thought to use the survey model citywide. She said,

"People always knew there was some vague benefit to trees, but you could never quantify it. But once you have the methodology to equate trees with dollars, now you're talking. It's no longer about hugging trees because they're good, but because you have hard data in a language more effective in the public dialogue."[iii]

That pretty much says it all. The campaign worked because the advocates thought carefully about the best cost-benefit strategy for making their case. They didn't want to appeal only to people's love of trees but wanted to make a good economic argument in their favor and, with a little ingenuity, ended up doing just that.

All that said, don't get too hung up if you can't figure out a way to put an exact dollar figure on your idea. What you need to know fundamentally is how the idea would work structurally in order for policy makers and their aides to help you understand whether the concept would be doable. For instance, state workers might be able to let the public know about *that* during the same hours when they process applications for some other service.

As you go through this process—of talking with and listening to people, sorting through what's been done in other places, and documenting the problem—you will invariably find some people (perhaps yourself) who have been directly affected by the issue. It is important to gather their stories because that is what puts a "human face" on your issue and makes it compelling. For instance, when we hear a news story about a natural disaster, the reporters usually start out by talking about the magnitude of the hurricane or the height of the waves, but what draws us into the tragedy are the stories of people who have been affected by that disaster. We look at them and think, "That could have been me," or "That woman on the raft looks just like Aunt Betty—hey, wait a minute; it *is* Aunt Betty!" The facts of any case always need to be balanced by the impact of the problem or, in some cases, more optimistically, the magnitude of the benefits that people would gain, if something were to change. Be sure at the very least to get quotes from people even if they don't feel comfortable allowing you to use their full name or picture.

There's one more important point to add about identifying advocacy issues. At the nonprofit organization level there can be situations when staff people disagree about whether or not a problem is such a big deal that it needs to be addressed through policy or legislative change. People within organizations resist the idea of working on broad policy changes for a variety of reasons. We've touched on some of these in previous chapters—for instance, being ignorant of the legal rights nonprofits have to lobby, thinking that lobbying might be a misuse of the agency's funds, or having a belief that lobbying isn't within the mission of the organization. At other times there may be leaders at an agency that don't believe the issue you have identified is affecting enough people that it warrants a push for change. These folks might feel that the time you spend trying to arrive at a legislative or policy solution will take you away from your primary job responsibilities. You'll go around in circles with that discussion until you engage in some basic fact finding to verify your instincts.

Fact finding to build your case might involve steps such as surveying caseworkers at your organization and others like it to see how many are encountering *that* problem on a regular basis, or conducting focus groups with community members or clients to see how many are dealing with *that* problem, or going door-to-door to survey how many neighbors have *that* problem. You'll want to be sure that you gather information using reliable survey methods to ensure that the results aren't challenged later on. If you haven't taken a survey methods course or took one so long ago there's mold growing on your textbook (assuming you didn't sell it for $2.50 at the end of the semester), then the best thing to do is to ask someone who has good survey skills for help in designing your protocol. If you're working on a project outside the hallowed halls of academia, you'll find that it's not hard to locate a friendly professor who will volunteer to help (start with the social work, political science, public administration, urban studies, or nonprofit studies department). It doesn't have to be overly complicated, but it does have to be unbiased and accurate. It would be wonderful if your boss gave you permission to work on gathering this information—if not, you may have to do it on your own time.

The time you spend documenting the extent of the problem will serve you well later on. First, if you are able to document that there is in fact *that* problem, your supervisor, upper-level managers, board members, or whomever it is that you need to convince that it's important for you or your organization to work on this issue will be more likely to give you the go-ahead. The best way to follow up with those who are resisting the idea is to ask people who confront the issue regularly or who are directly affected by it—to approach them. For example, several case managers might bring up the issue in a staff meeting. Alternatively or in addition, you could have community members or clients raise the issue in other ways. That way, it's not just you saying this is a problem (with the eye roll and deep sigh from the higher-ups that says, "There goes Pat *again . . .*"); you're having other people voice their concerns. Your data will back up the extent of the problem.

Even if they still don't go along with the idea that your organization should lobby on this issue, the process of reaching out to other organizations to see if their clients are also having *that* problem may uncover someone else who is enthusiastic about taking it on (ideally with agency leaders who agree to do something about the situation). Or, that someone else might end up being a client or community member who realized through your outreach that he or she wasn't the only one dealing with *that* problem. Ultimately, the information you've gathered will be useful in the advocacy campaign. As we've already said, legislators love facts, figures, and stories from real people to illustrate an issue.

Research the Issue: How They Did It

Speaking of real people, let's go back to Carolyn, the advocacy student, and her idea about pets and domestic violence. In response to the reaction from her classmates, Carolyn felt there was something to this idea that was worth exploring further. She decided to approach it from a different perspective by calling the director of the Rancho Coastal Humane Society/Animal Safehouse Program to get her opinion. She wondered what had led the Humane Society to establish an Animal Safehouse Program (ASP) in the first place. The executive director was resolute: She told Carolyn that the creation of the safe house in 1997 was the result of a horrible trend witnessed by colleagues working at battered women's shelters throughout the county.

According to the society's website,

> Victims of domestic violence and their children will often stay with a batterer because they fear their pet will be neglected, injured or killed if left behind. Concern for a beloved companion animal's welfare prevents or delays more than 50% of battered individuals from escaping domestic abuse, continuing to endanger themselves, their children and their pets. Our program provides a support service to domestic violence shelters which are unable to accept pets. We provide temporary shelter for the pets of victims of domestic violence, allowing battered individuals to escape abuse and seek safety. Because of this assistance, no one is forced to choose between abandoning a beloved pet and staying in an abusive relationship. With help from our Animal Safehouse Program, survivors and their children can seek shelter, medical treatment and counseling, knowing their pets are safe.
>
> We actively collaborate with domestic violence shelters, the San Diego Domestic Violence Council, the San Diego County Board of Supervisors, the County of San Diego Department of Animal Services, city and municipal animal shelters, the San Diego Family Justice Center,

San Diego Domestic Violence Response Teams, social services, mental health services, law-enforcement, educational facilities, military and many other agencies and individuals who want to eradicate abuse and help break the cycle of family violence.[iv]

A few additional calls to the partner organizations mentioned on the website convinced Carolyn that her original instincts were right: This was an issue that needed to be addressed. She brought her research back to the class, and it was compelling enough to convince two other students, Gretchen Pelletier and Renee Scherr, to join her and Darla on the project.

Once they agreed that a problem existed, the team faced the question of what should be done to fix it. The director of the Humane Society had suggested adding pets to temporary restraining orders and injunctions for victims of domestic violence. Would that work? The team wrestled to figure out what exactly they would be asking the legislature to do.

The group members began by pursuing independent scavenger hunts for similar legislation that had passed in other states, statistics on the relationship between domestic violence and animal abuse, and legal advice on how restraining orders work. Afterward they came together to share what they found—building on each other's work and assigning different portions of the research to various group members for follow-up.

As the weeks went on, the materials piled up: academic publications on domestic violence; reports and newsletters from both battered women's shelters and animal shelters; copies of similar bills that had been passed in New York, Maine, and Vermont; and stories of women who had seen their pets victimized by their abusers or feared it would happen. In particular, research done by Frank Ascione, a college professor, kept surfacing. One of the team members contacted him by e-mail, and he readily agreed that his work could be used to back up the campaign's efforts. Then, according to Gretchen, who chronicled her own and the group's journey through this project in a retrospective reflection piece,

On Nov. 12, we met with another USD student [Sarah Speed] who is in the Law program. We were put in touch with her through a networking circle that reached to the East Coast and back via phone conversations with a Maine attorney, [a group called] United Animal Nation and American Society for the Prevention of Cruelty to Animal contacts. Sarah had already been researching this issue on her own (the *legal specifics* of adding pets to restraining orders) . . . we met with her to discuss whether her solution matched ours.

Sarah provided us with a rationale for approaching the issue through an amendment to the California Family Code and Penal Code. We tested the legal language in a meeting with Steve Allen, Director of Legal Services, Center for Community Solutions, who provided excellent counsel. Further discussions honed the "fix" that we took to Sacramento.

All of this leads to the third item on our list: creating a fact sheet.

1. Identify an issue.

2. Research the issue.

3. **Create a fact sheet.**

4. "Brand" the issue.

5. Map out possible supporters and detractors.

6. Form a coalition.

7. Develop educational materials.

8. Launch a media campaign.

9. Approach elected officials.

10. Monitor progress on the issue.

Create a Fact Sheet: How It's Done

The fact sheet is the most important piece of information you'll need for your campaign because it is the CliffsNotes© summary of the issue you care about so deeply. It is a single powerful piece of paper that you will leave in the hands of every person with whom you'll meet to talk about your issue including potential coalition members, legislators and their aids, policy makers, and members of the media. You'll use it too to persuade your friends and members of your organization to get behind your effort. No one needs to tell you that it's hard to get people's attention for more than a few fleeting minutes (if that), and, therefore, your fact sheet had better be short, to the point, and compelling. The person reading your fact sheet needs to be able to glance down and absorb it without needing a long explanation from you about what it means.

Even though they are listed here as two separate steps, you'll develop the brand for your campaign (Step 4) at the same time you create your fact sheet (Step 3). As will be explained in the following chapter, the way you choose to name your campaign more often than not emerges from the facts you choose to frame your case.

There is both an art and a science involved in putting together a fact sheet. The art involves making it easy for someone to pick up and absorb the key points without getting eye strain. You need to have a clear heading, a clean typeface, bullets, and boxes; make strategic use of boldface and underlining; and, generally, put together something that is neat, tidy, and eye-catching. If you have a friend who is talented at graphic design, an appealing logo can help draw attention to your cause.

The science involves distilling all that you have learned about your issue into a single two-sided sheet. That isn't easy because once you've taken the time to learn all you can about the issue, you'll have a lot of information stuffed into all those nooks and crannies in your brain, which sometimes makes it difficult to pull out the most compelling elements of your presentation.

Those members of your group who have a hard time synthesizing it all can put their minds to developing the longer version of your fact sheet, which will be a companion white paper/case statement/policy paper (take your pick and call it what you want). Just like those nerdy kids in high school, some people in the world are in positions of power by virtue of having been elected or selected to serve the public who really do want to read about your issue in detail. These are the same people who didn't even think about shelling out $9.99 for the *Beowulf* study guide and actually read the whole thing from cover to cover. Those people will want to read through your position paper in its entirety; however, you'll still need to get their attention first by waving a fact sheet in front of their face. Keep in mind, though, that your position paper should not resemble a major dissertation on the topic: It too needs to be fairly concise and well referenced. You can still include things in it that simply cannot fit on a fact sheet such as copies of legislative language that was used in other states, bills that are similar to what you are proposing, bigger charts and graphs that document the issue, photos of the problem, and, of course, more detailed narrative.

As for the fact sheet, make sure it includes the following elements:

1. A title for your campaign (again, we'll talk about the importance of naming your issue in the next section).

2. A brief statement of the problem.

3. Facts that document the problem (which are footnoted on the flipside of the sheet so that the reader knows you didn't invent them).

4. A clear statement about your proposed solution (please be sure to put this on the front page).

5. A compelling human-interest story (or quotes) illustrating the problem.

6. A list of organizations that have signed on to support your issue (this part of your fact sheet will need to be revised and updated as your coalition grows—see Step 6).

7. The name and contact information of at least one person associated with your campaign. This is the person the legislator (or his or her aide), policy maker, and/or media person can contact for additional information and follow-up. It almost goes without saying: Make sure the e-mail address you list isn't from an old AOL account that you never check anymore and that the telephone number you list isn't the one you gave away to your grandmother when you upgraded your cell.

8. The website address for your campaign.

Create a Fact Sheet: How They Did It _____

As you can see, this is where the list of ten items that were covered at the beginning of the chapter begins to make a U-turn; how can you put together a fact sheet when you haven't even named the issue or begun to pull together the other members of your coalition? The truth is you need to start with a draft and work up to those other items on the list. Your fact sheet will evolve just as your campaign will evolve—you'll make several drafts along the way just as our students did as they were devising their campaign. Take a look for yourself at the first, second, and third versions of the animal team's fact sheets to see the evolution of their work (Figures 5.1, 5.2, and 5.3).[1]

Figure 5.1

Protecting Every Family Member From Domestic Violence

Adding animals to California's Family Code 6211 for protection against domestic violence.

It is estimated[i] that a victim of domestic violence, typically a woman, will make X calls to a protective agency before finally leaving her abuser.

An estimated 25% to 40% of domestic violence victims are unable to escape their abusers because they worry about what will happen to their pets or livestock should they leave.[ii]

Child victims are particularly vulnerable to threats to their pets. Batterers know this, and often threaten or harm the family animals to coerce a child into sexual abuse or to force them to remain silent about abuse.[iii]

A California loophole that helps abusers use family pets against the family: In the state of California, the companion animals of domestic violence victims do not receive full protection from batterers who are ordered, under a temporary restraining order (TRO) or injunction, to stay away from his/her victims. Pets fall loosely under "property" in the language of the TRO or injunction.

Why this is a problem: Animals are not recognized in the California Family Code as needing greater protection than other "property" in the home or in the immediate proximity of a human victim, e.g. a car. However, if the pet is not in the victim's home or with the victim, a batterer can gain access to that animal without fear of violating a restraining order.

Current legal definition: Because the California Family Code defines "domestic violence" as violence of one person inflicted on another, when filling out the forms to get a TRO (or injunction), victims must list pets as property (if, in their agitated state, they remember). However, if pets are property then there is an issue of ownership; some judges will not make a decision affecting property rights in a temporary restraining order, while other judges simply find the inclusion of pets unnecessary. If California were to adopt a law which mandates a penalty for violating a restraining order protecting pets (as was recently passed in Maine), then pets could be lawfully removed from the home when the abused person chose to leave and the abuser could not hurt the animals without retribution enforceable at law.

Fear, intimidation, control, threats: In addition to physical harm, these are very real, insidious and corrosive weapons that abusers use against their victims, and pets are often the tool.

---

[1]Figures 5.1, 5.2, and 5.3 were created by Gretchen Pelletier, Renee Scherr, Carolyn Smyth, Sarah Speed, and Darla Trapp.

Victims of domestic violence must be empowered with real protection – including legal consequences for abusers who come near their animals, wherever and with whomever they are.

Three examples of vulnerability under the current family code:

- San Diegan Yvonne Stromer's pet beagle, Baby, lives with a foster family while Yvonne and her son Matthew get their life back together after leaving her abusive husband. Away from her and the house, Baby is not technically under Yvonne's protective restraining order. Yvonne's husband has used threats against Baby in the past to intimidate and control her, and she has no doubt that he would do it again.
- Melinda S. boards her horse Nancy with a family that keeps her for free, ten miles from Melinda's home. Melinda cannot afford to move Nancy, even though her husband, who has a history of animal abuse going back to childhood, knows where Melinda's horse is.
- Jamie G. lives alone with her dog, Fritz, her companion and protector. Because she works long days, Jamie hires a neighbor's son to walk Fritz in the afternoon, though she knows that once Fritz is 100 yards away from home (and her), he is vulnerable to her angry and abusive ex-husband.

The solution: California is in a position to stand at the forefront among the leading progressive states in the U.S. in the protection of the entire family, by including companion animals. Along with the ASPCA, the United Animal Nation, San Diego Family Justice Center, and [others], University of San Diego Students Advocating for Protection propose that the following changes be made to the current California Family Code [I'm not clear; are we switching this out, per Steve's input?]:

Cal Fam Code § 6211 (2006)

§ 6211. "Domestic violence"

"Domestic violence" is abuse perpetrated against any of the following persons:

(a) A spouse or former spouse.

(b) A cohabitant or former cohabitant, as defined in Section 6209.

(c) A person with whom the respondent is having or has had a dating or engagement relationship.

(d) A person with whom the respondent has had a child, where the presumption applies that the male parent is the father of the child of the female parent under the Uniform Parentage Act (Part 3 (commencing with Section 7600) of Division 12).

(e) A child of a party or a child who is the subject of an action under the Uniform Parentage Act, where the presumption applies that the male parent is the father of the child to be protected.

(f) Any other person related by consanguinity or affinity within the second degree.

(g) *An animal under the care, custody, control or is owned, leased, possessed, kept, or held by any of the above persons defined in subsections a through f.*

By adding this language to the California Family Code, we not only establish a safe, enforceable distance between all members of the family and the abuser, we also create awareness of this prosecution tool amongst victims, victims' advocates, law enforcement, shelter intake personnel and the courts.

Three states have passed legislation *this year* protecting animals through temporary restraining orders and/or injunctions:

- **New York** (date) (language of legislation)
- **Maine** (date) (language of legislation)
- **Vermont** (date) (language of legislation)

(Continued)

Figure 5.1 (Continued)

People, pets and protection: sad facts

- 85% of women and 63% of children entering 50 of the largest shelters for battered women in the United States discussed incidents of pet abuse in the family.[iv]
- 71% of pet owning women in shelters reported that a pet had been threatened, injured or killed by their abuser.[v]
- 49% of pet-owning victims who fled their abusers and sought shelter continued to worry about their animals after entering shelter.[vi]

Just as we are now aware that domestic abuse is a circle that must and can be broken in families, it also follows that children learn about the treatment of animals – bad and good – through models perpetuated by adults.

- 62% to 76% of batter-perpetrated pet abuse incidents occur in the presence of children.[vii]
- 32% of pet-owning victims of domestic abuse reported that one or more of their children had hurt or killed a pet.[viii]
- A 1983 study noted that children were reported to be abusive to animals in more than a third of a sample of pet-owning families referred to New Jersey's Division of Youth and Family Services for suspected child abuse.
- Violent offenders incarcerated in a maximum-security prison were significantly more likely than non-violent offenders to have committed childhood acts of cruelty towards pets.[ix]

Restraining orders are not a perfect answer, but they are a tool that empowers victims of violence by allowing them to prosecute. Legislated protection for pets empowers victims, decreases the power of abusers and protects the animals that we, as human beings, are responsible for.

Join the "Protecting Every Family Member From Domestic Violence" *Advocates:*

- American Society for the Prevention of Cruelty to Animals (ASPCA)
- Rancho Coastal Humane Society
- United Animal Nation
- Add as we go along!

Endnotes

[i]We need a fact here, and a source.

[ii]Arkow, P. (1994). Animal abuse and domestic violence: Intake statistics tell a sad story. *Latham Letter 15*(2), 17.

[iii]Loar, L. (1999). "I'll only help you if you have two legs," or, Why human services professionals should pay attention to cases involving cruelty to animals. In, Ascione, F.R. & Arkow, P., eds.: *Child Abuse, Domestic Violence, and Animal Abuse: Linking the Circles of Compassion for Prevention and Intervention,* West Lafayette, IN: Purdue University Press, 1999, pp. 120–136.

[iv]Ascione, F.R. 1997. The abuse of animals and domestic violence: a national survey of shelters for women who are battered. *Society and Animals, 5*(3): 205–218.

[v]Ascione, F.R., Weber, C.V. and Wood, D. S. (1997). The abuse of animals and domestic violence: A national survey of shelters for women who are battered. *Society & Animals 5*(3). 205–218.

[vi]Favor, C.A. and Strand, E.B. (2003). Domestic Violence and Animal Cruelty: Untangling the Web of Abuse. *Journal of Social Work Education 39*(2), 237–253.

[vii]Favor and Strand (2003).

[viii]Ascione, F.R. (1995). Domestic violence and cruelty to animals. Paper presented at the Fourth International Conference on Family Violence, Durham, NH, July 24.

[ix]Merz-Perez, L., Heide, K. and Silverman, I. (2001). Childhood Cruelty to Animals and Subsequent Violence against Humans, International Journal of Offender Therapy and Comparative Criminology, Vol. 45 No. 5, 556-573.

Figure 5.2

The link between animal abuse and domestic violence:

* 85% of women and 63% of children entering 50 of the largest shelters for battered women in the United States discussed incidents of pet abuse in the family[4]
* 71% of pet owning women in shelters reported that a pet had been threatened, injured or killed by their abuser.[5]
* 49% of pet-owning victims who fled their abusers and sought shelter continued to worry about their animals after entering shelter.[6]
* 62% to 76% of batter-perpetrated pet abuse incidents occur in the presence of children.[7]
* 32% of pet-owning victims of domestic abuse reported that one or more of their children had hurt or killed a pet.[8]
* A 1983 study noted that children were reported to be

Protect *Every* Family Member From Domestic Violence

Advocates for the addition of animals to California's Family Code 6211 for protection against domestic violence.

A victim of domestic violence will make an average of 8 calls to a protective agency before leaving an abuser.[1]

An estimated 25% to 40% of domestic violence victims are unable to escape their abusers because they worry about what will happen to their pets or livestock.[2]

Batterers know that child victims are particularly vulnerable to threats to their pets, and often threaten or harm the family animals to coerce a child into sexual abuse or to force them to remain silent about abuse.[3]

A loophole helps abusers use pets against the family: In California, companion animals of domestic violence victims do not receive full protection from batterers who are ordered, under a temporary restraining order (TRO) or injunction, to stay away from his/her victims. If the pet is not on the victim's property or with the victim, a batterer can gain access to that animal without fear of violating a restraining order.

Proposed solution: We propose the following changes be made to the California Family Code:

Cal Fam Code § 6211 (2006)
§ 6211. "Domestic violence"

"Domestic violence" is abuse perpetrated against any of the following ~~persons~~:

(a) A spouse or former spouse.

(b) A cohabitant or former cohabitant, as defined in Section 6209.

(c) A person with whom the respondent has had a child, where the presumption applies that the male parent is the father of the child of the female parent under the Uniform Parentage Act (Part 3 (commencing with Section 7600) of Division 12).

(e) A child of a party or a child who is the subject of an action under the Uniform Parentage Act, where the presumption applies that the male parent is the father of the child to be protected.

(f) Any other person related by consanguinity or affinity within the second degree.

(g) An animal under the care, custody, control or is owned, leased, possessed, kept, or held by any of the above persons defined in subsections a through f.

Why this is needed: Because the California Family Code defines "domestic violence" as violence of one person inflicted on another, when filling out forms for a TRO (or injunction), victims must list pets as property. However, if pets are property then there is an issue of ownership; some judges do not make decisions affecting property rights in a TRO, while others find the inclusion of pets unnecessary. If California were to adopt a law which mandates a penalty for violating a restraining order protecting pets, pets could be lawfully removed from the home when the abused person chose to leave and the abuser could not hurt the animals without retribution enforceable at law.

Examples of vulnerability under the current family code:

* San Diegan Yvonne Stromer's pet beagle, Baby, lives with a foster family while Yvonne and son Matthew get their life back together. At the foster home, Baby is not technically under Yvonne's protective restraining order. reatened and harmed Baby in the past, and Yvonne

abusive to animals in more than a third of a sample of pet-owning families referred to New Jersey's Division of Youth and Family Services for suspected child abuse.

* Violent offenders incarcerated in a maximum-security prison were significantly more likely than non-violent offenders to have committed childhood acts of cruelty towards pets.[9]

The ex-husband has threatened and harmed Baby in the past, and Yvonne fears he would do it again.

- Melinda S. boards her horse ten miles from Melinda's home. Her husband, who has a history of animal abuse going back to childhood, knows where Melinda's horse is.
- Jamie G. lives alone with her dog, Fritz, her companion and protector. Because she works long days, Jamie hires a neighbor's son to walk Fritz. Once Fritz is 100 yards away from home (and her), he is vulnerable to her angry and abusive ex-husband.

Three states have passed legislation this year protecting animals through temporary restraining orders and/or injunctions . . .

- New York
- Maine
- Vermont

. . . and California has an opportunity to join them at the forefront!

Protect Every Family Member from Domestic Violence is *endorsed by:*

- American Society for the Prevention of Cruelty to Animals (ASPCA)
- Rancho Coastal Humane Society
- United Animal Nation
- Join us!

Sources:

[1]# and source to come.

[2]Arkow, P. (1994). Animal abuse and domestic violence: Intake statistics tell a sad story. *Latham Letter* 15(2), 17.

[3]Loar, L. (1999). "I'll only help you if you have two legs," or, Why human services professionals should pay attention to cases involving cruelty to animals. In, Ascione, F.R. & Arkow, P., eds.: *Child Abuse, Domestic Violence, and Animal Abuse: Linking the Circles of Compassion for Prevention and Intervention*, West Lafayette, IN: Purdue University Press, 1999, pp. 120–136.

[4]Ascione, F.R. 1997. The abuse of animals and domestic violence: a national survey of shelters for women who are battered. *Society and Animals*, 5(3): 205–218.

[5]Ascione, F.R., Weber, C.V. and Wood, D. S. (1997). The abuse of animals and domestic violence: A national survey of shelters for women who are battered. *Society & Animals* 5(3). 205–218.

[6]Favor, C.A. and Strand, E.B. (2003). Domestic Violence and Animal Cruelty: Untangling the Web of Abuse. *Journal of Social Work Education* 39(2), 237–253.

[7]Favor and Strand (2003).

[8]Ascione, F.R. (1995). Domestic violence and cruelty to animals. Paper presented at the Fourth International Conference on Family Violence, Durham, NH, July 24.

[9]Merz-Perez, L., Heide, K. and Silverman, I. (2001). Childhood Cruelty to Animals and Subsequent Violence against Humans, International Journal of Offender Therapy and Comparative Criminology, Vol. 45 No. 5, 556–573.

Figure 5.3

The link between animal abuse and domestic violence:

* 83% of directors of the largest shelters for battered women in the U.S. indicated women (63% for children) entering the shelters discussed incidents of pet abuse in the family[3]
* 71% of pet-owning women in shelters reported that a pet had been threatened, injured or killed by their abuser.[4]
* 49% of pet-owning victims who fled their abusers and sought shelter continued to worry about their animals after entering shelter.[5]
* 62% to 76% of batterer-perpetrated pet abuse incidents occur in the presence of children.[6]
* 32% of pet-owning victims of domestic abuse reported that one or more of their children had hurt or killed a pet.[7]
* A 1983 study noted that children were reported to be abusive to

Protect *Every* Family Member From Domestic Violence

Advocates for the addition of animals to California's Family Code 6211 & Penal Code Section 136.2 (g) for protection against domestic violence.

An estimated 25% to 40% of domestic violence victims are unable to escape their abusers because they worry about what will happen to their pets or livestock.[1]

Batterers know that child victims are particularly vulnerable to threats to their pets, and often threaten or harm the family animals to coerce a child into sexual abuse or to force them to remain silent about abuse.[2]

A loophole helps abusers use pets against the family: In California, companion animals of domestic violence victims do not receive full protection from batterers who are ordered, under a temporary restraining order (TRO) or injunction, to stay away from his/her victims. If the pet is not on the victim's property or with the victim, a batterer can gain access to that animal without fear of violating a restraining order.

Proposed solution: We propose the following addition be made to the appropriate California codes:

Family Code Section 6211 (Domestic Violence)

This section shall be amended to add "an animal under the care, custody, control or is owned, leased, possessed, kept or held by any of the above persons defined in subsections a through f." It should also be revised to state "Domestic violence" is "abuse perpetrated against any of the following" omitting the term 'persons' effectively includes the following subsections within the definitions and allows the inclusion of animals.

Penal Code Section 136.2 (g) (Protective and Restraining Orders)

This section shall include the protection of any animal that is owned, leased, possessed, kept or held, or in the care, custody or control of the person or persons requesting the Order from contact, with the intent to annoy, harass, threaten, take, or commit acts of violence, by the defendant.

Why this is needed: The intent of the bill is to add 'animals' to the domestic violence section of the California Family Code as in many domestic violence cases, a spouse will threaten the safety of the family pet as a means of intimidation and control. If there is no evidence that the pet has been subjected to an act of cruelty, the perpetrator cannot be charged with violation of Penal Code 597 (the anti-cruelty statute).

It is also the intent of the bill to add 'animals' to the California Penal Code on restraining or protective orders. Family disputes are not the only area where there are threats, acts of cruelty, torture, death or a 'disappearance' of a pet. Oftentimes an irate tenant will target a landlord's pet in retaliation for an eviction (or an employee against an employer).

Examples of vulnerability under the current family code:

* San Diegan Yvonne Stromer's pet beagle, Baby, lives with a foster family while Yvonne and her son get their life back together. At the foster home, Baby is not technically under Yvonne's protective restraining order. The ex-husband has threatened and harmed Baby in the past, and Yvonne fears he would do it again. *(Yvonne is available for interviews.)*

(Continued)

Figure 5.3 (Continued)

animals in more than a third of a sample of pet-owning families referred to New Jersey's Division of Youth and Family Services for suspected child abuse.

* Violent offenders incarcerated in a maximum-security prison were significantly more likely than non-violent offenders to have committed childhood acts of cruelty towards pets.[8]

- Melinda S. boards her horse ten miles from Melinda's home. Her husband, who has a history of animal abuse going back to childhood, knows where Melinda's horse is.
- Jamie G. lives alone with her dog, Fritz, her companion and protector. Because she works long days, Jamie hires a neighbor's son to walk Fritz. Once Fritz is 100 yards away from home (and her), he is vulnerable to her angry and abusive ex-husband.

Three states have passed legislation this year protecting animals through temporary restraining orders and/or injunctions . . .

- New York
- Maine
- Vermont

. . . and California has an opportunity to join them at the forefront!

Protect Every Family Member from Domestic Violence *is supported by*:

- California Partnership to End Domestic Violence
- American Society for the Prevention of Cruelty to Animals (ASPCA)
- SPCA Los Angeles
- United Animal Nation
- Rancho Coastal Humane Society
- Humane Society of the United States

Questions?   *Carolyn Smyth*, 619-XXX-XXXX (DV & animal rights); *Darla Trapp*, 858-XXX-XXXX x111 (DV & legal); *Renee Scherr*, 619-XXX-XXXX (other states' legislation); *Gretchen Pelletier*, 619-XXX-XXXX (media); *Sarah Speed*, 619-XXX-XXXX (legal & legislation). Also see "For Further Information" sheet.

Sources:

[1]Arkow, P. (1994). Animal abuse and domestic violence: Intake statistics tell a sad story. *Latham Letter 15*(2), 17.

[2]Loar, L. (1999). "I'll only help you if you have two legs," or, Why human services professionals should pay attention to cases involving cruelty to animals. In, Ascione, F.R. & Arkow, P., eds.: *Child Abuse, Domestic Violence, and Animal Abuse: Linking the Circles of Compassion for Prevention and Intervention*, West Lafayette, IN: Purdue University Press, 1999, pp. 120–136.

[3]Ascione, F.R. 1997. The abuse of animals and domestic violence: a national survey of shelters for women who are battered. *Society and Animals, 5*(3): 205–218.

[4]Ascione, F.R., Weber, C.V. and Wood, D. S. (1997). The abuse of animals and domestic violence: A national survey os fhelters for women who are battered. *Society & Animals 5*(3). 205–218.

[5]Favor, C.A. and Strand, E.B. (2003). Domestic Violence and Animal Cruelty: Untangling the Web of Abuse. *Journal of Social Work Education 39*(2), 237–253.

[6]Favor and Strand (2003).

[7]Ascione, F.R. (1995). Domestic violence and cruelty to animals. Paper presented at the Fourth International Conference on Family Violence, Durham, NH, July 24.

[8]Merz-Perez, L., Heide, K. and Silverman, I. (2001). Childhood Cruelty to Animals and Subsequent Violence against Humans, International Journal of Offender Therapy and Comparative Criminology, Vol. 45 No. 5, 556–573.

*Logo design courtesy of Ken Crump, Animal Cancer Center, Colorado State University

As you can see, the fact sheets changed over time as the research progressed. Later on, when we talk about how to identify and build your coalition, you'll see how you will want to update your fact sheet regularly as you keep adding the names of prominent individuals and organizations that are backing your effort.

Chapter Questions

1. What are some ideas you have for an advocacy campaign that could positively impact your own nonprofit or another in your community?

2. How would you go about researching the feasibility of your idea?

3. What are some high-profile lobbying campaigns that are being talked about in your community or state?

4. What movie made Bo Derek famous?

Endnotes

i   Hall, M. T. (2010, June 29). Chelsea's law adds treatment, assessment. *The San Diego Union Tribune*. Retrieved March 16, 2011, from http://www.signonsandiego.com/news/2010/jun/29/chelseas-law-adds-treatment-assessment/

ii   Durose, M. R., Langan, P. A., & Schmitt, E. L. (2003, November 16). *Recidivism of sex offenders released from prison in 1994*. Retrieved March 16, 2011, from http://bjs.ojp.usdoj.gov/index.cfm?ty=pbdetail&iid=1136

iii   Kilgannon, C. (2003, May 12). Get that oak an accountant; study puts a dollar value on work done by city's trees. *The New York Times*. Retrieved March 16, 2011, from http://www.nytimes.com/2003/05/12/nyregion/get-that-oak-accountant-study-puts-dollar-value-work-done-city-s-trees.html

iv   Rancho Coastal Humane Society. (2010). *Animal Safehouse Program*. Retrieved March 16, 2011, from http://www.rchumanesociety.org/programs/safehouse.asp

6

Ten Common Elements of Successful Advocacy Campaigns

Steps 4 to 7

Pat Libby

To recap where we've been thus far along our journey through the 10 steps, you've seen the big 10 laid out in list form, and read all about how to identify an issue, do research on it, and put together a fact sheet. In this chapter we'll walk you through Steps 4 to 7, which include branding the issue, mapping out possible supporters and detractors, forming a coalition, and developing educational materials. We've got a lot of work to do, so let's get started on figuring out how to name and frame the issue, which is otherwise known as giving it a "brand."

1. Identify an issue.

2. Research the issue.

3. Create a fact sheet.

4. **"Brand" the issue.**

5. Map out possible supporters and detractors.

6. Form a coalition.

7. Develop educational materials.

8. Launch a media campaign.

9. Approach elected officials.

10. Monitor progress on the issue.

"Brand" the Issue: How It's Done _____

The way you name and frame your campaign often emerges from the facts you choose to highlight your issue. And, how you present your issue has everything to do with how well it will "sell" in the marketplace of ideas. You need to figure out how to package your issue so that people hearing it for the first time will understand it (or think they do) and remember what it's all about. Although we tend to think of advocacy as waging a campaign that is focused on persuading elected or appointed officials to do something, chances are those officials will be more inclined to act if they hear from the general public—especially those citizens who reside in their district because that's ultimately who they have the responsibility of representing. Therefore, the name of your issue needs to be able to be easily communicated to a broad audience.

Really good *frames* have a way of positioning your issue so that people who might normally look at things from one perspective are drawn instead to consider your point of view because of how you've described it. Matt Bai, a political pundit who writes commentary for *The New York Times Magazine* has described framing as "choosing the language to define a debate and, more important, with fitting individual issues into the contexts of broader story lines."[i] A really good name for an issue can also serve a dual function of framing it as well.

Here are a few examples of good "names and frames" that you may already be aware of from local and national advocacy campaigns:

Death Tax

Partial Birth Abortion

Living Wage

In each of these cases, the names of those advocacy campaigns provided a frame for an issue that shifted or tried to shift debate on the topic by asking people to look at it in a different light. Let's look at the so-called "living wage" as an example. What is it?

Interestingly, a living wage is defined mostly by what it isn't, which is the minimum wage, much in the same way that nonprofits are defined by what they're not. Although the term was first coined in the early 1870s,[ii] it was repopularized more than 100 years later when in the mid-1990s activists in Baltimore began to clamor for minimum wages that would allow a worker to afford a decent quality of life. They managed to pass the first living wage ordinance in the United States, which required that businesses receiving contracts from the city pay a set wage that was above the minimum. The point was and is that people who work full-time shouldn't have to live in poverty and that government could make policy that would do something about it.

Today approximately 150 living wage campaigns have passed throughout the country, mostly at the municipal level, with the state of Maryland having the distinction of being the only state with a living wage law.[iii] What that means for the fine citizens of Maryland is that as of October 1, 2007, state government contractors and subcontractors have been required to pay wages that are significantly higher than the $7.25 federal minimum wage (the federal minimum was $6.15 per hour when this law was passed). Instead, organizations that do business with the state of Maryland pay $8.50 or $11.30 per hour, depending upon whether they are located in a higher- or lower-cost area of the state. All future living wage increases are slated to be adjusted to the Consumer Price Index. It's pretty cool stuff. In fact, most economic analyses of the living wage ordinances nationwide indicate that the benefits to workers and their families vastly outweigh any negative impact on business.

The point here is that the advocates who named and framed this campaign could have called it anything. They could have come up with a long wordy name or with a name that wouldn't have had such broad appeal. What if, for example, they had called it the "Move workers out of poverty" campaign? That wouldn't have quite the same righteous ring to it as "living wage." It is important for you to think strategically about the name of your campaign and what it will mean, at a glance, to people who are listening to it for the first time.

The name of your campaign is its calling card. Oftentimes legislators or other policy makers will refer to the name of your campaign in shorthand, so it's good to invent something that is concise and memorable.

"Brand" the Issue: How They Did It

In the case of our USD student group, they wrestled with whether to frame the issue as an animal rights issue or as a domestic violence issue. Their collective fear was that if it were framed as an animal rights issue, it wouldn't be taken as seriously. The name they came up with, "Protect *Every* Family Member from Domestic Violence," does push it in the direction of animal rights as it implies the animal is a member of the family. While most people tend to see their pets as full-fledged members of their families[1] (including me and my blanket-hogging dog, Frank), I also know that some people look at Frank and just see a mutt. Our honest assessment of the name given to the campaign conducted by our students is that they could probably have come up with something stronger, and at the very least, something that focused on the domestic violence aspect of the problem rather than pet abuse. Other than that, they did run a near perfect advocacy campaign as you'll see. The idea is to make the name and the frame of your campaign as palatable to as many people as possible. Another name the team batted around was "Protecting Pets, Protecting People," but it's kind of a tongue twister.

---

[1]According to a 2010 Harris Interactive Poll, 65% of Americans report buying their pets holiday gifts.

Step 5 involves mapping out possible supporters and detractors. Some people call this a Positional Map or a Strategy Map.

1. Identify an issue.

2. Research the issue.

3. Create a fact sheet.

4. "Brand" the issue.

5. **Map out possible supporters and detractors.**

6. Form a coalition.

7. Develop educational materials.

8. Launch a media campaign.

9. Approach elected officials.

10. Monitor progress on the issue.

Map Out Possible Supporters and Detractors: How It's Done

For pretty much every issue in the world there are people who are in favor of it, those who are against it, and those like Rhett Butler who "frankly . . . don't give a damn." Rhett aside, within those first two categories—the people for and against the issue—there are lots of shades of gray. What is meant by that is that there are some people who will do just about anything to make sure that your issue moves forward and others who will be whole-heartedly committed to doing just the opposite. What you want to do is to think carefully about which people and organizations are represented along the continuum of possible supporters and detractors. The reason the word *continuum* is used here is because on both sides of the "for" and "against" equation there will be a wide variety of people and organizations that are willing to get involved. They will run the gamut from hard-core believers that will drive the effort, to those that will do *something* to help, to people who *might* be willing to pitch in, to those that agree with the cause but not to the extent that they'd do any heavy lifting (although they might lend their name to the effort). There will also be people and organizations that will be peripherally affected by the issue but not enough to make a stink.

What you want to do during this process is to literally map out these players. You might start with a big wall chart for brainstorming purposes and then move to a format where you can move the players as the campaign progresses. At the beginning, ask yourselves,

a. Who do we think is going to be strongly in favor of the idea and can be enlisted to help it move along?

b. Who do we think may be somewhat in favor of the idea and could be convinced to do something to actively support it?

c. Who do we think is going to be actively against it and why? What arguments will they use to thwart the idea?

d. Who do we think might be somewhat against the idea and could be possibly neutralized if we could think of how to talk about the idea in a way that addresses or minimizes their concerns?

You can develop a chart that has headings like "Love Our Issue," "Middle of the Road (or We Just Don't Know)," and "Strong Opposition" and scribble in the information on a big sheet. Alternatively, you can go to the web and download a free Force Field Analysis tool from MindTools (http://www.mindtools.com/pages/article/newTED_06.htm) that will help you develop your map.

As you fill in the names on the chart, be sure to step back and take a look at who is in the middle and who is closest to the middle. What you want to do is to see if you can figure out arguments that will move those middle people over to your side. You'll also fill in the names of people and organizations you think will never come to see things the way you do, but might be willing to move closer to your viewpoint if you deal with their concerns. If you are able to be honest with yourselves and think carefully about the arguments the opposition might have, you may be able to put together research to refute or address their objections. At the very least, you won't be caught off guard when detractors come up with arguments against your idea (and you'll be well prepared with your own defense). That's why earlier on it was suggested that your advocacy teams be composed of people who have differing views or, even better, different affiliations across the political spectrum. If you have a diverse team, then, as you're working through all of the steps described thus far, you'll be well aware of what might lie ahead because your group will have already talked about it openly (and maybe even argued a bit, which is fine too).

It is worth taking a minute here to talk about what kinds of people and organizations should be on your supporter list because you want to be sure to think beyond the usual suspects. What happens a lot in nonprofit advocacy campaigns is that organizations tend to recruit other nonprofits that are just like their own as their only allies. That's not good for a variety of reasons including the fact that policy makers sometimes view nonprofit advocates as acting in their own self-interest (which is the height of irony since most of us who work in the sector make great sacrifices to do so). What they often think, though, is this: "Sure Pat's working hard on that campaign because she won't have a paycheck if her clients don't receive services." For this reason and others, think in terms of putting together a cross-sector coalition—one that involves people and organizations from the business community, public sector, and other nonprofit subsectors (for example, environmental organizations working in collaboration with nonprofit housing development groups). The reason that's important is because it doesn't make your effort seem as self-serving since it involves so many different types of people and organizations. The longer the list of your supporters, the stronger your campaign will be. Once that task is done, the map will ideally evolve over time as you meet with and add key players that dot your landscape.

In addition, you will have to create a separate map that will show your possible legislative allies and detractors. You'll need to go back to the research you did in Step 2 that identified who sponsored similar types of legislation in the past and who opposed it for what reasons. That information will be vitally important to helping you address the concerns of those legislators and opposition groups before they are raised this time. In addition, this research might unearth organizations you may not be aware of that supported the idea and worked toward its passage.

If there's never been a similar legislative or policy proposal, you'll have to do some simple biographical research on each of the people you plan to approach. If you look at the websites for your elected officials, you'll find them to be chock full of information about their interests and accomplishments. You'll also learn about the committees they sit on and the organizations they are members of. For those people who were elected more recently, you can look up articles that detail the key issues they talked about during their election campaigns. All of those clues will help your group determine who is likely to lend a hand (or oppose your idea). It will be worth its weight in gold if you have an understanding of the terrain before you wade into that territory.

The last word on this topic draws the conversation back to naming and framing your issue. It almost goes without saying that if you take the time to figure out the potential arguments against your issue and who will be making them, you can use those insights to help you develop a name and frame for your campaign. A good name and frame will help you neutralize those objectives before they are even uttered.

Map Out Possible Supporters and Detractors: How They Did It

As you can see from the fact sheet our students put together, their coalition consisted of both domestic violence prevention organizations and animal rights groups. It wasn't a cast of thousands, but it did represent both sides of the issue. The positional map the team developed was actually very simple in part because, interestingly, the students didn't have a lot of real opposition to what they were trying to accomplish (which is rare). Obviously, the more money or resources involved, the more complex the map. For their campaign the map looked like Figure 6.1.

Figure 6.1

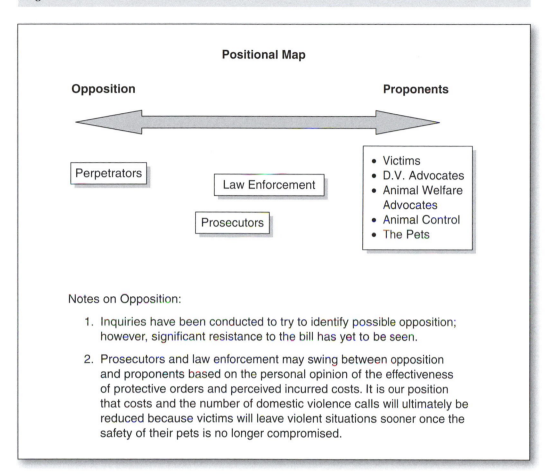

Positional Map

Opposition   Proponents

Perpetrators

Law Enforcement

Prosecutors

- Victims
- D.V. Advocates
- Animal Welfare Advocates
- Animal Control
- The Pets

Notes on Opposition:

1. Inquiries have been conducted to try to identify possible opposition; however, significant resistance to the bill has yet to be seen.

2. Prosecutors and law enforcement may swing between opposition and proponents based on the personal opinion of the effectiveness of protective orders and perceived incurred costs. It is our position that costs and the number of domestic violence calls will ultimately be reduced because victims will leave violent situations sooner once the safety of their pets is no longer compromised.

We'll move next to Step 6, *form a coalition.*

1. Identify an issue.

2. Research the issue.

3. Create a fact sheet.

4. "Brand" the issue.

5. Map out possible supporters and detractors.

6. **Form a coalition.**

7. Develop educational materials.

8. Launch a media campaign.

9. Approach elected officials.

10. Monitor progress on the issue.

Form a Coalition: How It's Done

By now it should be as plain as the nose on your face that when you are putting together your positional map, you're simultaneously thinking through whom you can convince to jump on board your campaign.

There are three main points about coalition building that have already been touched on in the discussion about previous steps that deserve a little more airtime. They are:

1. Look for unusual bedfellows when forming your coalition.

2. Not every member of your coalition needs to work on the issue in the exact same way.

3. Be sure to enlist coalition members that reside in the district of the legislators you are seeking to lobby.

The "odd bedfellows" argument is this: The more broad-based your coalition is, the more likely it is to attract legislators or policy makers who have views that are equally wide ranging and, ideally, across the political and ideological spectrum. It is an unfortunate fact that both Congress and our state legislatures are increasingly polarized along party lines. Too often we hear about an issue that is being promoted by one party and one party only. It makes sense that if you are able to draw political support from both sides of the aisle, there will be a much greater likelihood that your issue will move on to become law. If your coalition involves people and organizations that can easily connect to policy makers across the gamut of parties and beliefs, then you're halfway home.

This is still true if, for instance, your state legislature happens to be dominated by one party. After all, not all Republicans or Democrats think alike (never mind those who are independent, Green, or Libertarian!). As a case in point, you can have Democrats who support the death penalty, those who oppose the death penalty, and those who favor the death penalty but only if it's administered in a certain way for select types of crimes. The important thing here is to make sure that your coalition has people and organizations on it that can speak directly to politicians who share their worldview. If you think about it, it's really a matter of human nature. As sympathetic as we might be to an issue, our sympathies increase if there are people just like us who are backing that issue or who have been directly affected by it. If you consider your own reactions to things, you know that's the case.

Let's take the example of you watching a local newscast about children who are brutally bullied at school in a district where policies don't allow the principal to take what you would consider to be appropriate action like automatically suspending the thug for a minimum of a week and mandating counseling. You are much more likely to want to jump off your sofa and do something about it if you, your child, or someone else you know ended up repeatedly on the wrong side of a bully's act (especially if that bully walked away with no repercussions). Perhaps you'll get together with other parents and meet with the principal, address your local PTA, petition the school board for harsher penalties for kids who bully others, seek funding for a bully prevention program, or do something else to address the issue. If you haven't been touched by that kind of situation, you may feel bad while you're watching the news clip, but it's unlikely that you'll think much more about it after you see the commercial featuring the dancing tortilla chips.

The fact is there are so many things that pull on our heartstrings it becomes impossible to act on each and every thing that needs fixing in the world. Naturally we focus on those things we care most about and believe we have the power to change. Legislators are like that too and, as you would expect, are drawn to those people and causes that they can relate to for one reason or another or that have an impact on the community they serve.

In September 2005 the state of California passed legislation that the Governor subsequently vetoed, legalizing same-sex marriage (this was several years before the ballot measure and court action about same-sex marriage in California). As Dean Murphy wrote in a *New York Times* article on the subject,

> The bill, which defines marriage as between "two persons," won final legislative approval Tuesday night in the State Assembly by only a narrow margin, 41 to 35, after a coalition of gay, Latino and African-American groups successfully fended off conservative opposition to it by framing the issue as one of civil rights, not religious values. It passed by a single vote in the State Senate last week, meaning that neither house had a sufficient majority to override a veto.[iv]

As you can imagine, an African American legislator who might not himself be gay or have (or know of) gay friends, family members, or professional colleagues might look at the issue differently if he were lobbied by people he knew or could relate to who spoke about the legislation as a civil rights issue.

A second point has to do with divvying up the work. At the very beginning of your effort there will be a core group of people who seize the day and say, "We must do something about this!" These individuals will begin the steps outlined in this book (or do something along these lines) and gather support as they go along the path of trying to create legislative or policy change.

As you and members of your group talk to more and more people about the issue, some of the new people you engage will feel equally impassioned by the idea and will spend many hours dedicated to conceptualizing and carrying out the campaign from start to finish. Others may be willing to pick up different tasks along the way such as making sure your group is in compliance with the city, county, or state regulations regarding lobbying, doing the research, or playing the role of topic expert for research that has already been done; writing up that research in a user-friendly format; persuading others to join the campaign; designing campaign materials; getting other organizations to endorse or sign on to your campaign; organizing public education events to spread the word; developing talking points for the media; putting together a website for the campaign; creating public education materials; mobilizing members of their own organization to act; visiting with policy makers; and so forth. The key here is to realize that your coalition members will play different roles depending upon their time and interest in the issue. *Don't be distraught if everyone isn't doing an equal amount of work.* Do devise a plan of action that minimally identifies the following:

1. A rough timeline for the campaign and the steps that need to be done along the way. If you are trying to get a bill passed, you'll need to refer to other chapters in this book to chart out key junctures in the policy-making process so that you can make sure you're prepared for each of those steps (e.g., when is the budget prepared by each entity? When do hearings take place?). If you are working on a city or county campaign, you'll need to understand what the time frame is for that process as well.

2. The core members (you can also call yourself the "steering committee") of the campaign and what decisions the group will be entrusted to make as you move along. You will have to think carefully too about how decisions get made: by a majority vote of the group or by consensus? If you are voting, does each member have an equal vote, or do organizations that represent a greater number of people who are affected by the issue have more voting power? As new members of your coalition are added, what decision-making powers will they have? For instance, who gets to vote on the name of your campaign?

3. Which organizations and individuals will be responsible for each step in the process? Who will hold them accountable for following through on their commitments? Does the work done in subcommittees need to be ultimately approved by the core campaign group?

4. Who is the primary point person(s) that policy makers and their aides speak to when they have questions about your issue?

5. Who is entrusted to speak to the media?

If you are clear from the beginning about who is responsible for what, you will minimize feelings of resentment along the lines of "so-and-so thinks she's 'all that' and in charge" while "what's-his-name isn't doing 'jack' like the rest of us." Going back to our situation with the school bully, it's perfectly OK if someone's only role is to come testify at the school board meeting, or even dash off an e-mail to school board members in favor of the proposal that you've drafted outlining stronger penalties for bullies. In some coalitions, having powerful people or organizations lend their names to your effort is huge in and of itself.

Whatever you do, please make sure that all coalition members have signed on to your campaign in writing and understand exactly what is required of their participation. You want to be absolutely sure beyond a shadow of a doubt that your fact sheet lists only those people and organizations that have officially agreed to back your cause. The last thing in the world you need is for any individuals or groups to claim that you are using their names without permission. That type of charge could potentially undermine all your work. Similarly, if you get to a point where one member of your coalition wishes to resign because she or her organization doesn't agree with your tactics, please take the time to listen to her concerns and, if no resolution can be found, graciously allow her to back out. You want to have people and organizations behind you who have no reservations about what you are trying to accomplish and how you are conducting your campaign.

Running an advocacy campaign is a true team effort as long as you recognize how teams really operate. You have star players like Babe Ruth, who are out front doing the heavy lifting game after game while other team members come in only to pinch-hit or steal bases. Some spend most of the time sitting on the bench and aren't called in to play until someone else is injured. They're all proud to wear the uniform and be part of the effort. And they all appreciate the fans in the stands who cheer them on as they make their way through a competitive season. Get the point?

Finally, as was mentioned briefly above, you want to make sure that your coalition contains members who live in the district of the person you plan to lobby. Ideally those people will have had previous contact with that elected official and will understand the key issues that are important to him. You'll also want to make sure that those people are registered to vote! That really does matter to the elected official for reasons that will be discussed further in the next several steps.

1. Identify an issue.

2. Research the issue.

3. Create a fact sheet.

4. "Brand" the issue.

5. Map out possible supporters and detractors.

6. Form a coalition.

7. **Develop educational materials**.

8. Launch a media campaign.

9. Approach elected officials.

10. Monitor progress on the issue.

_____ Develop Educational Materials: How It's Done

So let's talk about those fans. Step 7 is all about mobilizing and educating people.

In the previous chapter we talked about issues that are staring you in the face because so many people within your community or clients you serve have been affected by the thing you are trying to address. You will need to mobilize those people and their friends and family to help you make your case. To do that, begin with an inventory of your coalition members. How many of your members belong to organizations that have an active membership? How do they communicate with those members—at weekly or monthly meetings, at informal gatherings like potlucks and picnics, via a regular newsletter, through the Internet, through e-mail, or on a social networking site? Of your coalition members, which organizations will be able to spread the word about your cause most broadly and effectively? How many people can all of you reach through your combined network?

Some of the people contacted through your coalition are going to be eager to talk from direct experience about the problem or opportunity you are proposing; others are going to be willing to write letters, make phone calls, or send e-mails or faxes that speak to the issue. Many will have extensive social media networks that you can plug into to identify and mobilize supporters (Chapter 11 discusses this in detail). You'll want to get an idea of how many people from each organization will be willing to make each of those types of contacts (e.g., how many people will be willing to meet with policy makers, tell their stories to the press, make calls, or rally their troops online?). There will hopefully be representatives from your coalition who will be willing to reach out to other community organizations to educate their members and gather their support, or host public forums that promote the issue to an even broader audience. You will also want to make sure you have people from a variety of organizations playing similar roles to make sure that everyone who is willing to meet directly with a policy maker doesn't come from the same organization but rather comes from different organizations that are working for the cause. The total number of all those people who are willing to take action on behalf of your issue is quite important because you want to be able to say to the people you are lobbying that your group represents so many concerned citizens.

Why is all of this necessary? The honest truth is that lawmakers really do care when their constituents contact them (and "constituents" in this sense means people who reside within their districts and *vote*). And yes, they really do check to see if people who contact them about a particular issue are *registered* to vote. The reason they care is because if their constituents are happy with their job performance, those folks will go to the polls and reelect them. It doesn't matter if those being lobbied are appointed officials or aides to an elected official—they will still check to see if you are registered to vote. After all, their job security depends upon whether their boss, the elected official, stays in office. These staff people, no matter how high up they are on the food chain, act as a proxy for the elected person.

For instance, if I am an aide to a city council member or legislator and I don't listen to what the people in my district want (or, for that matter, listen politely), then they won't be happy with my boss, they'll express their unhappiness by voting for her opponent, and I'll soon find myself stocking shelves at Wal-Mart (well, maybe not, but I will be out of a job). You would think the one exception to this rule is when the politician is a lame duck, meaning that person can't run for office again because the law forbids it as is the case with term limits or if the politician has simply declared that he just doesn't want to run again for whatever reason. The fact is that politicians really do want to serve the greater good and sincerely care when people in their communities take the time to contact them about an issue regardless of how long they have been or will continue to stay in office.

Politicians and their proxies also care about the *way* in which their constituents communicate with them. If they receive a large number of faxes, postcards, or e-mails about a particular item and all of those faxes, postcards, and e-mails have the exact same wording printed on them, then that's really like getting a lot of junk mail. It's not nearly as good as a smaller number of personalized letters, postcards, or telephone calls that talk about different reasons why the issue matters. The rule is simple: The more personalized the interaction, the more it counts.

The biggest impact is when constituents take the time to schedule a visit with officials or their proxies to discuss the issue face-to-face. Sure, you can always try to drop in unannounced, but scheduled visits work much more effectively. What our students find most surprising when they travel to our state capitol to meet with state legislators, their aides, or other California policy makers (such as people in leadership positions in various departments that the State Cabinet comprises) is how willing the officials are to listen to the issue being presented. Honestly, it's a little sad that the students are perennially astonished by this phenomenon because that's what these policy makers get paid to do—to serve the people.

Part of this lovefest has to do, of course, with the excellent research and fact sheet the students have prepared, and how well they've framed the issue, thought through concerns others might raise, prepared the people they've brought with them to talk directly about the issue, and rehearsed their presentation to be able to answer the questions asked of them. The truth is, even if the students weren't so outstanding, public officials are always impressed when citizens take the time to come speak to them in person (and even more so if someone has to travel a distance for that purpose). That really matters. A lot. It matters because it shows how much you and your colleagues care about this particular thing.

If you live in or near your state capital, or are lobbying for a cause that has to do with county or state government, it's pretty easy to set up some face time with the policy makers (or, again, their proxies), and in Step 9 we're going to share some ideas with you about the best ways to approach them. To be frank, though, even if you live close by, most of *your* constituents—that is, those people you know who are most affected by the issue—won't go to an in-person meeting. They won't go for a variety of reasons—some have full-time jobs and can't get off work; others have difficulty getting around because they're frail and it's cold or they have kids to look after or whatever. Some might be scared or embarrassed to speak publicly about the issue. Others care about the issue enough to help you out but don't feel so strongly about it that they're willing to devote all that much time to making change happen. That's fine as long as you are able to inspire these people to take *some* type of action. This is where your mobilization and education work comes in. Your job is to figure out how to energize as many people as possible to weigh in on your side and to make sure those people spin the issue the way you want it spun.

The key to mobilizing people is making it easy for them to participate in your campaign. That involves two important steps: first, distilling what you've learned in your research into digestible, easy-to-understand nuggets of information that quickly educate your members about why it's important to act and how they can convince others this thing is important. The second step involves making sure that it's fairly effortless to take action.

Essentially, all you need is the information that's already contained in your handy-dandy fact sheet and specific directions on what to do and how to do it. You'll want to give them options for contacting their elected officials such as the ones already mentioned ad nauseam in this section—sending faxes, calling, e-mailing, writing letters, and paying visits—making sure they understand the relative importance of each of those options. You'll need to be clear on the talking points that your constituents should use and let them know that their personal stories make a real difference. You'll also want to ask them to sign up for regular alerts that they'll receive either by e-mail, tweets, or telephone about what new action they can take as the issue moves through the process.

An example from the Massachusetts Coalition for the Homeless is demonstrated in Figure 6.2.

Figure 6.2

**MASSACHUSETTS
COALITION
FOR THE HOMELESS**

May 24, 2010

Please Contact Your State Senator Today:
Help Improve the Senate's Version of the
Fiscal Year 2011 State Budget

Support the following amendments to the Senate Ways and
Means Committee's budget recommendations!

Quick Links	Dear Pat,
Coalition's home page Coalition's Senate budget page Senate amendments Senate Ways & Means Committee's proposed budget website SWM Executive Summary Coalition's budget comparison chart	Last week, the Senate Committee on Ways and Means ("Senate Ways and Means" or "SWM") unveiled its fiscal year 2011 budget recommendations for the Commonwealth. Under the leadership of Chairman Steven Panagiotakos, the Senate Ways and Means Committee calls for $27.88 billion in FY'11 spending. As we reported, many of the line items we follow would see their funding levels maintained or slightly increased to accommodate increased demand. At the same time, however, some of the programs we follow most closely, including the Emergency Assistance family shelter and services account, would be severely cut by the SWM budget.
Join Our Mailing List	Last Thursday and Friday, Senators submitted 724 amendments to the SWM budget. At the beginning of this week, Senators can sign on as co-sponsors of those amendments, in advance of this week's budget debate. The Senate is scheduled to debate this proposed budget and consider floor amendments starting Wednesday (with a pre-debate caucus of Senate Democrats scheduled for tomorrow morning).
Join the Coalition for our HeARTs for Humanity event!	
Join us for a benefit cocktail party and art raffle in Boston's South End on Thursday, June 17th! Follow this link for more details: HeARTs for Humanity	Please contact your State Senator today to ask her/him to support the following amendments, so as to improve the Senate version of the budget. Ask your Senator to contact the amendment sponsors' offices to sign their name to these amendments. To find out who your Senator is, please go to www .wheredoivotema.com. For a list of Senators and their contact information, please click here.
Are you on Facebook? Now the Coalition is, too!	Thank you again for your advocacy with and for families and individuals who are at-risk or experiencing homelessness!
Join us by clicking on this link: MCH Facebook Page	**The Senate's FY'11 Budget Recommendations for Housing, Shelter, Homelessness Prevention, and Benefits Programs: Senate Ways and Means Budget and Proposed Amendments** Please follow this link to access the Coalition's chart comparing the Senate Ways and Means Committee's FY'11 recommendations with the Governor and House of Representatives' proposals for FY'11 and the current FY'10 appropriations: Budget Comparison Chart To access the complete SWM budget recommendations, please go to the Senate Ways and Means Committee's FY'11 Budget Recommendations. To access the complete list of Senate amendments, please go to Senate amendments. To learn more about the Coalition's FY'11 budget work, please go to the Coalition's FY'11 Priorities

(Continued)

Figure 6.2 (Continued)

Support These Key Amendments to Housing, Homelessness, and Benefits Line Items*

Please note that the links below will bring you to the page on which the amendments are listed (Economic Development, Health and Human Services 1, and Health and Human Services 2). From there, you can scroll or search to find the amendment text on the page.

Emergency Assistance Family Shelter and Services Program (EA, Line Item 7004-0101):

Amendment 341, **sponsored by Chairwoman Susan Tucker:** This amendment would increase the notice time from 45 days to 90 days before changes could be made in EA program eligibility or benefits. It also would prohibit the Department of Housing and Community Development (DHCD) from giving such notice before December 5, 2010, so as to allow the Legislature time to take action after returning to formal sessions on January 5, 2011. In addition, this amendment would ensure that EA eligibility is not reduced due to a potential decrease in the 2010-2011 federal poverty guidelines. The language would direct DHCD to base eligibility on 115% of the 2009 federal poverty guidelines, or a later-issued standard that is higher. The House already has adopted identical language. This amendment would help protect children and families experiencing homelessness. This amendment is co-sponsored by Senators Candaras, Eldridge, Spilka, and Walsh.

Please click here for a fact sheet on Amendment 341.

Amendment 334, **sponsored by Chairwoman Susan Tucker:** This amendment would change language in the proposed EA line item, clarifying that the $3.5 million in earmarked funds should be used to help to "more rapidly move families into permanent sustainable housing."

Department of Housing and Community Development Administrative Account (Line Item 7004-0099):

Amendment 349, **sponsored by Chairwoman Susan Tucker:** This amendment would protect households that receive a short-term subsidy from losing priority for a permanent housing subsidy. This amendment would cost nothing, and simply clarify that a priority that already exists is not lost due to the receipt of a short-term subsidy. This language is especially important at a time when the DHCD has issued more than 1,200 short-term vouchers to help families exit shelter and thousands of additional households are receiving temporary rental assistance through the federally funded Homelessness Prevention and Rapid Re-housing Program (HPRP). The House already has adopted similar language. This amendment is co-sponsored by Senators Candaras, Eldridge, Spilka, and Walsh.

Please click here for a fact sheet on Amendment 349.

Emergency Aid to the Elderly, Disabled and Children Program (EAEDC, Line Item 4408-1000):

Amendment 556, **sponsored by Chairwoman Gale Candaras:** This amendment would increase the notice time from 60 days to 90 days before changes could be made in EAEDC program eligibility or benefits. It also would prohibit the Department of Transitional Assistance (DTA) from giving notice before December 5, 2010, so as to allow the Legislature time to take action after returning to formal sessions on January 5, 2011. This amendment would help protect extremely low-income elders and persons with disabilities. The House already has adopted identical language. This amendment is co-sponsored by Senators Spilka and Walsh.

Please click here for a fact sheet on Amendment 556.

Transitional Aid to Families with Dependent Children Program (TAFDC, Line Item 4403-2000):

Amendment 549, **sponsored by Chairwoman Gale Candaras:** This amendment would increase the notice time from 60 days to 90 days before changes could be made in TAFDC program eligibility or benefits. It also would prohibit DTA from giving notice before December 5, 2010, so as to allow the Legislature time to take action after returning to formal sessions on January 5, 2011. This amendment would help protect extremely low-income families with children. The House already has adopted identical language. This amendment is co-sponsored by Senators Spilka and Walsh.

Please click here for a fact sheet on Amendment 549.

Department of Transitional Assistance Administrative Account (Line Item 4400-1000):

Amendment 658, **sponsored by Chairwoman Patricia Jehlen:** This no-cost amendment would require DTA to produce a report this year setting forth the design and costs of a DTA-based, early warning, homelessness prevention program for families and individuals participating in DTA programs. This "No Place Like Home" program is generally described in Senate Bill 43/House Bill 169, "An Act to Prevent Homelessness Among Recipients of Transitional Assistance." Having this report will move the state one step closer to giving DTA the tools needed to help the low-income families and individuals it serves to remain housed and avoid homelessness. This amendment is co-sponsored by Senators Eldridge, Fargo, and Spilka.

Please click here for a fact sheet on Amendment 658.

(Continued)

Figure 6.2 (Continued)

	Residential Assistance for Families in Transition Program (RAFT, Line Item 7004-9316): Amendment 325, **sponsored by Chairman Jamie Eldridge:** This amendment would increase RAFT funding to $2.5 million for FY'11, so as to help more children and families avoid or exit homelessness. This amendment is co-sponsored by Senators Fargo and Jehlen. **Shelter and Services for Unaccompanied Adults (Line Item 7004-0102):** Amendment 289, **sponsored by Senator Jack Hart:** This amendment would increase the appropriation by $350,000 so as to match the final House amount of $37,643,335.
	While there are several amendments that we oppose, we ask for your particular help in opposing the following amendments: We urge the rejection of Amendment 359, **sponsored by Senator Robert Hedlund,** related to **state-funded public housing (Line Item 7004-9005),** as it would lead to increased homelessness by barring U.S. citizen and lawfully present children and their immigrant parents from state public housing if the parents cannot prove that they have an immigration status that qualifies for a federal public housing subsidy. We also urge the rejection or redrafting of Amendments 645 and 654, **sponsored by Senator Stephen Buoniconti,** related to **EA (Line Item 7004-0101) and TAFDC (Line Item 4403-2000),** so as to protect and support vulnerable families who are experiencing homelessness and other very low-income families.
	Thank you for your advocacy! To share feedback with us about your outreach to your Senator, or for more information, please contact the Coalition at 781-595-7570: Kelly Turley (x17 or kelly@mahomeless.org) or Leslie Lawrence (x16 or leslie@mahomeless.org). Thank you again! We will be back in touch soon to let you know the outcome of these amendments and how housing, homelessness, and benefit programs fare in the final Senate version of the fiscal year 2011 budget. We also will keep you informed of the progress as the budget continues to make its way through the Conference Committee and full Legislature in the month ahead. Thank you again!
	mchalert Massachusetts Coalition for the Homeless

Please join us in raising money to help end homelessness, just by searching the Internet or shopping online with GoodSearch.

GoodSearch for the Massachusetts Coalition for the Homeless by following this link: http://www.goodsearch.com/?charityid=849550.

Source: Massachusetts Coalition for the Homeless. Reprinted with permission.

As you can see, the coalition has made it easy for its members to quickly understand the key points of the legislation and to take action. If you spend some time looking around on websites of other advocacy organizations, you'll find more good examples of techniques that are used to mobilize, educate, and inspire people.

Chapter Questions

1. If you could rename the Protect *Every* Family Member campaign, what would you call it?

2. Can you think of at least one other current name and frame that is popularly used to promote an advocacy campaign?

3. What names have you discussed for the advocacy campaign you propose? Why did you discard some names, and why did others seem to work better?

4. Develop a first draft of a positional map for your proposed campaign that has a minimum of 10 high-profile individuals or organizations listed.

5. Look up a legislative committee that is operating at the state level and research how its members voted last session on a particular issue. How easy or difficult is it to map their positions?

6. Name three ideas for educating and mobilizing members of your organization about your proposed advocacy campaign.

Endnotes

i   Bai, M. (2005, July 17). The framing wars. *The New York Times Magazine.* Retrieved March 17, 2011, from http://www.nytimes.com/2005/07/17/magazine/ 17DEMOCRATS.html

ii   Glickman, L. B. (1999). *A living wage: American workers and the making of consumer society*. Ithaca, NY: Cornell University Press.

iii   Jen Kern, Director, ACORN Living Wage Resource Center, personal communication, February 29, 2008.

iv   Murphy, D. (2005, September 8). Schwarzenegger to veto same-sex marriage bill. *The New York Times*. Retrieved March 17, 2011, from http://www.nytimes.com/2005/09/08/national/08arnold.html

7

Ten Common Elements of Successful Advocacy Campaigns

Steps 8 to 10

Pat Libby

W e're in the thick of it now. We've figured out that our issue is real and meaningful, done research that backs up our feelings with data, boiled that research down to a double-sided fact sheet, and created a poignant name for our campaign. We've also put our heads together to figure out who will be for and against us and what their arguments will be, assembled a coalition of folks who are willing to do some work to advance our cause, and developed a set of straightforward educational materials that our coalition members can distribute to their clients, friends, and community. Boy, we've come a long way! Our next steps are to publicize the issue in the media after which we'll approach our elected officials and begin the lobbying process. Let's get going on learning how to launch a media campaign.

1. Identify an issue.

2. Research the issue.

3. Create a fact sheet.

4. "Brand" the issue.

5. Map out possible supporters and detractors.

6. Form a coalition.

7. Develop educational materials.

8. **Launch a media campaign**.

9. Approach elected officials.

10. Monitor progress on the issue.

Launch a Media Campaign: How It's Done _____

One way of getting citizens to weigh in on your issue is to raise awareness of it in the media, Step 8.

There are two primary reasons you want to get media coverage for your issue, and they feed off of one another. First, the more people know about the issue, the more likely they'll be to throw their support behind your effort. You might attract some people who have no interest in joining any formal campaign yet are willing to call their local official and say, "I read about that thing in the paper, and I feel strongly that the law needs to be changed." Second, the more press you get, the more apt policy makers will be to pay attention to your cause because they'll see the issue is gaining visibility, which may mean increased public support and increased scrutiny of what they will do about it.

It isn't the case that any press is good press because it is critical that you control the message that is being spread about your issue (just tune into Rush Limbaugh on any given day, and you'll see what can happen when a media message gets spun out of control). The best way to control the message is to make triple sure that you have checked all of your facts to ensure they are accurate, make sure that all of your listed supporters are indeed supporters, and know that the people who have been affected by your issue are of good character, are well prepared to speak about the issue, and, most important, are prepared to field some potentially ugly questions.

What works particularly well is if you are able to get a news story printed that you can make copies of and include as part of the packet of materials you'll bring to your meeting with legislators (or their aides or policy makers—in other words, whomever you're lobbying). Somehow seeing your cause in print makes it seem like a much bigger deal, and it is because through the media you've been able to convey your message to a broader group of people. If you can get a photo of your issue, that's an added bonus. Ideally, if you time things just right, you can get the story to appear within a week of your visit.

So where do you begin? Jeff McDonald, a former student of ours who is also a reporter at *The San Diego Union-Tribune*, has given our students lots of great advice on how to deal with the media. Here are some of his tips:

1. Know and understand your local media outlets.
   - Be sure to do an inventory of what's out there—radio, TV, Internet, and print (include weeklies and community magazines in addition to the major newspaper in your area).
   - Watch the weekend news pages and morning shows to keep track of where they do live broadcasts and feature stories. Get in touch with the editors who hand out those assignments and think about creative approaches that will get their attention (for instance, for the newspaper, information that you've discovered in the course of researching your campaign might be startling enough to produce a headline. For TV, it might be a story about a person who has been affected by your issue).

- Figure out which news organizations and reporters cover what types of stories. For example, you don't want to pitch a "feel-good" story to an investigative reporter, and you don't want to sell an in-depth story to a weekly magazine or TV station as these types of venue are much more likely to want something light.

- Look for the bylines of the reporters who write stories on topics that are similar to yours and invite them to meet with you and other members of your organization. Position yourself as someone who can be called upon to be quoted as an expert on your issue. Tell them why your issue matters and give them the facts. Keep in contact with those people when important developments happen in your campaign. They may not be interested in your idea when you first pitch it, but as it gathers steam with community events or at the legislative level, they might be willing to give it some coverage. Remember to be polite and professional when speaking with these folks. If you yell at them because they choose not to cover your issue at first, then they'll never cover any story related to your efforts.

2. Make sure your press releases are well written and well targeted.

   - Be concise—a single page is best with a brief description of the issue and a web address for follow-up. Make sure you have included the contact information for someone who will be easily available and able to answer questions. And, like your fact sheet, if you have assembled a group of organizations that have signed on to be part of your coalition, be sure to list them.

   - Give at least two weeks' notice before scheduled events.

   - Remember that press releases are "glorified sales pitches"—they aren't stories. The idea is to "sell" the reporter on the idea of investigating or covering the story, not to write it for him.

   - Target your press release to specific individuals and follow up the press release with a telephone call to make sure it has been received (but don't hound the reporter!).

   - Remember, it's OK to target multiple media organizations at the same time. If you're sending a press release, they'll know that that's your media strategy. Alternatively, you can target a single reporter at the largest newspaper in your area to offer her an "exclusive," which is saying that you are allowing that reporter to cover the story before anyone else. If you decide to go the "exclusive" route, you cannot ethically send the press release or talk about the story with any other media outlet once the reporter decides to write or otherwise produce your story.

3. Develop specific events for your campaign that are designed to attract TV and other news coverage.

   - Organize walks, runs, benefits, cleanups, or other events that draw attention to your issue.

- Make a public announcement of your study, your poll, or other research you have done or uncovered that speaks to the importance of your issue.
- Use your coalition to turn out people and attention. The media is more likely to cover your event if more than one organization is involved in hosting it. The bigger the crowd, the more newsworthy the event.

4. When reporters call . . .

- Make sure you have developed "talking points" in advance so that you are able to "stay on message."
- Be sure to always tell the truth. If a reporter asks a question about your issue and you don't know the answer, it's fine to admit what you don't know. You can ask the reporter why she wants to know that particular piece of information in the hope that you can answer it with another, and, if she still isn't satisfied, you can let the reporter know that you'll get back to her once you do have an answer.
- If you want to give a reporter background on the story yet you don't want to be quoted on that information, you can say to him, "This information that I'm about to tell you now is 'off the record.'" For example, you may want to tell him about someone who has done something so egregious against your cause that you want to have it known but you don't want to be quoted talking about that person's actions. Just be careful, though, that you have thoroughly checked your facts before going down that path so that the reporter can verify what happened.
- Be sure to always return a reporter's call. Invite her to tour your agency or to meet with members of your community.

In addition to these tips, Jeff also suggests recruiting someone with marketing, media, or public relations experience to your campaign or to the board of directors of your nonprofit. People with those skills know how to craft messaging that can be easily understood by the public, have lots of connections with other media folks, and are quite good at handling crisis situations should one arise during the course of your campaign. If things are moving so quickly you don't have time to recruit that type of person, you can look for ways to pitch your story by doing a web search for articles that were generated in other states or localities that launched similar campaigns (assuming, of course, your issue was vetted elsewhere).

You need to keep in mind that relationships with the media are a lot like relationships with anybody else—it takes some time to build trust. The people you're working with from the press need to know that you're a solid citizen and not selling them a bunch of bad information. That's why ideally it's good to begin cultivating relationships with editors and reporters long before you need them to write or produce a story.

Figure 7.1 is an example of an effective press release developed by yet another group of students (Travis Degheri, Kelly Holmes, Annamarie Maricle, and Frances Meda).

Chapter 11 of this book is devoted to social media and Internet advocacy. It contains tons of information on other important ways of promoting your campaign.

Figure 7.1

PRESS RELEASE
Contact: Frances Meda
Cell: XXX-XXX-XXXX
Email: @yahoo.com

For Immediate Release

Grassroots Coalition Working to Stop Drug Sales to Minors

The San Diego group DXM: 18 and Over the Counter is meeting with state lawmakers in Sacramento on Monday, January 10th to fight for legislation to stop the sale of cough medicine containing dextromethorphan (DXM) to minors. This proposed bill will have NO COST to taxpayers and PROTECT CHILDREN from abusing over-the-counter cough medicines.

DXM: 18 and Over the Counter is leading a grassroots effort to stop children from abusing DXM, the most common drug in 140 cough and cold medicines sold over the counter. More than 400,000 children in California abuse cough remedies made with dextromethorphan every year. DXM: 18 and Over the Counter seeks to ban the sale of products containing DXM to minors.

Here are the facts:

- Annually, more than 400,000 Californians, ages 11 to 17, abuse DXM to get high.
- Overdoses can cause seizures, comas, brain damage and even kill a first-time user.
- Between 2004 and 2007, emergency room visits due to DXM abuse soared by 70 percent.
- Teens who abuse DXM believe it's a "safe high" because it is legal and readily available in the same stores that sell gum and soda.
- Prohibiting the sale of medicines containing DXM will protect children.

DXM: 18 and Over the Counter has already met with Assemblywoman Toni Atkins to discuss the proposed legislation. For more information contact Frances Meda at (XXX) XXX-XXXX or by email at 18andoverthecounter@gmail.com.

Follow the DXM:18 and Over-The-Counter Coalition:

Twitter: @DXM18andOver
http://facebook.com/pages/18-and-Over-the-Counter/160938723950766
18andoverthecounter.blogspot.com

Source: Student project. Thank you to Travis Degheri, Kelly Holmes, Frances Meda, and Annamarie Maricle.

Launch a Media Campaign: How They Did It _____

Here is a sample of some of the media the students generated for their campaign:

BILL SEEKS TO SAVE PETS FROM ABUSE IN DISPUTES

Submitted by administrator on Mon, 06/25/2007 – 13:03

By JIM SANDERS
Sacramento Bee
Monday, June 25, 2007

Man biting dog?

To keep that from happening, pets soon may be eligible for restraining orders to keep a human away.

Proposed California legislation is targeting a twisted form of domestic violence in which abusers attack loved ones by hurting or killing their pets.

The measure, which appears headed for passage, states that "perpetrators often abuse animals in order to intimidate, harass or silence their human victims."

The bill would allow judges to include pets in protective orders they issue, thus granting temporary custody or ordering abusers to keep their distance.

"Victims of domestic violence have delayed leaving their homes, delayed seeking safety, because their abuser said, 'You take one step out of the house and I'll kill your dog,'" said Democratic state Sen. Sheila Kuehl, who crafted the bill.

Kuehl, who said she knows of one woman who returned home to find her cat hung from the front door, said she wants to ban some abusive humans from contact with loved ones' pets.

Under her bill, a judge may grant a restraining order – so there can be no biting, kicking, beating, scratching, stealing, mauling, threatening or selling of the animals.

The measure was approved by the Senate, 31–7, and last week it cleared the Assembly Judiciary Committee, 10–0. Gov. Arnold Schwarzenegger has taken no position.

No formal opposition has surfaced, but some people warn that the legislation could lead to false or exaggerated claims to spite a former lover.

Statistics are not readily available on the number of pet injuries or deaths linked to human domestic violence. But Stephanie Bamberger, managing attorney for WEAVE, formerly known as Women Escaping A Violent Environment, said it is common for clients to fear for their pets' safety.

"I think it certainly would give the protected person a little more peace of mind that they could protect the animals they love," she said of the bill.

Eighty-five percent of women and 63 percent of children entering 50 of the nation's largest shelters for battered women cited incidents of pet abuse in a 1997 study by the Humane Society of the United States.

"There are many cases where a spouse will actually kill, beat or torture a pet in front of the children," said Beverlee McGrath, California legislative specialist for the Humane Society.

Yvonne Creswell, 32, of San Diego told lawmakers that an abusive former partner threatened to "get rid of my dog" or "let her go free on the streets."

"I knew during the 18 months that I endured his violence that I would not leave unless I could take my animals with me," she said.

Cruelty to animals already is illegal, but enforcement occurs only after harm is done.

To protect themselves against abuse, domestic-violence victims can obtain restraining orders for themselves and human family members – but not necessarily pets.

Animals are not cited in family law as property to be protected. Judges conceivably could include them in restraining orders, but many do not, Kuehl said.

"Then, when you call the police and say, 'He's threatening to kill my dog,' you really don't have any basis for officers to come out," Kuehl said.

The measure would allow endangered pets to be protected by court order for days, weeks or years. The bill would cover any type of animal. Violators could be charged with a misdemeanor.

New York, Vermont and Maine passed similar laws last year.

(Jim Sanders can be reached at jsanders@sacbee.com.)

Other press included:

FloridaPets.net. (2007, June 26). *Bill seeks to save pets during domestic violence cases.* Retrieved March 19, 2011, from http://floridapetsnet.blogspot.com/2007/06/bill-seeks-to-save-pets-during-domestic.html

Gardner, M. (2007, April 23). *Animals get legislature's attention.* Retrieved March 19, 2011, from http://www.signonsandiego.com/news/state/20070423-9999-1n23animals.html

Hsu, A. (2007, May 10). Groups move to protect women and their pets [Radio broadcast]. *All Things Considered.* Retrieved March 19, 2011, from http://www.npr.org/templates/story/story.php?storyId=10119810

Knufken, K. (2007). *USD students campaign for four-legged victims of domestic violence.* Retrieved March 19, 2011, from http://www.sandiego.edu/usdmag/?p=1319

Law.com. (n.d.). *Legislator wants to open more (doggie) doors to courthouse.* Retrieved March 19, 2011, from http://www.law.com/jsp/article.jsp?id=1172743393016&pos=ataglance

Martinez, L. (n.d.). *USD students lend helping paw for new pet safety legislation.* Retrieved March 19, 2011, from http://www.sdnews.com/view/full_story/302169/article-USD-students-lend-helping-paw-for-new-pet-safety-legislation?

McDonald, J. (2007, March 5). *More nonprofits learn benefits of lobbying: Projects created by class now bills.* Retrieved March 19, 2011, from http://www.signon sandiego.com/news/politics/20070305-9999-1m5lobby.html

Sanders, J. (2007, June 25). *Bill seeks to save pets from abuse in disputes.* Retrieved March 19, 2011, from http://www.scrippsnews.com/node/24581

State of California Legislative Counsel. (n.d.). *Bill information* [SB 353]. Retrieved March 19, 2011, from http://www.leginfo.ca.gov/bilinfo.html

Now on to Step 9 and things are getting exciting!

1. Identify an issue.

2. Research the issue.

3. Create a fact sheet.

4. "Brand" the issue.

5. Map out possible supporters and detractors.

6. Form a coalition.

7. Develop educational materials.

8. Launch a media campaign.

9. **Approach elected officials.**

10. Monitor progress on the issue.

Approach Elected Officials: How It's Done _____

In many ways this is the moment you've been waiting for! You've done your "due diligence"—you know your facts and figures cold, you've got a nifty fact sheet and companion white paper, you've done your best to name your issue so that it will be well framed, you've built a broad-based coalition, you know who your opposition might be and what arguments they are likely to make against your idea, and you've checked the laws of your state (or city or county) to make sure you understand whether you have to be registered as a lobbyist. So now what?

You need to figure out who rules over and holds the keys to your kingdom. In other words, who are the legislators or policy makers who have jurisdiction—power and influence—over the subject area under which your issue falls? Governing bodies at the federal and state level, and many at the local level, operate according to a fairly easy-to-understand committee structure. For instance, for the state of California, you can go online and look up the names of all of the types of committees that operate in the legislature (which you can also do if you live in Idaho, Alaska, Mississippi, Maine, and all 50 states for that matter).

There are several different types of committees. Standing committees oversee policy areas ranging from agriculture to water; other standing committees are fiscal committees such as those responsible for the budget. There are also "select committees" that deal with more narrow issues than those discussed in the standing committees and generally do not have the authority to hear/pass/kill bills. Finally, there are joint committees, which contain members of both houses. Whoa, Nellie: "Both houses?" What the heck does that mean?

To revisit a bit of what Howard explained in Chapter 4, the system works like this: Whether you're operating at the state or federal level, each chamber of the legislature comprises two branches (with the exception of Nebraska, which has only one chamber). These chambers have different names: One is called "The Senate" and the other is called "The House," which is shorthand for the House of Representatives (alternatively it can be called "The Assembly" or "House of Delegates" depending upon where you live). Each branch is referred to as a separate house. That's how you get to the saying "both houses" of the legislature or, on the federal level, both houses of Congress (on the federal level the "representatives" elected to the House side are called Congressmen or Congresswomen). Regardless of whether the legislative body operates at the state or federal level, there are always fewer Senators than House Members because Senators represent a larger number of people and, therefore, have more power than a Representative, an Assembly Member, a Delegate, or a Congressperson.

What you need to do is figure out which legislators serve on the particular committee where your issue would be considered. Legislators are more apt to carry a bill if the topic matches the committee on which they serve because that way they have more control over the process.

As you can imagine, it's not hard to figure out who chairs those committees, what types of issues (or legislation) they've considered during the past several years, and how the committee and the individuals who are on it voted on those items. Your job is to get to know the players (on paper first), and to then figure out whether anyone on the committee was elected from a district where you or one of your coalition members lives. Elected officials will almost always be gracious about talking to the public and, of course, will be even more so if you and/or members of your coalition vote in their district. That's why it's good to have a broad-based coalition—ideally you'll want some members of your group to be connected to the district of each person you want to approach.

Simply put, your strategy needs to target the key players. If you use the example of the bill our students worked on having to do with both animal welfare and domestic violence, you'll want to meet with as many members as possible of the committee that would ultimately hear such a bill. Which committee? There is no Domestic Violence Committee, and the only "animal" committee was the Agriculture Committee—not really the direction the students wanted to go! Take a look at Howard's discussion of bill assignments in Chapter 4 and check out the jurisdictions of the standing committee. The students' bill was about family law (even though some circumstances of domestic violence involved situations with informal families), and a check of the jurisdictions shows that the Judiciary Committee hears family law. Indeed, that is where the bill went in both houses. What does all this mean? Your targeting should direct you to contact members (i.e., the legislators who sit on that committee) of the committee that will most likely hear the bill.

After you've done your homework on who's who, the next step is to pick up the phone and call the office of your elected officials to schedule an appointment. The thorough background research you did prior to making that call will enable you to say something like "I'm calling on behalf of the XYZ coalition. We're planning a trip to the state capitol on such and such a date and would like to make an appointment to meet with Senator So-and-So because he's a big supporter of XYZ issues. We'd like to discuss some thoughts we have on strengthening the XYZ laws." You will be more likely to get an appointment if you can quickly demonstrate your familiarity with the work of the Senator by showing that you know about his work to successfully pass or attempt to pass legislation on a topic that is related to your cause. If he's a newly elected official, you can draw upon the interests that are stated on his website including those organizations for which he's volunteered.

The purpose of your appointment will be to set up a time to meet with your elected (or appointed) official or his or her designee. Now you might be saying, "Designee?! No way; I'm putting a ton of work into this campaign, and I don't want to meet with Senator Libby's legislative assistant—I want to meet with the Senator herself" (hmmm, "Senator Libby," I like the way that sounds . . .). Chances are that if the Senator is available when you plan to visit, she may be willing to meet with you—at least for a while and depending too on how far you've traveled to come see her. More likely, you'll meet with someone in her office, a legislative aide who is knowledgeable about your topic or other policy areas related to the topic. If you do a good job, that staffer will end up being your internal advocate. Being an internal advocate means the aide will keep your issue in the forefront of the Senator's mind, remind her about your key talking points, update her on things like how many new organizations are signing on to your coalition every week, and, if you're able to develop a good relationship with her, clue you in on various opportunities and obstacles for getting your legislation passed.

The lesson here is not to minimize your chances of meeting with anyone who works for a big cheese. In most cases you'll find that staff to city council members and legislators are pretty smart (the higher ranking the office, the more experienced the aide tends to be), and, if the elected official is interested in your issue, that staffer will be able to give you tremendous guidance on how to shape your campaign. In fact, when you work in a state where legislators have term limits, legislative aides may know more about how the system works than the legislators themselves because they've been in the building longer!

In small states such as Rhode Island, Delaware, Maryland, Connecticut, and Massachusetts, no one lives that far from the state capitol. In those states there's really no excuse not to visit your state legislators in their own offices. If you do live far away from the place where your elected or appointed official works, then you have several options that, to be honest, aren't terrific. Your elected officials will have an office in your district, and you can set up an appointment to meet with them there. The only problem with that is that policy people—that is, the legislative aide whose job it is to understand and work on the policy issues affecting your cause—are housed at the state capitol and don't tend to spend that much time in the district. You can get lucky at times by developing a good relationship with someone in your local legislator's office who can subsequently arrange for you to meet with the policy aide when he's in town. It is always best when you have direct contact with both the legislator and her policy person.

The office holders themselves do hold regular district meetings and often enjoy coming out to see you if you have something interesting to show them. They are generally pretty good about that and like seeing your organization in action if you plan well in advance. Still, it's just not the same as being up close and personal at the state capitol where business gets done. It's also an amazingly cool experience to lobby at your state capitol in part because the capitol buildings themselves are incredibly interesting places to visit. Therefore, if the issue is something that you care about deeply, you've got to find a way to make the journey by plane, train, or automobile. Realize, though, that the investment of time and money will be well worth it, assuming you've done your homework first.

So here you are. You've done your background work, and you have set up and confirmed appointments in advance with as many legislative offices as possible prior to your visit. You've made copies of all of your materials, and coordinated your schedules to know that you've set aside enough time in between appointments to get from one meeting to another (or have decided that, if need be, you'll split up the team if appointments run over). You've practiced your talking points, ironed your clothes (or, at least, made sure they aren't stained), borrowed a briefcase from a friend, gotten a cheap airfare or pooled your pennies to take the Greyhound bus, and then, finally, you've arrived! You've made it! It's huge! It's beautiful! It's scary! Now what?

You'll find your way to the legislator's office and begin your first meeting. You and your colleagues will begin the meeting by thanking the person (whether it's the elected official or her proxy) for meeting with you. You'll then thank the Senator (Assembly Member, Representative, Delegate) for her long-standing support of XYZ issues. Why do you acknowledge the Senator's work in this area? You acknowledge it because it shows you are familiar with the Senator's work and the causes that are dear to her heart. It will also make the Senator and her staff more receptive to hearing what you have to say. You'll then use your fact sheet to briefly present your case—pointing out the key facts of your problem, your proposed solution, and the coalition of organizations that have signed on to your effort. Be sure to ask directly if the Senator would be willing to author a bill of this nature.

The person with whom you're meeting will probably ask you a number of questions about your issue. Be sure to tell the truth. If you don't know the answer to something, let the person know that you're happy to find out what it is and get back to him. You'll find most often that whomever you're speaking with will be giving you his undivided attention (except for perhaps a few random interruptions). People will probably be quite gracious too even if they disagree with what you have to say.

Let's say, though, for the moment, that you meet with Senator Lewis and she *loves* your idea and understands immediately why it's important. It's just that, well, she thinks it needs to be modified somewhat in order to make it palatable to the other senators on her committee and, eventually, to the other senators in the legislature. That scenario is more likely to happen than not. Often you'll walk in with a *big* idea (although it may not seem so big at the time) and come out with a much smaller version of that idea. It might not even happen at the first office. For instance, as much as Senator Lewis was able to wax poetically about your idea, Senator Rosenstein wasn't nearly as crazy about it and didn't think it would fly at the committee level without some modifications. Then Senator Briggs added her 10 cents, and before you knew it, your idea looked a lot different than what you thought when you first woke up that morning. Listen to what everyone has to say and think carefully about whether these compromises will work for you—don't negotiate away those things that are vitally important to your cause but do consider what's possible. You may have to start at a different point and build up to what you want over a series of years. Passing legislation requires negotiation, cooperation, conciliation, and patience. It's like the words to that old Rolling Stones song, "You can't always get what you want. But if you try sometimes you just might find you get what you need."[i]

Problems arise when advocates go into an elected official's office *demanding* that something happen. Advocates sometimes think that if they arrive with a hoard of people, picket signs and TV cameras in tow, then they will be sure to "win" their case. Actually the opposite may happen. The elected official might be so offended by your behavior that he slams the door on your point of view and on the people who have been affected by the situation you are trying to address. If you were in his situation, you might do the same; no one I know responds well to that kind of pressure.

There is an old saying "It's easier to catch flies with honey," which means that it's easier to attract someone to your point of view when you're being nice. No matter how tempted you may be, do not, under any circumstances, raise your voice in an argumentative or whiny tone to the people you are lobbying. It just won't get you anywhere. It is critically important that you act respectfully to the elected and appointed officials who serve our communities for the simple reason that if you are disrespectful to one, others who may have views that are much more similar to yours will be reluctant to work with you because they'll be wary of your behavior (word travels fast). You may feel in your heart of hearts that your issue is *the* most important issue of the day and become frustrated if your local official doesn't agree. Remember, though, she's probably met with many other individuals and groups who feel similarly about the issue they've brought for consideration. Don't stomp your feet, try not to cry, keep it together, and make every effort to act professionally at all times.

Thankfully we live in a country where we are allowed to express our views freely, and sometimes your elected officials have opinions that are vastly different from your own. When that is the case, the best thing to do is to work as hard as you can to educate them about the situation as you see it using the solid research you've taken the time to put together. If you are able to develop a relationship with that person over time, you might be surprised at how your mutual respect might evolve into support for the things you care about down the road.

Even with all of your advanced planning, there will be times when you are lobbying at your state capitol when you realize that you want to drop in on someone you hadn't made an appointment to go see. It might be because that adorable aide in Senator Muller's office said, "Did you guys set up an appointment to talk to Senator Deitrick? She's really hot on this topic." And somehow you hadn't known that—perhaps because she was just sworn into office a few weeks earlier and you couldn't get much background information on her interests. It's OK to drop in on people without an appointment. You may get lucky and even be able to meet with Senator Deitrick herself. Sometimes you'll run into people on the elevator whom you didn't expect to see and lobby them. A few years ago a group of our students snagged a state assemblyman on the plane trip back to San Diego. Ironically, they hadn't been able to get an appointment with him for earlier in the day and now had him cornered on the flight! The moral of the story is bring along plenty of extra information packets.

After the meeting, act like ambassadors for Emily Post and write thank-you notes to each of the legislators and the aides who took time to meet with you. Equally important, make sure that if people have agreed to sponsor your idea as a piece of legislation, you get back to them as soon as humanly possible with the information they need. Letters from your constituents to various members of the committee will also be welcomed. And don't forget to keep generating positive press for your idea and for the legislator who has agreed to author your bill.

_____ Approach Elected Officials: How They Did It

Prior to their trip to Sacramento the students did some local legwork by contacting the office of San Diego's District Attorney and members of the local

county board of supervisors. Their reasoning was that if high-level local officials endorsed the idea, that would carry weight in the state capitol (and they
were correct). They almost succeeded in getting the endorsement of the local
District Attorney (she said yes, but then an aide vetoed the idea for reasons they
still don't understand to this day) but did get an endorsement from one County
Board Supervisor. They then referenced the supervisor's endorsement in a pre-
liminary conversation with Senator Sheila Kuehl's office (that conversation was
initiated by their law school buddy, Sarah Speed, who was working in collaboration with Jill Buckley, Senior Director of Legislative Services for the American
Society for the Prevention of Cruelty to Animals, otherwise known as the
ASPCA, and Beverlee McGrath of the Humane Society of the United States).
Kuehl was selected as a possible sponsor because of her past record of legislative accomplishments on behalf of domestic violence victims.

As Gretchen, one of the student group members, tells it,

> During our visits to the various legislative aides and one senator, I can-
> not recall a single question that could not be answered by pointing to
> the position paper. Verbally, we took turns elaborating on the issues;
> our class cohorts let our coalition partners who had also traveled to
> Sacramento (Sarah Speed, Jill Buckley of the ASPCA, and Madeline
> Bernstein of the Society for the Prevention of Cruelty to Animals Los
> Angeles) handle the first visits. Once we gained confidence, we were
> able to take over the messaging, and our "professional" partners began
> mimicking our language, most significantly the framing of the issue as
> a domestic violence issue, not animal rights. Our group of seven was
> received very positively at each of our stops, and I believe that the sheer
> number of us had an impact.
>
> By the end of the day, we were able to circle back to Senator Kuehl's
> office and report that other legislative offices might author the bill if she
> would not. We created a buzz, and by the next morning we learned that
> Senator Kuehl wanted to author it! [See Figure 7.2.] We were amazed.

1. Identify an issue.

2. Research the issue.

3. Create a fact sheet.

4. "Brand" the issue.

5. Map out possible supporters and detractors.

6. Form a coalition.

7. Develop educational materials.

8. Launch a media campaign.

9. Approach elected officials.

10. **Monitor progress on the issue.**

Figure 7.2

January 10, 2007

Protect Every Family Member From Domestic Violence
4477 Marseilles Street, San Diego, California 92107

Mandi Bailhache, Legislative Aide
Assemblymember Betty Karnette, 34th District
California State Capitol
P.O. Box 942849
Sacramento, CA 942849-0054

Dear Mandi,

Thank you again for meeting with our group this past Monday afternoon, especially with the capitol so busy with the pending health care announcement. Your encouragement and comments such as, "who *wouldn't* support this!" left us feeling confident, as it echoed the sentiments of virtually every office we visited.

  Yesterday we were told that Senator Sheila Kuehl will be authoring this important piece of legislation, and we are delighted that you will be able to offer Ms. Karnette your personal take on it, after having met with us.

  I would like to note that Tam Ma in Senator Kuehl's office pointed out that we had the wrong Family Code number on our position paper. Instead of Family Code #6211, it should be 6320. (We had been going back and forth on the best code for the intended results.)

Thank you again for your time and encouragement.

Sincerely,

Gretchen Mathys Pelletier
619-XXX-XXXX

University of San Diego Students Advocating for Protection

Carolyn Smyth, 619-XXX-XXXX (DV & animal rights); Darla Trapp, 858-XXX-XXXX x111 (DV & legal); Renee Scherr, 619-XXX-XXXX (other states' legislation); Gretchen Pelletier, 619-XXX-XXXX (media); Sarah Speed, 619-XXX-XXXX (legal & legislation)

_____ Monitor Progress on the Issue: How It's Done

Even though we've arrived at Step 10, finding someone to author your bill is actually the beginning of a new stage of your journey. Once you do, you'll work closely with your legislator's office to follow the yellow brick road that was outlined to us by the state of California (again, your state will have a similar map) to help your bill wend its way through the legislature. And, if you are fortunate to get your bill passed, you will have to dedicate some time to making sure it is properly implemented (the subject of the last chapter in this book).

The students will tell you about their experience here.

Monitor Progress on the Issue: How They Did It_____

Once Senator Kuehl became the bill's author, it took on a life of its own, with the team pushing (or, more accurately, cheering it on) from further back. It was assigned a new name—SB 353—which made it easy to track online.

As the bill moved through the approval process, starting with the Senate, then on to the Assembly, then back to the Senate, slight modifications were made, though the essence of the bill remained untouched. E-mails swirled between team members keeping one another appraised of the progress. Frustratingly for the team members, a great debate was ongoing about the California prison system at the same time that SB 353 was ready for its final vote in the approval. The team had to watch as the bill was scheduled for a vote . . . and then overlooked . . . time and again. Finally, however, it was passed by a unanimous vote.

When the Senate and Assembly were finished and SB 353 was approved by both, the team started an e-mail blitz to Governor Schwarzenegger's office. "We drafted a script e-mail to the Governor, and copied it to everyone we knew—friends, business associates, our moms . . ." As a warm-fuzzy, no-cost issue, it wasn't difficult to garner support and enthusiasm.

The "Governator" signed it, and SB 353 became law. Here's a copy of the e-mail they received:

October 16, 2007

Thank you for your e-mail in support of SB 353. I appreciate hearing from my fellow Californians on issues that are important to them, and I welcome your input on legislation that affects the future of California.

I am pleased to inform you that I signed this bill after extensive consideration and thorough deliberation of arguments from both supporters and opponents of this issue. You may read the final language of this bill on the Official California Legislative Information website: www.leginfo.ca.gov.

Again, thanks for voicing your opinion on this issue. Taking the time to communicate your views and offer suggestions is essential to good citizenship and good government. I value the comments of people like you who are engaged in the improvement of our great state.

Sincerely,

Arnold Schwarzenegger

The List That's Not a List

At the very beginning of Chapter 5, you were presented with "the list." By now, you can see that it is a little misleading to call it a "list" because the steps flow into one another and back again.

One of my students[ii] created the flowchart in Figure 7.3, which has helped clarify the process for some practitioners and completely confounded others. The chart provides another perspective on how to look at the process.

As you can see, it's a circuitous process. While the chart may look fancy, each piece by itself is easy to understand and, more important, to do. The

Figure 7.3

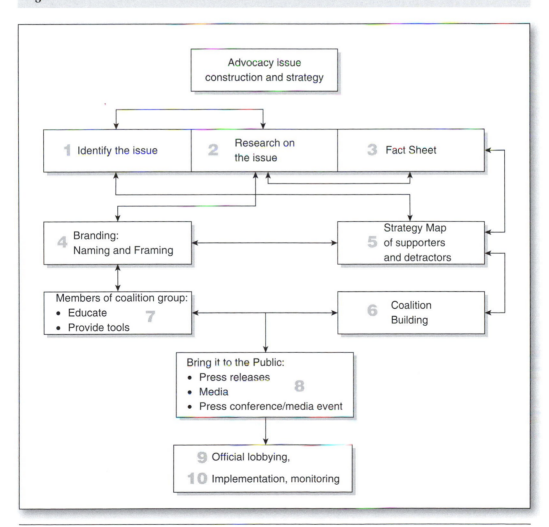

Source: Chart created by Jon Glasoe. Reprinted with permission.

great thing is that when you put it all together you come up with a first-rate advocacy campaign.

The last chapter in this book is devoted to an in-depth discussion of the steps you need to take to make sure that once your bill passes, it is enacted properly. It's not enough simply to get a law on the books; it's critical that you ensure that it is being implemented.

Chapter Questions

1. What are the most prominent media outlets in your community? What strategy will you use to approach newspeople at those outlets with your story?

2. What creative ideas do you have for an event that could highlight your advocacy campaign?

3. What is your strategy for identifying which legislators (or other elected officials) you'll approach with your idea?

4. How will you involve people who have been affected by the issue in your campaign?

5. Can you find a map of how the legislative process works in your state?

6. What do you think of the final diagram of the 10-step process? Does it make more or less sense than the list of the 10 steps?

Endnotes

i The Rolling Stones. (1969). You can't always get what you want. On *Let It Bleed* [Studio album]. London: Olympic Studios.

ii Thank you to Jonathan Glasoe for creating this masterpiece!

8

The 10 Steps in Action

A Case Study of the Strategy and Process

Pat Libby and Maureen Carasiti

E very year we ask a group of students from the previous year's advocacy class to come in at the beginning of the semester to share their stories about the project they worked on (and, in some cases, are still working on, which is a testament to their diligence). We do this not because we are lazy and want to get out of having to prepare a lecture for that week (although, come to think of it, that is an added bonus) but because we think that having one group of students teach another is incredibly powerful. It tells our students that people just like them who knew little or nothing about advocacy to begin with can be amazingly successful. It also sets the bar high in terms of showing the students what we expect they will accomplish.

In this chapter we're going to share the story of a team of students who worked on a campaign to protect people with developmental disabilities. We'll start off by introducing their story to you. For the most part, though, the documents they created for their campaign will speak for themselves. This chapter will walk you through the first seven steps used by the team. Chapter 9 will continue their story.

1. Identify an Issue

As Snoopy would say, it was a dark and stormy night (OK, that part isn't true). At the beginning of each advocacy course, we ask students to present their ideas for possible campaigns. One semester, one of those students, Maureen Carasiti, made an emotional appeal to the class for a group to work with her on a project to curb abuse of adults with developmental disabilities by their paid caregivers. Maureen had registered for our course specifically to address this problem, which she had witnessed with alarming regularity during her 25 years of service in the field.

> In my work I had seen abuse occur flagrantly and way too frequently. Although I was fully present and aware of the gaps in the system that enabled the problem to become so pervasive, I lacked the experience and knowledge of how to modify those systems or inspire legislative action to address this problem. For those reasons I enrolled in the advocacy course.

In a nutshell, the problem was this: When caregivers working with adults with developmental disabilities[1] were terminated for suspected patient abuse—something that took place as the result of a detailed multistep process that involved the agency documenting the abuse and having an investigation of said abuse by outside regulators—there was nothing in place to prevent those same caregivers from being rehired immediately by another agency. So you have a situation where someone is doing something that is not illegal but just plain mean, like pulling a patient's hair or giving her a bath in freezing cold water. The supervisor catches the caregiver in the act, writes her up, and calls for an outside investigation; the investigation occurs; and the person is written up for "substantiated abuse," is fired, and then one month later reappears at another DD agency working with clients in the same capacity. Even worse, Maureen had seen dismissed employees working at another agency alongside the clients they had formerly abused—forcing the clients to see their abusers again and again on a regular basis. This was a problem she and other agency executive directors talked about all of the time. She thought: Why can't there be a central database that has a list of all of these horrible people so that agencies can avoid hiring them? Maureen was so frustrated by this problem that she was practically in tears when she made a plea to her classmates to help with this idea.

In summary the issue was this:

- Abuse against people with developmental disabilities is high and often committed by caregivers. Unless prosecuted criminally, there is no system by which abusive caregivers can be tracked. Therefore, they are able to move easily from agency to agency, perpetuating the cycle of abuse.
- While state agencies do investigate reported incidents of abuse, and often substantiate those allegations, they may never get prosecuted criminally. There is no comprehensive system that compiles findings and allows convenient access to that information.

Now you may think that what happened next was that a group of her peers raised their hands and said, "Sign me up, Maureen—I'll help you," but

---

[1]Adults with developmental disabilities are commonly referred to by professionals in the field as the "DD" population—an abbreviation we'll use here.

that wasn't the case at all. To be honest, we were surprised they didn't. They didn't because they didn't fully understand the issue and they had questions about the legality of the remedy Maureen was proposing. Not one of them was initially persuaded to join her.

As Maureen tells it,

> I was certain and confident that once I shared the problem of abuse, the entire class would want to join in this effort. Wrong! As I think back now, my voice for advocacy really began with them. I was in a position where I needed to convince my fellow classmates that something needed to be done to address the problem of abuse.

Jessica Towne-Cardenas, a classmate who ultimately became a member of Maureen's project team, argued that this type of reporting system might violate civil rights and employment privacy laws. While she was sympathetic (as the department director of a domestic violence program), she just couldn't see her way around "blacklisting" people who hadn't committed actual crimes.

Maureen was undaunted. Through passion and persistence she succeeded in persuading Jessica and two other classmates (Becky Lee [Launder] and Paige Simpson) to, at the very least, work with her on *researching* the issue. Writing later about the experience, Jessica said, "I'm very thankful that she dug her heels in and said, 'No, I'm doing this project, and I'm just going to keep talking to you until you come with me.'" Originally Jessica and her classmates thought "there was no way we could develop this idea."

2. Research the Issue

Yet, the more they looked into it, the more they realized that there was a way. By involving the group in the process of researching the issue, Maureen gained allies. The more they read about caregiver abuse, the more enraged they became. The more enraged they became, the more motivated they were to help with the issue. Jessica described her "aha" moment like this:

> I learned about the Child Abuse Index and the California Nurses Association Registry and found out that California is already tracking and reporting to potential employers abuse cases that are never prosecuted. Well, how about that? Now we had a legal backbone for this registry to stand up against privacy laws. Talk about oppression— adults with DD are segregated from society, have a huge amount of prejudice against them, and the state government protects children and the elderly and not adults with DD! This is a huge gap in the system. After seeing the registries both nationwide and especially those in California, it really started to be evident that this registry could exist and needs to exist.

The students' research also revealed the existence of registries for this *exact* purpose—for people working with the DD population—in Ohio, Idaho, Vermont, Louisiana, Wisconsin, and New Mexico. Reams of more research eventually were condensed into a comprehensive white paper that is contained in the next section.

Of course, facts alone didn't by themselves carry the day. Another team member, Paige, said she joined the project because she had gotten to know Maureen in another class and was "impressed by her passion for her work." It wasn't so much the topic that initially attracted Paige (although she was sympathetic to it); it was more the sense that her classmate was a good woman, trying to do something she cared about deeply. Writing later about the group, she added this:

> Our group was slow to form because of uncertainty around the topic. This was helpful because it caused us to be more critical from the start and throughout the process. Educating ourselves and forming arguments for our proposal was excellent and vital preparation for taking it public. Ultimately any initial awkwardness among group members was overcome by the fact that we did good work together.

As the team members began their work, each took responsibility for learning more about the topic. Becky, the fourth team member, said, "Prior to beginning this class, I had no idea of even the definition of *developmentally disabled*. Now I feel as if I could be called an 'expert' on the subject."

In the early stages of the project, the team sought out various individuals and groups for their expertise and experience with the issue of abuse and its impact on people with developmental disabilities. These folks greatly assisted the team in the overall conceptualization of the campaign. They were critical to supporting and strengthening the team's research efforts by presenting the students with valuable contacts to other people who had helpful ideas or interest in joining the cause.

3/4. Create a Fact Sheet/"Brand" the Issue _____

Based on their research—including conversations with many people who were affected by the issue—the group decided to name its campaign the Registry to End Abusive Caregiver Hiring, and thus The REACH Project was launched. As you can see, it's a simple, straightforward name and frame given to a very complex issue (although, as you can imagine, it wasn't easy to develop). By naming the campaign "REACH" the advocates ensured that they, their allies, and legislators and their aides could have a quick way of referencing both the issue and the legislative effort. You can just imagine advocates and legislators using that shorthand to refer to the issue, can't you?

Let's take a look at the campaign here starting with the fact sheet that was created (see Figure 8.1). The fact sheet is the synthesis of research on the topic

Figure 8.1

The REACH Project

REGISTRY TO END ABUSIVE CAREGIVER HIRING

Protecting people with developmental disabilities through streamlined, accessible abuse reporting

Alarming Statistics

Individuals with developmental disabilities (DD) are...

- **11 times** higher risk of being sexually assaulted.[3]

- **13 times** higher risk of being robbed.[3]

- Higher risk for being re-victimized. Two studies found that **50% of sexually assaulted, DD woman had been victimized 10+ times.**[3]

Background: In California, over 220,000 individuals with developmental disabilities receive care in residential and day programs, independent and supported living, and at-home, private care.[1] Sadly, these individuals are 2 – 5 times more likely to experience severe, long-lasting, and repeated abuse than the non-disabled—in the very settings responsible for their well-being.[2]

Characteristics of Vulnerable Populations
(children, elderly and developmentally disabled)

- Dependent on others for basic needs
- Impaired cognitive ability
- Over-trusting authority figures
- Difficulty communicating effectively

How California Protects Vulnerable Populations
beyond criminal background checks

CHILDREN	ELDERLY	DD
Child abuse registries track substantiated and alleged abuse investigations.	Nursing homes are staffed by certified nurses, whose quality care is tracked in the nurse aide registry.	No protection.

The PROBLEM:
44% of abusers make contact with their victims as unlicensed, direct care workers.[4] If caught, investigated, and/or fired, many abusers move on to another agency—because they can. Current California privacy laws prevent prospective employers from accessing information about abusers. Without such knowledge, employers continue to hire abusive caregivers and the cycle continues.

The SOLUTION:
Create a registry that tracks cases of substantiated abuse and flags care givers that have established patterns of inconclusive abuse to be accessible by prospective employers. Currently, registries are available for children and the elderly in California but are absent for individuals with developmental disabilities. Why leave this vulnerable population any more vulnerable?

(Continued)

Figure 8.1 (Continued)

The REACH Project

REGISTRY TO END ABUSIVE CAREGIVER HIRING

Other states with abuse registries protecting the developmentally disabled:

- Delaware
- Idaho
- Iowa
- Ohio
- Wisconsin
- Louisiana
- New Mexico
- Vermont

All 50 states have abuse registries protecting children and elderly.

Benefits of the Registry

- The registry will address a critical need to protect individuals with developmental disabilities and the agencies that care for them statewide. It will also afford this population the same protection offered to other vulnerable populations in California.
- Currently, 56% of people with developmental disabilities in California are under the age of 21. The number of people being diagnosed with a developmental disability increases yearly. Instituting a registry now will improve the adult care system receiving these youth in the near future.[5]
- A registry will help reduce the workload of state and private agencies that spend a significant amount of time and resources conducting investigations.

FAQ's...

Q: Who will create and monitor the registry?
A: A consultant will create the database. An inter-agency employee will oversee the registry, data input and related events.
——

Q: Who will contribute information to the registry?
A: All those conducting non-criminal investigations: Department of Health Services, Community Care Licensing and Adult Protective Services.
——

Q: What information will be included in the registry?
A: Investigating agency, name of abuser, other identifier, type of abuse, findings, date of findings.
——

Q: What information is accessible in the registry?
A: All substantiated findings. Records of individuals with 3+ abuse investigations in a 5 year period will be flagged.
——

Q: Who can access the data collected?
A: Data will be publicly accessible (in part to benefit those seeking private, in-home care). Licensed care agencies will be required to check all prospective employees against the registry before hiring but will retain hiring discretion. It is recommended that agencies check their employee list against the registry every six months.
——

Q: How can the registry be accessed?

A: The data is available through an online database.
——

Q: How will the database be financially supported?
A: The database will be user fee-based or supported through grants.
——

Q: Don't criminal background checks address this issue?
A: No, most cases of abuse are never formally prosecuted.
——

Q: Should the registry be merged with an existing registry, such as the CNA registry?
A: No. Differences in licensure and logistics (i.e. reporting features) make the Child Abuse Index and CNA registry incompatible with what REACH proposes.

The REACH Coalition

Home of Guiding Hands	Casa de los Amigos
Developmental Services Continuum, Inc.	United Cerebral Palsy—San Diego
Independent Options, Inc.	Developmental Services Network (DSN)
Noah Homes, Inc.	Toward Maximum Independence, Inc.
Seeds Educational Services, Inc.	Unyeway
San Diego Regional Center	Horrigan Enterprises
H&W Independent Solutions, Inc.	Charles I Cheneweth Foundation
P.R.I.D.E. Inc.	Casa de Amparo
Humboldt Community Access and Resource Center	Mountain Shadows Support Group, Inc.
Country Hills Healthcare Center	Peppermint Ridge Friends and Family
CPSRC Inc. Adult Development Center	Orpas Corporation
St. Madeleine Sophie's Center	ARC—San Diego
Supporting Alternative Solutions, Inc.	Teri, Inc.
	Your name here!

References:
[1] http://www.dds.ca.gov/FactsStats/CMF.cfm November 2006.
[2] Sobsey, D. (1994). Violence and abuse in the lives of people with disabilities: The end of silent acceptance? Baltimore: Paul H. Brookes Publishing Co
[3] http://ucicorrections.seweb.uci.edu/ppt crime_victims_dis.ppt#260,4,Defining Developmental Disabilities (DD)
[4] Sobsey and Doe 1991 Patterns of Sexual Abuse and Assault. *Journal of Sexuality and Disability*, 9 (3), 243-259.

Contact REACH to join the coalition!
www.calreachproject.org   CAL_ReachProject@yahoo.com

done by the team. It includes all of the essential elements that were mentioned in Chapter 5.

The position paper which appears in the appendix (p. **182**) was distributed along with the fact sheet to the legislators (and their aides) with whom the team met. As you'll see when you read through it, it contains a synopsis of the research the team members did to build the case for the legislation they were proposing. The position paper spends considerable space documenting other states that have similar laws in place and how those laws operate.

As you can see, the team provided the policy makers with tremendous detail about why this particular piece of legislation was needed, how other states approached the implementation question, and additional resources policy makers and their aides could access for additional information (see Appendix on p. 202).

But, let's back up a minute. Before the students made their trek to Sacramento, they needed to map out a legislative strategy that included figuring out who and what the opposition might be.

5. Map Out Possible Supporters and Detractors

Maureen described the process as it was happening:

> Through our research and interviews with other service providers, disability service providers, disability advocates, licensing agencies, and consumers and their loved ones, we have not discovered anyone who is opposed to the REACH registry in terms of the goal to end caregiver abuse for adults with developmental disabilities. Everyone loves that idea because it is such an enormous problem and sees this as a very viable solution. However, there are some hot buttons around a few issues:
>
> 1. How the registry will be implemented. Who will be responsible for the work involved in creating and maintaining the registry? There are several agencies that could conceivably house the registry, but none seem willing to volunteer to take it on.
>
> 2. How the registry will be funded. There are several ways the registry could be funded, and there are supporters and opponents to each one. In essence, everyone wants someone else to fund it! Our suggestion is either that the costs be wrapped into licensing fees already paid to the state by service providers or that the registry be user-fee based like the Department of Justice Fingerprint Registry; that way providers could choose whether or not to reimburse that cost for employees.

3. Does it violate any privacy laws? We have not contacted labor unions or the ACLU about this issue, so we can only assume that they would oppose this type of registry. However, it is worth noting that privacy issues were not brought up in many of our conversations.

By thinking through the opposition, and doing the research on how other states had addressed some of the questions that could be raised by opponents or by legislators who were supportive of the issue but justifiably concerned about implementation issues, the team members were well prepared for their meetings in Sacramento.

There were, however, still more steps that had to be climbed before making the trip. One of those, as you know, involved mapping out the legislative strategy. Here's what the students told us:

The beginning stages of The REACH Project's legislative strategy involved researching legislators in the San Diego region to identify any representatives we could meet with locally that we thought might be receptive to the issue of abusive caregivers. The only San Diego legislator that seemed to fit the bill was Senator Christine Kehoe. In researching Senator Kehoe's and others' biographies, we started to get an idea of the different committees that legislators sit on, and this helped us pinpoint more accurately which legislators had a history of sponsoring legislation on or general interest in advocacy for issues regarding abuse, public health and safety, and/or dependent adult or elder care.

Our focus primarily brought us to the following committees: Developmental Disabilities and Mental Health, Committee on Public Safety, Subcommittee on Aging & Long Term Care, and Committee on Human Services. Through these committees, and additional information in legislator biographies, the coalition settled on the following legislators to meet with in Sacramento:

- o Patty Berg, Assembly Member—Aging & Long Term Care Committee Chair, Subcommittee on Budget Review for Health & Human Services
- o Karen Bass, Assembly Member—Majority Floor Leader, Human Services Committee
- o Sheila Kuehl, Senator—Developmental Disability & Mental Health Budget Fiscal Review, Subcommittee on Aging & Long Term Care
- o Elaine Alquist, Assembly Member—Human Service Committee
- o In San Diego: Christine Kehoe, Senator—Developmental Disability & Mental Health Committee, Budget & Fiscal Review Committee

Initially phone calls to request meetings were made; however, we found that every office asked for a written request for a meeting. Consequently letters summarizing the issue and the REACH registry were faxed or e-mailed as requested in early December along with the fact sheet. The following week follow-up phone calls were made . . . and then made again. It was surprising how many follow-up calls and e-mails were necessary before we succeeded in setting an appointment (and some never did respond to our request for a meeting time).

In the meantime we built our coalition and continued our research. As our coalition grew, we received another list of legislators in early January from Protection & Advocacy, Inc. (PAI), an agency that works for the rights of and quality care for adults with developmental disabilities. That started round two of our meeting requests and phone calls with the following legislators who had worked with PAI in the past:

- John Benoit, Assembly Member—strong public safety background as a police officer
- Lois Wolk, Assembly Member—served as Chair of the Assembly Human Services Committee, focusing attention on improving disabled access and improving efforts to prevent child abuse and elder abuse. Her efforts earned her the Outstanding Advocate Award from the Easter Seals Society of California
- Hector de la Torre, Assembly Member—PAI has worked with this legislator in the past
- Joe Simitian, Senator—sponsor of an annual "There Oughta Be a Law" contest, protection of children at risk and children in foster care.

As mentioned above (and you already know this from reading Chapter 6), members of the REACH team also had a goal of enlisting as many coalition members as possible before they began meeting with legislators. That led them to Step 6.

6. Form a Coalition

This step is outlined in an excerpt from the project report submitted by The REACH Project team for the advocacy course requirement:

All phases of development of The REACH Project contributed to the evolution of our coalition. Our efforts began with the project's conceptual design in terms of identifying the issue, conducting research, branding the issue, mapping out possible supporters and detractors, and determining a vision for the future.

As The REACH Project took shape and our written materials were completed, we saw the potential impact that a larger coalition could have on empowering the movement and advancing our cause. We began regular communication with potential coalition members via written correspondence, phone and conference calls, and formal and informal meetings.

Starting locally in San Diego, we utilized Nonprofit Management Solutions [a nonprofit technical assistance center] to gain contact with agencies that provide services to people with developmental disabilities. An introductory letter was developed and sent to over 40 agencies via e-mail. We then reviewed the GuideStar website to identify additional agencies throughout the state of California, which we contacted as well. Shortly after these introductory e-mails were made, we began placing follow-up phone calls. It was through these personal interactions that further information could be discussed and explained.

As we succeeded in recruiting more members for the coalition, we became more effective in terms of persuading others to join. Getting people on board was relatively easy at times, because this issue was attractive to most and resonated deeply with many of the supporting agencies. Comments such as "Thank you for taking on this pervasive and long-standing problem" and "It is about time" reinforced our purpose and strengthened our advocacy voice. Still, at other times, we were surprised by those who chose not to get involved or even to voice an opinion on the matter. Fortunately, we were able to quickly discern and/or predict when we needed to approach an organization with a more well-defined political strategy.

Moving forward we developed a comprehensive plan to create momentum to build the coalition in order to build our power and influence. These methods included the development of a coalition member packet, assigning a coordinator to follow up with routine communication, social networking, and additional recruitment efforts such as securing speaking engagements at service industry meetings and conferences.

Due to their initial success, when the students took their first trip to Sacramento, they had convinced 16 separate organizations to join their coalition. Keep in mind this trip occurred only *four* months after Maureen first made her pitch in class! Eventually, The REACH Project attracted 24 coalition members.

7. Develop Educational Materials _____

The team soon discovered that a strong coalition increased the impact of their advocacy efforts and empowered others. "As we built a base of support, we were fairly confident that our members would become actively engaged to advance our purpose." And thus, a wide variety of educational materials were created by the team to inform members of The REACH Project coalition.

Figure 8.2 is a copy of the e-letter that the team sent to new coalition members.

Figure 8.2

Welcome to **The REACH Project Coalition!** Thank you for your dedication to this important cause.

The following information is a resource for you as you help advocate for legislation to be introduced in California that protects citizens with developmental disabilities by creating an accessible registry of abusive caregiver findings.

Many organizations do not realize the impact they can make on the California legislature. With minimal effort and time commitment, and by working **together**, The REACH Project Coalition can advance this issue through the State of California.

At present, there are two key tasks of The REACH Project Coalition.

- First, strength is in numbers. The greater number of organizations backing the idea, the more attention legislators will give The REACH Project. **As a coalition member, please recruit at least two organizations to join REACH**
- Second, we need as many voices to contact representatives in Sacramento. **As a coalition member, please make at least five contacts with members of the legislature.** This can be accomplished through letters, e-mails, snail mail and telephone calls.

These tasks can be accomplished with a few hours of service. Below are some ideas and resources to help you.

- **E-mail and Snail Mail legislators in Sacramento.** As noted above, we are asking you to write your representatives. We encourage you to craft your own message as the power of your voice is important. However, we have created a sample letter that is available for your reference. If nothing else, please edit the text to include your name and organization. The more letters the representatives receive, the more inclined they will be to support the advancement of The REACH Project. Feel free to share this letter with others within your organization and those who you recruit to join the coalition.

  {The sample letter to legislators was attached here. We'll include it at the end.}

- Call Legislators. Although e-mail and snail mail are effective in creating a paper trail, personal calls to legislators will create a more personal impact. Inform the legislators of the cause by sharing your stories. Since many nonprofit organizations do not have much experience advocating with legislators, feel free to utilize the following script when making your phone call.

  {The sample telephone script was attached here. We'll include it at the end.}

- **Recruit others!** The REACH Project is a grassroots initiative and we are asking you to find others to join our coalition. You may pursue your own contacts or, if you need suggestions, we encourage you to reference the 100+ contacts REACH has already made, and help follow-up with organizations that have not yet replied. Please contact us via e-mail and we will assign you a group of contacts to follow up with.

(Continued)

Figure 8.2 (Continued)

When recruiting, you may want to use the following letter to help introduce The REACH Project to a potential coalition member.

{The sample letter was attached here.}

- **Share Personal Stories.** The REACH Project is seeking personal letters of support from both individuals and organizations. If your organization or any of your consumers or their families wishes to write a letter, we feel this will make a strong impact on the state legislature. Please forward the letter to The REACH Project either electronically or by snail mail to Becky Lee (address provided).

The following resources are designed as an educational tool to help The REACH Project explain the issue of caregiver abuse. We encourage you to use this document to briefly explain the issue, e-mail to colleagues in the field, and/or spread the word of the coalition as you meet with others. As more members join the coalition, this document will be up-dated as needed.

{The fact sheet you saw at the beginning was attached here.}

Furthermore, The REACH Project has developed talking points when describing the issue to organizations unfamiliar with the initiative.

{Talking points were attached here.}

In the case an organization requests more information about the research and the full story of The REACH Project, please reference the position paper.

{The position paper which appears in the appendix was attached here.}

All of The REACH Project materials can be located at www.docs.google.com Username: CAL_REACHProject@yahoo.com. Password:reachproject

Please let us know if you have any trouble accessing the website. A special internet browser is required for Mac users.

Again, thank you for your support and desire to help further this initiative. We are confident with the commitment from your organization; you can make a difference. If you have any questions or need assistance, please feel free to contact us via e-mail.

The REACH Project Founders,

Becky Lee, Jessica Towne-Cardenas, Maureen Carasiti, Paige Simpson (with e-mail contact information provided).

And now, here are those cool attachments we promised to share starting with the sample letter to legislators.

Dear <<Senator_____ (or Assemblyman_____)>>

As a constituent of California, and a resident of X, I am writing to urge you to support The REACH Project, which aims to protect California's vulnerable citizens who have developmental disabilities.

REACH is advocating for the creation of a registry to track caregivers with a history of abuse, to prevent them from being reemployed where they may abuse again. This would be similar to the Child Abuse Registry and Certified Nurse Aide (CNA) Registry, which protect California's children and elderly who are cared for by licensed individuals in state-licensed programs. No registry currently exists to protect adults with developmental disabilities.

Research indicates people with disabilities are more likely to experience severe and repeated abuse than people without disabilities. Even more alarming, 44% of all offenders against people with disabilities make initial contact with their victims through the web of special services provided to people with disabilities (Sobsey & Doe, 1991). In California, employee privacy laws often protect abusers of adults with developmental disabilities to the detriment of victims, by making it difficult for prospective employers to access a caregiver's employment history. Employers have access to criminal records, but many abuse cases are not prosecuted legally.

Several states, including Minnesota, New Mexico, Vermont, and Illinois already have a registry similar to what REACH is proposing for California. By creating this registry, California would not only become a leader in the nation for the rights of the developmentally disabled, but would also be providing an urgently needed protection to its most vulnerable citizens.

I urge you to author legislation in support of the REACH Project. Please know that your support will protect hundreds of thousands of developmentally disabled individuals.

I look forward to hearing how you will support this important issue.

Sincerely,

<<Your Name Here>>

<<Your Contact Information Here>>

REACH Telephone Script

Hello,

I am calling to ask that you support The REACH Project, which helps protect California's vulnerable developmentally disabled population.

People with disabilities are more likely to experience severe and repeated abuse than people without disabilities. Even more alarming, 44% of all offenders against people with disabilities make initial contact with their victims through the web of special services provided to people with disabilities. The creation of a registry to track caregiver abuse will help to protect this vulnerable group.

Again, I urge you to support The REACH Project by introducing this concept to the California State legislature.

Note: If you are calling your legislator, be sure to stay on the line long enough for them to take your name and address so they can validate that you are a constituent.

(Continued)

Figure 8.2 (Continued)

REACH – Please join us! Letter to colleagues.

<Insert date here>

To <Whom it may concern>

I am writing on behalf of The REACH Project, a movement to protect California's vulnerable developmentally disabled population. We are advocating for the creation of a registry to track caregivers with a history of abuse, to prevent them from being reemployed where they may abuse again. This would be similar to the child abuse index and Certified Nurse Aide (CNA) registries.

Your organization is likely aware of the research that shows people with disabilities are more likely to experience severe and repeated abuse than people without disabilities. Even more alarming, 44% of all offenders against people with disabilities make initial contact with their victims through the web of special services provide to people with disabilities (Sobsey & Doe, 1991).

In California, employee privacy laws often protect abusers of adults with developmental disabilities over the victims. Other vulnerable populations, such as children and the elderly, have greater protection. California's Child Abuse Registry protects children who are cared for through the state licensed foster care and licensed day care system. The elderly who are cared for by licensed staff are protected by the CNA registry. All are protected when employees are subject to a live scan, but only in the case of criminal prosecutions. Many abuse cases never make it this far.

Several states, including Minnesota, New Mexico, Vermont, and Illinois already have a registry similar to what REACH is proposing for California. By creating this registry, California would not only become a leader in the nation for the rights of the developmentally disabled, but would also be providing an urgently needed protection to its most vulnerable citizens.

REACH is working closely with legislators to introduce this issue as a bill. As you know, there is power in numbers. Your support will help further this very important cause when we speak with legislators.

May we add your organization to our list of supporters? An information fact sheet is attached for your reference. Please contact me if you have any further questions about the initiative or if you are interested in setting up a meeting to discuss the issue further.

Thank you very much for your attention to this matter. I look forward to following up with you in the next week.

Sincerely,

<Insert your name here>

REACH Project

San Diego, California

<insert your e-mail address here>

<insert your phone number here>

The REACH Project Registry to End Abusive Caregiver Hiring

*Protecting people with developmental disabilities
through streamlined, accessible abuse reporting*

Talking Points

SUMMARY: People with developmental disabilities are being abused, and at alarming rates. Many times abusers come into contact with their victims as direct care providers. Currently, abusive caregivers are able to move easily between agencies because of information barriers. The creation of a registry will remove these information barriers by tracking abuse findings, making this information accessible to prospective employers, and preventing abusers from victimizing again.

- Abuse against people with developmental disabilities is a critical public safety and human rights issue in California. It affects over 220,000 individuals with developmental disabilities in this state as well as the families, friends, professionals, and communities who love and support them.

- Individuals with developmental disabilities are severely challenged or lacking in areas such as self-care, learning, and mobility. Their impairments are the result of conditions that arise before the age of 18 and are life-long, such as mental retardation, cerebral palsy, or Down syndrome.

- The abuse problem affecting people with developmental disabilities is threefold:

  o The incidence of abuse, including repeat abuse, is disturbingly high. For example, people with developmental disabilities are 11 times more likely to be sexually abused than the non-disabled. And, 50% of women with developmental disabilities who are sexually abused are victimized over 10 times.

  o Tragically, 44% of the abusers who victimize people with developmental disabilities are the caregivers responsible for their wellbeing.

  o Abusive caregivers are moving easily from agency to agency, perpetuating the cycle of abuse.

- Several gaps in the system provide abusers with mobility and threaten individuals with developmental disabilities.

  o One, fingerprint scans and background checks only reveal criminal prosecutions, which are not frequent in abuse cases due to underreporting, a high burden of proof, and the fact that many forms of abuse do not qualify as a criminal offense. Thus, many abusers are not identified in this process.

  o Two, most direct care workers serving people with developmental disabilities are not licensed, unlike those serving children or the elderly. Without licensure, individuals are not as accountable for meeting certain standards of training and performance. Future employers do not have the "stamp of approval" that licensing provides, when making hiring choices.

(Continued)

Figure 8.2 (Continued)

     ○ Three, due to California's strong privacy laws, prospective employers cannot legally ask specifics of previous employers about a person's work history. This ironically protects the privacy of abusive employees at the expense of their potential victims.

     ○ And four, California currently operates the Child Abuse Registry and Certified Nursing Assistant registry, which track abusive caregivers of children and the elderly. Neither registry addresses abusive caregivers of adults with developmental disabilities. They are left unprotected.

- California Assembly Bill X will establish a registry to track abusive caregivers victimizing individuals with developmental disabilities. This registry will offset the limitations of fingerprint scans, overarching privacy laws, and a lack of caregiver licensure that put people with developmental disabilities at risk. It will also ensure equity of protection among vulnerable populations in California.

- While the registry will be new, its content is not. It will come from abuse investigations already being conducted by the Department of Human Services, Community Care Licensing, and Adult Protective Services, which license <u>provider agencies</u>. Currently, the findings remain isolated and are not easily accessible. The registry will change this.

- The registry logistics will be based on best practices. Its features include public accessibility balanced with privacy safeguards. Substantiated records will be the primary release but established patterns of suspected abuse—when individuals have three or more allegations in a five-year period—will also be flagged.

- The cost of creating a registry is negligible, particularly when compared to the human rights benefits gained. Also, over time the cost of conducting abuse investigations will be reduced by the removal of repeat abusers from the system.

- Other states, including Louisiana, Wisconsin, New Mexico, and Ohio have registries in place to protect people with developmental disabilities. California should be at the forefront of human rights with them. Our support is vitally important in the protection of those who simply cannot protect themselves.

    For more information, contact Paige Simpson at Cal_reachproject@yahoo.com

    | The REACH Project Registry to End Abusive Caregiver Hiring |

Protecting people with developmental disabilities
through streamlined, accessible abuse reporting

Talking Points – Anecdote

Bob, a resident in a group home, refuses to get off of the couch to attend a community event when encouraged verbally by Mary, an unlicensed, direct care staff member. Frustrated, Mary forcefully pulls Bob off the couch, pushes him out the front door, and calls him a "baby." Bob and his friend Sally, who witnessed the event, are visibly upset. Mary is later separated from the agency for substantiated findings of abuse. Shortly thereafter,

Mary interviews for a position at Bob's day care program and may once again be responsible for his care.

What happens next?

- As in many cases of abuse, Mary's abuse findings are not likely to have enough legal relevance to be prosecuted in a court of law. Fingerprint scans and background checks for future employment will not reveal Mary's past and prevent her from being hired. *The cycle continues.*

- Unlike in the care of children or the elderly, most direct care workers who work with the developmentally disabled are not licensed and/or certified. Therefore, no licensing/certifying agency oversees or reports on Mary's employment viability. Once again, her prospective employer does not have access to her history or quality of care. *The cycle continues.*

- Even if Mary provides a list of past employers, due to overarching privacy laws, the prospective employers cannot inquire directly about her past performance. Ultimately, Bob's day program will have no way of knowing Mary's history of abuse except through self-disclosure. Will she tell the truth? *The cycle continues.*

Mary is hired. What will happen with Bob?

For more information, contact Paige Simpson at Cal_reachproject@yahoo.com

What a breathtaking tour through the first seven steps! Not bad work for a bunch of rookies. In the next chapter, we'll see how it all turned out.

_____ **Chapter Questions**

1. What was the best part of The REACH Project strategy? In particular, what did the team do that you might not have thought of on your own?

2. If you were working on The REACH Project, what would you have done differently?

3. Does the state in which you live have laws in place that protect vulnerable populations (i.e., seniors, children, and/or adults with developmental disabilities) from being abused? If so, what do those laws look like?

4. What lessons did you learn from The REACH Project that you will incorporate into your own legislative campaign?

5. What became more or less clear about the first seven steps after reading this chapter?

Chapter 8 Appendix _____

REGISTRY TO END ABUSIVE CAREGIVER HIRING
The REACH Project

Background

In California, over 220,000 individuals with developmental disabilities (DD) receive care in residential and day programs, independent and supported living, and at-home, private care.[1] Sadly, these individuals are 2 to 5 times more likely to experience severe, long-lasting, and repeated abuse than those who are not disabled—in the very settings responsible for their well-being.[2] Of further concern is the fact that 44% of abusers make contact with their victims as unlicensed, direct care workers.[3]

Abuse of the DD population encompasses physical, sexual, verbal, and financial abuse, as well as neglect, abandonment, abduction, isolation, and deprivation of needed goods and services. Adults with DD are at significantly higher risk of being abused than the non-DD population due to many factors:

- They are often segregated from the mainstream population, either individually or as a group. Studies show that crime rates are high for individuals with disabilities residing in group homes and other segregated facilities.[4]
- They are heavily dependent on caregivers (which may include those in professional settings, family, and friends) for basic needs including medical treatment and personal hygiene involving feeding, dressing, and bathing.
- They are cognitively impaired to varying degrees, and because of this they may be easily persuaded, eager to please, confused by a caregiver's abusive behavior, overtrusting of authority figures, unable to articulate abuse to others, and/or unaware of their rights.

All of these characteristics lead to a huge power differential between caregivers and consumers (individuals with DD receiving care). Abuse in all forms is related to power and control, whether it is adult to child, male to

_____

[1] California Department of Developmental Services. (2008). *Client master file.* Retrieved March 18, 2011, from http://www.dds.ca.gov/factsstats/cmf.cfm

[2] Sobsey, D. (1994). *Violence and abuse in the lives of people with disabilities: The end of silent acceptance?* Baltimore: Paul H. Brookes.

[3] Sobsey, D., & Doe, T. (1991). Patterns of sexual abuse and assault. *Journal of Sexuality and Disability, 9*(3), 243–259.

[4] Sobsey, D., & Mansell, S. (1990). The prevention of abuse with people with developmental disabilities. *Developmental Disabilities Bulletin, 18*(2), 51–56.

female, or a caregiver supporting an individual with developmental disabilities. This tip in the balance of power leads to a higher risk of all forms of abuse. Research indicates that abuse within the DD population is prevalent and the offenses are extreme. According to the University of California–Irvine presentation "When Justice Sleeps: Violence and Abuse Against the Developmentally Disabled," people with developmental disabilities are at

- 13 times higher risk of being robbed,
- 11 times higher risk of sexual assault, and
- significantly higher risk of being revictimized (two studies showed that 50% of women with DD who had been sexually assaulted had been victimized 10+ times).[5]

Additionally, the study estimates that people with developmental disabilities are victims of an estimated 5 million crimes each year. Compare this to 1 million domestic violence, 0.8 million "elder abuse," 3 million child abuse, and 8,000 hate crimes (annually).[6]

Scenarios

Caregiver abuse can take many forms and have varying consequences for the victims, caregivers, and employers. Consider the following scenarios:

A. A direct care staff member in an intermediate care facility threatens Mary, a resident, with a cigarette lighter, in order to "persuade" her to take a bath. Mary sustains no physical injury but undoubtedly sustains emotional trauma, as do two peer witnesses. The caregiver is fired, but her whereabouts are unknown. The caregiver was never prosecuted criminally, so she cannot be tracked by the legal system. She is an unlicensed care provider, so there is no agency to monitor her employment conduct.

B. Bob, a resident in a group home, refuses to get off of the couch to attend a community event when encouraged verbally by a direct care staff member. Frustrated, the staff person then forcefully pulls Bob off the couch, pushes him out the front door, and calls him a "baby." The caregiver is separated from the agency. Then, the same caregiver gets a job at Bob's day program and is responsible once again for Bob's care. Bob is anxious about being around the caregiver. What happens next?

---

[5]Petersilia, J. (n.d.). *When justice sleeps: Violence and abuse against the developmentally disabled* [PowerPoint presentation]. Mental Retardation Research Center, University of California–Irvine. Retrieved March 18, 2011, from http://ucicorrections.seweb.uci.edu/ppt/crime_victims_dis.ppt#260,4

[6]Ibid.

(Continued)

- As in many cases of abuse, neither of these is likely to have enough legal relevance to be prosecuted in a court of law. Fingerprint scans and background checks for future employment will not reveal either caregiver's past. *The cycle continues.*
- Unlike in the care of children or the elderly, most direct care workers working with adults with developmental disabilities are not licensed and/or certified. Therefore, no licensing/certifying agency oversees their employment viability. *The cycle continues.*
- The caregivers may be interviewed by other facilities, which will have no way of knowing their pattern of abuse except through self-disclosure. The caregivers may choose to lie. Or, if they do list past employers, due to overarching privacy laws, the prospective employers cannot inquire directly about past performance. *The cycle continues.*

The Problem

The high incidence of abuse in the developmental disability community, and the frequency of its incidence by caregivers, is appalling. Even worse is the fact that abusive caregivers are easily able to move on to another agency and abuse again. This is possible because current California privacy laws prevent prospective employers from easily accessing information about potential employees' past history of abuse and/or abuse investigations unless they are convicted of abuse in a formal court of law. While state agencies do investigate reported incidents of abuse, and often do substantiate those allegations that may never get prosecuted criminally, there is not a comprehensive system that compiles findings and allows convenient access to them. Further, other vulnerable populations, such as children and the elderly, have safeguards in place that adults with developmental disabilities do not.

As noted, one hiring safeguard that is in place for employers in DD agencies is the Department of Justice fingerprint clearance, which reports abuse history of unlicensed caregivers if they have been convicted of abuse crimes. This safeguard, however, has its limitations. As in all forms of abuse, most cases go unreported[7] to law enforcement, and those that are reported are rarely prosecuted due to lack of evidence. Unless a crime is reported by the victim or someone else on the victim's behalf, someone witnesses the abuse, and/or the abuse is severe enough to prove the validity of the incident, the chances of an abuser being convicted in court are slim, leaving no accessible history for a potential employer.

Also, it can be extremely difficult to secure criminal prosecution in abuse cases because many forms of abuse do not leave evidence; thus the only proof is one person's word against another's—not a strong case for the prosecution. This is further complicated by the segregation and cognitive and verbal impairments of individuals with DD. As well, not all forms of abuse are appropriate for criminal prosecution. Some common forms of abuse that go "under

---

[7]One study found that 40% of the crimes against people with mild and mental retardation went unreported to police and 71% of crimes against people with more severe mental retardation went unreported [see Wilson & Brewer (1992). The incidence of criminal victimization of individuals with an intellectual disability. *Australian Psychologist, 2,* 114–117].

the radar" include the withholding of food, threats (physical and verbal), humiliation and other forms of emotional abuse, hair pulling, shoving, and the use of very hot or very cold water for bathing.

Beyond criminal prosecutions, there are other impediments that DD agencies face in accessing vital information regarding caregiver hires. All state licensing agencies including Community Care Licensing and Department of Health Services, Adult Protective Services, and the state Ombudsmen [Office of the State Long-Term Care Ombudsman] currently investigate reported abuse allegations in the agencies that they license. Findings are declared substantiated or unsubstantiated and shared with the submitting agencies, which then determine whether a suspected caregiver will remain employed, receive further training, or be terminated from employment. Finalized findings are filed by the investigating agency and are not centralized or easily accessible to hiring agencies. This galvanizes the vulnerability and risk of abuse for the DD population and makes it possible for abusive caregivers to move easily from setting to setting.

Protective mechanisms that are absent for adults with developmental disabilities are in place for other vulnerable populations, such as children and the elderly. The following figure shows a comparison of the characteristics of vulnerable populations followed by a comparison of how these populations are currently protected.

The Solution

To protect people with developmental disabilities, The REACH Project—Registry to End Abusive Caregiver Hiring—advocates for the creation of a registry that supports streamlined, accessible abuse reporting in California. Other states, including Ohio, Idaho, Vermont, Louisiana, Wisconsin, and New Mexico, have already instituted such registries. Establishing REACH will bring California to the forefront of this human rights movement with states that are already leading the way in taking action to protect people with developmental disabilities and the agencies that care for them.

The following are proposed details of REACH, based on best practices research from other states' registries geared toward the DD community, California's Child Abuse Registry, and CNA (Certified Nurse's Aide) registries.

Who will create and monitor the registry?

- A consultant will be contracted to create an electronic database; all data to be included will date to the start of the registry.
- An interagency employee will be appointed to oversee the registry, data input, and related events.

Who will contribute information to the registry, and what information will be included?

- The Department of Health Services, Community Care Licensing, and Adult Protective Services will contribute information regarding the

(Continued)

(Continued)

Figure 8.A

Characteristics	Vulnerable Populations		
	Children	Elderly	Developmentally Disabled
Difficulties Communicating Effectively	X	X	X
Overtrusting of Authority Figures	X	X	X
Immature or Impaired Cognitive Ability	X	X	X
Dependent on Others for Basic Needs	X	X	X

How California Protects Vulnerable Populations Beyond Criminal Background Checks

Children	Elderly	Developmentally Disabled
Child abuse registries track both substantiated and alleged abuse investigations for those working in the foster care and licensed childcare programs.	Certified nurses whose quality of care is tracked in the nurse aide registry staff most nursing homes and residential facilities.	No protection

outcomes of abuse investigations involving unlicensed, direct care workers.

- Pertinent information to be included:
  o Name of investigating agency
  o Name of alleged abuser
  o At least two of the following identifiers: the alleged abuser's birth date, home address, and/or driver's license number
  o Date of the incident
  o Type of abuse (following the State of California definition of abuse)
  o Findings (substantiated or inconclusive)
  o Date of findings

What information is accessible?

- All information collected in the registry with regard to substantiated cases of abuse.
- Because substantiating abuse can be very difficult, the database will

be designed so that persons with three or more inconclusive investigations in a five-year period will be flagged. Information collected in the registry with regard to these cases will be shared after a flag is applied.

Who can access information and how?

- The registry will be searchable through an online database. Users will search by the care workers' first and last names plus up to two identifiers to help ensure proper identification.
- Licensed care providers will be *required* to check the registry for all prospective employees. (They still retain hiring discretion, however.) It is recommended that they recheck existing employees against the registry every six months in case of findings that emerge after their hire.
- The registry will be accessible by the public so that persons seeking individuals for private, in-home care of people with DD have access to this information as well as licensed care providers. (Individuals will not be able to add to the registry.)

How will caregivers be protected?

- When alleged abusers are notified of the findings of an investigation (in which they received due process to contest), they will be alerted to their inclusion on the registry and the extent of public access to this information if the case is substantiated. If the findings are inconclusive, they will be notified of their inclusion in the registry and the public's limited access to this information (available only if they have more than three inconclusive cases in a five-year period).
- Alleged and substantiated abusers have the right to appeal the inclusion of their name on a registry by sending a written petition to the interagency person overseeing the registry. Appeals will be held on a quarterly basis and reviewed by an interagency committee to include members of the licensing agencies and the licensed care providers.
- Alleged and substantiated abusers have 30 days within receipt of the notice that they are to be included on the registry to appeal it. Otherwise they must wait five years to petition for removal again.

How will licensing agencies and licensed care providers be protected?

- A provider that reports allegations of abuse, neglect, or exploitation or that declines to hire an employee because the employee is included in the registry is presumed to be acting in good faith and will be immune from liability as to that employee for both civil and criminal culpability.

(Continued)

(Continued)

If, however, the provider acted in bad faith or with malicious purpose, the provider is not immune from liability as to that employee.

How will the registry be supported financially?

- Costs could be covered by state licensing agencies through fees already imposed on care providers or could be user-fee based such as the Department of Justice fingerprint clearance process. Grants may also help cover costs.
- Over time, state licensing agencies, other investigating agencies, and provider agencies will save money by avoiding the hiring of caregivers with abusive histories leading to costly investigations.

The Benefits

The benefits of REACH (Registry to End Abusive Caregiver Hiring) are significant and necessary. By establishing a registry to protect adults with developmental disabilities, California will be responsibly addressing a critical need of a vulnerable group of citizens—citizens who deserve to be protected under the law. At present, a majority of California's DD population is under 21 years of age, and the number of individuals being diagnosed is growing each year.[8] By creating this registry now, California will be better prepared to protect what will be a major influx into the adult DD care system in the near future. It will also afford this population the same protection offered to other vulnerable populations in California. Lastly, a registry will help reduce the workload of state and private agencies that spend significant time and resources conducting investigations. We believe it should be a high priority of the State of California to grant the public access to an online registry of unlicensed, direct care workers with substantiated or repeated allegations of abuse to ensure effective hiring practices and the protection of individuals with developmental disabilities.

---

[8]Statistics provided by the California Department of Developmental Services show that the number of persons with certain developmental disability status (1, 2, and 8) rose from 127,134 in 1994 to 201,051 in 2004. Additionally, in 2004, 56.7% of persons with developmental disabilities were under the age of 21 (http://www.dds.ca.gov/FactsStats/Home.cfm).

Enclosure A.

Review of Legislation

The table below provides information on several states with registries that protect individuals with developmental disabilities (DD). This information is not always easy to find, as the DD population is often not addressed or is subsumed into other categories.

State	Current Law
Delaware	The State of Delaware provides both an Adult Abuse Registry and a CNA Registry. The Adult Abuse Registry is comparable to what REACH is proposing. It tracks abuse records for unlicensed direct care workers. Patterns of abuse allegations are noted as well as substantiated cases. It requires all employers providing care, whether to children or the elderly or the developmentally disabled, to check the Adult Abuse Registry before hiring. Entries to the Adult Abuse Registry may be submitted to an appendix portion of the CNA Registry. Title 16 Health & Social Services/3000 Division of Long Term Care Residents Protection/3101 Adult Abuse Registry. http://www.state.de.us/research/AdminCode/title16/3000/3101.shtml#TopOfPage
Idaho	Idaho is part of a Federal Pilot Project: Background Checks for Direct Access Employees and Contractors of Long Term Care Facilities and Providers. As part of this, the Office on Aging sends a list of all individuals who are listed as perpetrators of substantiated abuse, neglect or exploitation to the criminal history unit, which maintains a registry. This serves a dual purpose. When a name is received, the database is first checked to see if a criminal history background check has previously been conducted on the individual. If so, the Commission on Aging forwards all of their records about the investigation. The Criminal History Unit then puts an alert on their criminal history record that a substantiated action was found. The last known long term care provider is contacted to see if the caregiver was terminated. If so, an alert in the Criminal History Unit records prevents the individual from going to a second agency, as the second agency has to confirm the individual has a viable background check. If the individual is still working at the facility, we can require the individual go through another background check when a denial can be issued. Per Mond Warren, State of Idaho http://www3.state.id.us/oasis/2006/S1327.html#daily
Iowa	HF 2588 – Criminal & Abuse Registry Checks – Makes it illegal for a nursing home, residential care facility (RCF), intermediate care facility for the mentally retarded (ICF/MR) and an intermediate care facility for mental illness (ICF/MI) to hire a person with a criminal record or record of child or dependent adult abuse. Requires these facilities to conduct criminal and abuse registry checks before hiring a person. Goes into effect on 7/1/2006. http://www.infonetiowa.com/current_issue/active_bill_list.php
Louisiana	OTIS – Online Incident Tracking Long Term Care – In this database, substantiated abuse and neglect cases as well as unsubstantiated ones, are documented. A particular facility, client or alleged abuser's name can be pulled out of the database to see if the particular individual or entity has been involved in X-amount of cases and if there is a pattern to help do further investigation. This database is maintained in an IBM-AS400 system, which is shared by all at Health Standards Section in a mainframe. Regular Session, 2005, House Bill NO. 528, Act No. 483. Per Hank Choate, Louisiana Department of Health

(Continued)

(Continued)

New Mexico	The Employee Abuse Registry Act was unanimously approved legislation (SB 590) that went into effect on January 1, 2006. This act created an adult abuse registry housed by the Department of Health that tracks abusive, unlicensed persons providing direct care for individuals with developmental disabilities as well as the elderly. All potential employers must check hires against the registry. http://legis.state.nm.us/Sessions/05%20Regular/bills/house/HB0626.pdf or http://dhi.health.state.nm.us/elibrary/NewItems/EAR_Rule.pdf
Ohio	Sub. S.B. 171 of the 123rd General Assembly (as passed by the General Assembly) required the state of Ohio to create a registry of MR/DD employees found to have abused, neglected, or misappropriated the property of individuals with mental retardation or a developmental disability. It also established due process procedures governing the registry and prohibits a person or government entity from hiring, contracting with, or employing as an MR/DD employee an individual who is included in the registry. http://lsc.state.oh.us/analyses/fnla123.nsf/All%20Bills%20and%20Resolutions/BD8C7D50FEA3630D852568F50040FF72
Vermont	Adult Protective Services is tasked with receiving and investigating allegations of abuse, neglect and exploitation of vulnerable elderly and disabled adults in Vermont. Investigations are conducted to determine the validity of allegations and when warranted include the coordination of protective services to address critical safety concerns. The APS Program maintains a registry of substantiated perpetrators of abuse and performs checks of that registry for employers that provide care and services to vulnerable adults. http://www.leg.state.vt.us/statutes/fullsection.cfm?Title=33&Chapter=069&Section=06911
Wisconsin	The Wisconsin Caregiver Misconduct Registry is a record of the names of nurse aides and other non-credentialed caregivers with a substantiated finding of caregiver misconduct (abuse or neglect of a client or misappropriation of a client's property). Registry information should be reviewed regularly to determine appropriate hiring and employment decisions. Through this program, three reports are offered publicly: Monthly Additions of Findings 2005-6; Wisconsin Caregivers With Findings Reported from Other States; Names Removed From Wisconsin Nurse Aide Registry. http://dhfs.wisconsin.gov/caregiver/misconduct.htm and http://www.legis.state.wi.us/statutes/1999/99Stat0146.pdf

*It is also interesting to note that within California, the Adult Protective Services of Orange County has an Elder and Dependent Adult Abuse Registry in place to protect these populations from repeated abuse, neglect, or exploitation. According to their website, the Orange County Elder and Dependent Adult Abuse Registry received nearly 5,500 reports of elder and dependent adult abuse in 2005, elder and dependent abuse reports have increased by 127% from 1994 to 2005, and between 450 and 550 reports are received at the Registry each month. For more information, go to http://www.ssa.ocgov.com/Elder_Disabled/Report_Abuse.asp

Enclosure B.

Sample Legislation: New Mexico

SENATE JUDICIARY COMMITTEE
SUBSTITUTE FOR SENATE BILL 590
47th legislature – STATE OF NEW MEXICO – first session, 2005

AN ACT

RELATING TO HEALTH; ENACTING THE EMPLOYEE ABUSE REGISTRY ACT; ESTABLISHING A REGISTRY OF PROVIDER EMPLOYEES WITH SUBSTANTIATED ABUSE, NEGLECT OR EXPLOITATION CHARGES.

BE IT ENACTED BY THE LEGISLATURE OF THE STATE OF NEW MEXICO:

Section 1. SHORT TITLE.–This act may be cited as the "Employee Abuse Registry Act".

Section 2. DEFINITIONS.–As used in the Employee Abuse Registry Act:

A. "abuse" means:

(1) knowingly, intentionally or negligently and without justifiable cause inflicting physical pain, injury or mental anguish; or

(2) the intentional deprivation by a caretaker or other person of services necessary to maintain the mental and physical health of a person;

B. "department" means the department of health;

C. "direct care" means face-to-face services provided or routine and unsupervised physical or financial access to a recipient of services;

D. "employee" means a person employed by or on contract with a provider, either directly or through a third party arrangement to provide direct care. "Employee" does not include a New Mexico licensed health care professional practicing within the scope of the profession's license or a certified nurse aide;

E. "exploitation" means an unjust or improper use of a person's money or property for another person's profit or advantage, pecuniary or otherwise;

F. "neglect" means, subject to a person's right to refuse treatment and subject to a provider's right to exercise sound medical discretion, the failure of an employee to provide basic needs such as clothing, food, shelter, supervision and care for the physical and mental health of a person or failure by a person that may cause physical or psychological harm;

G. "provider" means an intermediate care facility for the mentally retarded; a rehabilitation facility; a home health agency; a homemaker agency; a home for the aged or disabled; a group home; an adult foster care home; a case management entity that provides services to elderly people or people with developmental disabilities; a corporate guardian; a private residence that provides personal care, adult residential care or natural and surrogate family services provided to persons with developmental disabilities; an adult daycare center; a boarding home; an adult residential care home; a residential service or habilitation service authorized to be reimbursed by medicaid; any licensed or medicaid-certified entity or any program funded by the aging and long-term services department that provides respite, companion or personal care services; programs funded by the children, youth and families department that provide homemaker or adult daycare services; and any other individual, agency or organization that provides respite care or delivers home- and community-based services to adults or children with developmental disabilities or physical disabilities or to the elderly, but excluding a managed care organization unless the employees of the managed care organization provide respite care, deliver home- and community-based services to adults or children with developmental disabilities or physical disabilities or to the elderly;

H. "registry" means an electronic database that provides information on substantiated employee abuse, neglect or exploitation; and

I. "secretary" means the secretary of health.

Section 3. EMPLOYEE ABUSE REGISTRY.–

A. The department shall establish an "employee abuse registry" of employees and enter into the registry names of employees with substantiated abuse, neglect or exploitation charges as determined by the department pursuant to the Employee Abuse Registry Act.

B. Before a provider hires or contracts with an employee, the provider shall inquire of the department's registry as to whether the employee is included in the registry.

C. When the department's registry receives an inquiry, the department shall inform the provider whether an employee is included in the employee abuse registry.

D. Providers that hire employees shall document that they have checked the abuse registry for each applicant being considered for employment or contract.

E. A provider shall not hire or contract with an employee in a direct care setting who is included in the employee abuse registry.

F. The department or other governmental agency may, at its discretion, terminate or not enter into or renew a contract with a provider that fails to comply with the provisions of Subsection E of this section.

G. A provider that reports allegations of abuse, neglect or exploitation or that fails to hire an employee because the employee is included in the registry is presumed to be acting in good faith and shall be immune from liability as to that employee. If, however, the provider acted in bad faith or with malicious purpose or discriminated against the employee, the provider is not immune from liability as to that employee.

H. After a period of five years, an employee placed on the employee abuse registry may petition the department for removal of the employee's name from the employee abuse registry. Petitions for removal shall be in writing and mailed or hand delivered to the department. Within thirty days of the department's receipt of a petition, the secretary shall issue a written decision on the petition and provide that decision to the employee in person or by certified mail. If the secretary denies the petition, the employee may, within ten days of receipt of that decision, request a hearing. If an employee requests a hearing, that hearing shall be conducted by an independent hearing officer. An employee aggrieved by the final decision following a hearing shall have the right to judicial review pursuant to the provisions of Section 39-3-1.1 NMSA 1978.

Section 4. INVESTIGATION AND SUBSTANTIATION OF ABUSE, NEGLECT OR EXPLOITATION BY THE DEPARTMENT.–

A. In addition to other actions required by law, the department shall review all reports of abuse, neglect or exploitation against employees of providers that are licensed by or under contract with the department and shall investigate such reports as necessary to determine whether there is a reasonable basis to believe that an employee committed abuse, neglect or exploitation.

B. If the department determines that abuse, neglect or exploitation has occurred, the department shall notify the employee and the provider of that determination, and such determination shall include a determination of whether the abuse, neglect or exploitation was the result of conduct by the employee, the provider or both.

Section 5. ADULT PROTECTIVE SERVICES DIVISION REPORT OF ABUSE, NEGLECT OR EXPLOITATION.–

A. The adult protective services division of the aging and long-term services department shall investigate allegations of abuse, neglect and exploitation consistent with its statutory responsibilities.

B. If the adult protective services division determines that abuse, neglect or exploitation has occurred, it shall notify the employee and the provider of that determination, and such determination shall include a determination of whether the abuse, neglect or exploitation was the result of conduct by the employee, the provider or both.

C. The adult protective services division shall report to the department of health any substantiated finding of abuse, neglect or exploitation made against an employee of a provider under waiver or other programs administered by the aging and long-term services department and not otherwise licensed by or under contract with the department.

Section 6. PLACEMENT ON REGISTRY AND HEARING PROCESS.–

A. If the department or the adult protective services division of the aging and long-term services department determines that abuse, neglect or exploitation by an employee has occurred, the department making that determination shall notify the employee and the provider, in person or by certified mail, of the following:

    (1) the nature of the determination of the abuse, neglect or exploitation;

    (2) the date and time of the occurrence;

    (3) the employee's right to a hearing;

    (4) the department's intent to report the substantiated findings, once the employee has had the opportunity for a hearing, to the registry; and

    (5) that the employee's failure to request a hearing in writing within thirty days from the date of the notice shall result in the department reporting substantiated findings to the registry and the provider.

B. If an employee requests a hearing, that hearing shall be conducted by an independent hearing officer of the department that made the determination of abuse, neglect or exploitation.

C. After expiration of the time period for requesting a hearing, or if a determination of abuse, neglect or exploitation is substantiated through the hearing process, the substantiated finding of abuse, neglect or exploitation shall be placed on the registry through a report of the appropriate department.

D. An employee aggrieved by the final decision following a hearing shall have the right to judicial review pursuant to the provisions of Section 39-3-1.1 NMSA 1978.

Section 7. ADOPTION OF RULES.–By January 1, 2006, the department of health and the aging and long-term services department shall jointly establish and adopt rules necessary to carry out the provisions of the Employee Abuse Registry Act, including procedures for determining abuse, neglect and exploitation that consider the severity of the alleged abuse, neglect and exploitation and procedures for reporting for the administrative hearing process and for sanctions for failure to comply with the Employee Abuse Registry Act.

Section 8. PENALTIES.–The department shall administer sanctions for a provider's failure to comply with the Employee Abuse Registry Act, including a directed plan of correction or civil monetary penalty not to exceed five thousand dollars ($5,000) per instance.

Enclosure C.

Sample Legislation: Ohio Bill Final Analysis

Sub. S.B. 171

123rd General Assembly

(As Passed by the General Assembly)

Sens. Spada, Gardner, Kearns, Drake, Prentiss, Johnson, Fingerhut, Armbruster, Brady, DiDonato, Hottinger, Latell, Mumper, Schafrath, Wachtmann, Watts, Latta, Cupp, Nein, White, Espy, McLin, Herington

Reps. Winkler, Willamowski, O'Brien, Smith, Metzger, Grendell, Core, Pringle, Calvert, Flannery, Clancy, Terwilleger, Austria, Distel, Allen, Jolivette, Krupinski, Widener, Evans, Redfern, Bender, J. Beatty, Sykes, Patton, Salerno, Damschroder, Hartnett, Aslanides, Olman, Mettler, Perry, Stevens, Britton, Womer Benjamin, Trakas, Harris, Robinson, Schuler, Amstutz, Verich

Effective date: * * *The Legislative Service Commission had not received formal notification of the effective date at the time this analysis was prepared.*

Act Summary

- Requires the Department of Mental Retardation and Developmental Disabilities to create a registry of MR/DD employees found to have abused, neglected, or misappropriated the property of individuals with mental retardation or a developmental disability.
- Defines an "MR/DD employee" as an individual who is employed by the Department, a county board of mental retardation and developmental disabilities (county MR/DD board), or an intermediate care facility for the mentally retarded or employed in a position that involves providing specialized services to an individual with mental retardation or a developmental disability.
- Establishes due process procedures governing the registry.
- Prohibits a person or government entity from hiring, contracting with, or employing as an MR/DD employee an individual who is included in the registry.
- Requires that suspected abuse or neglect of children with mental retardation and developmental disabilities be reported to the Department, a county MR/DD board, or a law enforcement agency.
- Requires the Department to maintain reports of major unusual incidents.

- Requires the Department to establish committees to review and investigate reports of abuse, neglect, and major unusual incidents.
- Limits the duty of the Department and county MR/DD boards to notify a law enforcement agency regarding reports of abuse or neglect.
- Coordinates the definitions of abuse and neglect for purposes of reporting and investigation.

Content and Operation

Registry of certain MR/DD employees
(secs. 5123.50 to 5123.54)

Under the act, the Department of Mental Retardation and Developmental Disabilities must establish a registry of MR/DD employees found by the Department to have engaged in abuse, neglect, or misappropriation of the property of an individual with mental retardation or a developmental disability.

For the purposes of the act, "MR/DD employee" means an employee of the Department or a county board of mental retardation and developmental disabilities (county MR/DD board); an individual who is employed by an intermediate care facility for the mentally retarded (ICF/MR) or provides services pursuant to a contract or as a volunteer with an ICF/MR; or an individual who is employed in a position that includes providing specialized services to individuals with mental retardation or a developmental disability. *"Specialized services" means a program or service designed and operated to serve primarily individuals with mental retardation or a developmental disability.*

"Abuse" is defined for purposes of the act as (1) the use of physical force that can reasonably be expected to result in physical harm or serious physical harm, (2) unlawful sexual conduct or sexual contact, or (3) purposely using words to threaten, coerce, intimidate, harass, or humiliate an individual. "Neglect" means, when there is a duty to do so, failing to provide an individual with any treatment, care, goods, or services that are necessary to maintain the health and safety of the individual. "Misappropriation" means depriving, defrauding, or otherwise obtaining property by any means prohibited by the Revised Code.

Procedure for reviewing reports
(sec. 5123.51)

In addition to its duties concerning reports of abuse and neglect of adults with mental retardation or a developmental disability, the Department is required by the act to review each report it receives of abuse, neglect, or misappropriation of property of an individual (child or adult) with mental retardation or a developmental disability that includes an allegation that an MR/DD employee committed or was responsible for the abuse, neglect, or misappropriation. The Department is prohibited from reviewing a report it receives from a public children services agency until the agency has completed its investigation of the report. The Department must either investigate the allegation or adopt the findings of an investigation or review conducted by another person or government entity and determine whether there is a reasonable basis for the allegation. If the Department determines that a reasonable basis exists, it must conduct an adjudication under Revised Code Chapter 119 (the Administrative Procedure Act).

The Department must appoint an independent hearing officer to conduct the adjudication hearing and may not hold the hearing until any criminal proceeding or collective bargaining arbitration regarding the same allegation has concluded. If the hearing concerns an employee of the Department who is represented by a union, the Department and a union representative must jointly appoint the hearing officer.

In conducting the hearing, the hearing officer must determine whether there is clear and convincing evidence that the MR/DD employee has done any of the following:

(1) Misappropriated the property of an individual with mental retardation or a developmental disability;

(2) Knowingly abused or neglected such an individual;

(3) Recklessly abused or neglected such an individual, with resulting physical harm;

(4) Negligently abused or neglected such an individual, with resulting serious physical harm.

The act requires that the hearing officer give weight to the decision in any collective bargaining arbitration regarding the same allegation.

The act provides that files and records of the Department's investigation are not public records, but the Department must provide copies of those files and records to the Attorney General, a county prosecutor, or a law enforcement agency on request.

Inclusion in the registry
(secs. 5123.51 and 5123.52)

In general, the act requires the Director to include in the registry the name of an MR/DD employee if the Director finds that there is clear and convincing evidence that the employee has done any of the things listed in (1) through (4) under "*Procedure for reviewing reports*" above.

The Director is not permitted to include in the registry an individual who has been found not guilty by a court or jury of an offense arising from the same facts and is not required to include an MR/DD employee if the Director determines that there are extenuating circumstances. The act requires that the

Director consider as an extenuating circumstance whether the use of physical force by an MR/DD employee was necessary as self-defense. In the case of an allegation concerning a Department employee, the Director of Health or that director's designee must review the hearing officer's decision to determine whether the employee should be included in the registry. The Director of Mental Retardation and Developmental Disabilities is required to include the employee in the registry on notice from the Director of Health.

When an MR/DD employee is included in the registry, the Director of Mental Retardation and Developmental Disabilities must notify (1) the employee, (2) the person or government entity that employs or contracts with the employee, (3) the individual who was the subject of the report that caused the employee to be included in the registry and the individual's legal guardian, if any, (4) the Attorney General, county prosecutor, or another appropriate law enforcement agency, and (5) if the employee authorized to engage in a profession, the entity responsible for regulating the employee's professional practice.

Prohibition employing or contracting with individuals included in the registry
(secs. 5123.52 and 5126.28)

The act prohibits any person or government entity from hiring, contracting with, or employing as an MR/DD employee an individual who is included in the registry established by the act. The prohibition does not apply if a collective bargaining agreement that is in effect on the act's effective date provides otherwise, but prevails over subsequent collective bargaining agreements. Except in cases of gross negligence or willful or wanton misconduct, a person or government entity that fails to hire or retain an individual as an employee because the individual is included in the registry is immune from civil liability. An individual who is fired because of being included in the registry is considered to be discharged for just cause for the purposes of unemployment compensation benefits.

The act prohibits the Department and county MR/DD boards from entering into a new contract or renewing a contract with a person or government entity that fails to comply with the prohibition on hiring, contracting with, or employing such individuals, until the Department or board is satisfied that the person or government entity will comply.

Inquiries regarding the registry
(sec. 5123.52)

The information contained in the registry is a public record. When the Department receives an inquiry regarding whether an individual is included in the registry, it must inform the person making the inquiry whether the individual is included in the registry.

The act requires a person or government entity to inquire whether an individual is included in the registry before hiring, contracting with, or employing the individual as an MR/DD employee.

Removal from registry for good cause
(sec. 5123.53)

An individual included in the registry may petition the Director for removal from the registry. The Director is authorized to remove an individual from the registry if good cause exists, which includes meeting rehabilitation standards the Department establishes by rule as required by the act.

Rule-making authority
(sec. 5123.54)

The act requires the Director to adopt rules under Revised Code Chapter 119 to implement the MR/DD employee registry. The rules must establish rehabilitation standards and specify other circumstances that constitute good cause for the purpose of removal from the registry.

Registry office
(sec. 5123.61)

Current law requires the Department to establish a registry office for the purpose of maintaining reports of abuse and neglect. The act requires that the registry office also maintain reports of major unusual incidents. The act does not define that term or give the Department the authority to define it. The Department is also required by the act to establish committees to review reports of abuse, neglect, and other major unusual incidents.

Reporting and investigation of abuse or neglect
(secs. 5123.61, 5123.31, 5126.32, and 5126.33)

Continuing law requires certain persons who have reason to believe that a mentally retarded or developmentally disabled adult has suffered any wound, injury, disability, or condition that reasonably indicates abuse or neglect to immediately report that information or cause it to be reported to a law enforcement agency or to the county MR/DD board. *This requirement applies to physicians, including hospital interns or residents; dentists; podiatrists; chiropractors; practitioners of a limited branch of medicine; hospital administrators and employees; nurses; employees of ambulatory health facilities; employees of home health agencies; employees of adult care facilities; employees of community mental health facilities; school teachers or school authorities; social workers; psychologists; attorneys; peace officers; coroners; clergymen; resident's rights advocates; superintendents, board members, or employees of a county MR/DD board; administrators, board members, or employees of residential facilities for persons with mental retardation or a developmental disability; administrators, board members, or employees of any other public or private provider of services to an adult with mental retardation or a developmental disability; members of citizen's advisory councils established at an institution of the Department; and persons rendering spiritual treatment through prayer in accordance with the tenets of a well-recognized religion. Members of the Legal Rights Service Commission and employees of the Legal Rights Service are exempt from the reporting requirement.* If the report concerns a resident of a facility operated by the Department of Mental Retardation and Developmental Disabilities, the report must be made to either a law enforcement agency or the Department. The law also permits any person with reasonable cause to believe that an adult with mental retardation or a developmental disability has suffered abuse or neglect to report that belief.

When the Department or the county MR/DD board receives a report of abuse or neglect, it is required to notify a law enforcement agency. *"Law enforcement agency" means the state highway patrol, the police department of a municipal corporation, or a county sheriff.* A county MR/DD board must also notify the Department. The law enforcement agency must investigate all reports of abuse or neglect of adults with mental retardation or a developmental disability and make a report of its findings to the Department or county MR/DD board. The Department must investigate reports regarding residents of facilities it operates and submit a report of its investigation to the law enforcement agency. A county MR/DD board is required to review reports of abuse and neglect it receives and submit a report to the law enforcement agency responsible for investigating the report and to the Department.

The act adds MR/DD employees to the persons required to report abuse or neglect. The act expands mandatory reporting to include reports concerning children with mental retardation or a developmental disability. The Revised Code currently requires that the Department and county MR/DD boards receive only reports of abuse and neglect that concern adults. Reports of abuse or neglect concerning children, including mentally or physically handicapped persons under age 21, are made to a public children services agency or county peace officer. The act requires that reports involving such children be made, in addition, to a law enforcement agency, county MR/DD board, or the Department. *If the law enforcement agency is also the county peace officer, the person would only have to make one report.*

Under the act, the Department is required to notify a law enforcement agency and the county MR/DD board is required to notify the Department and a law enforcement agency of a report only if the report includes an allegation of an action or inaction that may be criminal under federal or Ohio law.

Coordinating definitions for abuse and neglect reporting and investigations
(secs. 5123.50, 5123.61, and 5126.30)

As described above, county MR/DD boards must review reports of abuse or neglect concerning adults with mental retardation or a developmental disability. The Department must investigate reports of abuse or neglect involving residents of facilities it operates. For purposes of the county MR/DD board reviews, prior law defined "abuse" to mean any of the following:

An act, or a failure to act, that results or could result in emotional or physical injury to an adult, unless the act is done in self defense or by accident; An act that constitutes sexual activity as defined in the Criminal Code for sex offenses and would constitute a sex offense; Insulting or coarse language or gestures directed toward an adult that subject him to humiliation or degradation; An act that deprives an adult of real or personal property by fraudulent or illegal means. "Neglect" was defined as the failure of an adult or caretaker to provide goods and services necessary for an adult with mental retardation or a developmental disability to avoid physical harm. The Revised Code did not provide a definition of abuse or neglect for purposes of the Department's investigations of abuse or neglect reports.

The act establishes definitions for abuse and neglect that are applicable to investigations by the Department. The definitions are the same as those established under the act for the MR/DD employee registry (as described above), with the exception that "abuse" includes misappropriation as defined under the act for the registry. The act also makes the definitions of abuse and neglect that are applicable to Department investigations applicable to county MR/DD board investigations.

History

Action	Date	Journal Entry
Introduced	07-13-99	p. 887
Reported, S. Health, Human Services & Aging	03-16-00	p. 1464
Passed Senate (33-0)	03-16-00	p. 1468
Reported, H. Children and Family Services	05-10-00	p. 1937
Passed House (96-0)	05-16-00	pp. 1958-1959
Senate concurred in House amendments (33-0)	05-17-00	pp. 1732-1733

Enclosure D.

Additional References

Publications

Baladerian, N. (1991). Sexual Abuse of People with Developmental Disabilities. Sexuality and Disability, 7 (3), 323–35.

LaPlante, M.M., and Carlson, D. (1996). Disability in the United States: Prevalence and Causes, 1992. Based on the National Health Interview Survey, Disabilities Statistics Report (7). Washington, D.C.: National Institute on Disability and Rehabilitation Research.

Luckasson, R. (1992). "People with Mental Retardation as Victims of Crime," in *The Criminal Justice System and Mental Retardation* (R.W. Conley, R. Luckasson, and G.N. Bouthilet (eds.)). Baltimore, Md.: Paul H. Brookes.

Morrision, L., et al. (2003). Abuse and Neglect of Adults with Developmental Disabilities – A Public Health Priority for the State of California. Protection and Advocacy, Inc., State Council on Developmental Disabilities, USC University Affiliated Program, and The Tarjan Center for Developmental Disabilities, UCLA.

Petersilia, J. (2001). Crime Victims With Developmental Disabilities: A Review Essay. Criminal Justice and Behavior, American Association for Correctional and Forensic Psychology, Vol. 28, No. 6, 655–694.

Sobsey, D. (1994). Violence and Abuse in the Lives of People with Disabilities. Baltimore: Paul H. Brookes.

Sobsey, D., and Doe, T. (1991). Patterns of Sexual Abuse and Assault. Journal of Sexuality and Disability, 9 (3), 243–259.

Sobsey, D., and Mansell, S. (1990). The Prevention of Sexual Abuse in Persons with DD. Journal of Sexuality and Disability, 9 (3), 243–259.

Sobsey, D., Lucardie, R., and Mansell, S. (1995). Violence & Disability: An Annotated Bibliography. Baltimore, Md.: Paul H. Brookes.

Waxman, B.F. (1991). "Hatred: The Unacknowledged Dimension in Violence Against Disabled People," in Special Issue: Sexual Exploitation of People with Disabilities. Journal of Sexuality and Disability, Vol. 9, No. 3, pp. 185–99.

White, C., Holland, E., Marsland, D., and Oakes, P. (2003). The Identification of Environments and Cultures that Promote the Abuse of People with Intellectual Disabilities. Journal of Applied Research in Intellectual Disabilities, 16, 1–9.

Websites

American Bar Association, Commission on Law and Aging

http://www.abanet.org/aging
http://www.abanet.org/irr/hr/winter00humanrights/petersilia.html

California Department of Developmental Services

http://www.dds.cahwnet.gov/
http://www.dds.cahwnet.gov/factsstats/pdf/factbook_8th.pdf
http://www.dds.cahwnet.gov/general/info_about_dd.cfm
http://www.dds.cahwnet.gov/factsStats/Caseload_main.cfm
http://www.dds.ca.gov/factsStats/factsStats_main.cfm

California Department of Health Services

www.dhs.ca.gov/hisp/chs/OHIR/vssdata/tables.htm
http://www.dhfs.state.wi.us/caregiver/misconduct.htm
www.census.gov

California State Council on Developmental Disabilities

http://www.scdd.ca.gov/about_developmental_disabilities/Default.htm
http://www.scdd.ca.gov/who_we_are/council_members.htm

Joan Petersillia, Ph.D. (publications on disability topics)

http://www.seweb.uci.edu/users/joan/publications.html

Los Angeles Channel 2, CBS News

http://cbs2.com/local/local_story_333004656.html

National Center on Elder Abuse

http://www.elderabusecenter.org
http://www.elderabusecenter.org/pdf/2-14-06%20FINAL%2060+REPORT.pdf
http://www.elderabusecenter.org/pdf/research/apsreport030703.pdf

Office for Victims of Crime Online Directory of Crime Victim Services

http://ovc.ncjrs.org/findvictimservices

State of California Center for Health Statistics, Office of Health Information and Research

http://www.dhs.ca.gov/hisp/chs/OHIR/tables/

U.S. Department of Health and Human Services: Ensuring a Qualified Long-Term Care Workforce: From Pre-Employment Screens to On-the-Job Monitoring
(The Lewin Group, May 2006)

http://aspe.hhs.gov/daltcp/reports/2006/LTCWqual.htm#findings
http://bhpr.hrsa.gov/healthworkforce/reports/nursinghomeaid/appf.htm

University of California, Irvine

http://ucicorrections.seweb.uci.edu/ppt/crime_victims_dis.ppt#260,4,Defining
Developmental Disabilities (DD)

9 REACH the Final Steps!

Maureen Carasiti

As has been mentioned a few times in this book, the list of the 10 steps isn't really a list because sometimes things get done in a different order than you initially planned. Oftentimes, too, steps get revised along the way as momentum builds for your campaign (for instance, as you add more members to your coalition, your fact sheet will change, and the educational materials you design for those members might also change). In the case of The REACH Project, we should technically be on Step 8, launching a media campaign; however, the REACH team members didn't launch their media campaign until *after* their visit to the state capitol. Therefore, we will pick up the story with Step 9 and return to Step 8 afterward. Since Step 10 is implementation, that is left for Howard in Chapter 12.

9. Approach Elected Officials

In January at the start of the legislative season, we made our first trip to Sacramento, our state capital. The agenda for the day involved a tour of the capitol building (which was fabulous) and meetings with various legislators. Jessica Towne-Cardenas had scheduled appointments with the offices of three Assembly Members and one Senator (Assembly Members Patty Berg, Karen Bass, and John Benoit, and Senator Elaine Alquist). We were granted appointments ranging from 10 to 15 minutes with each.

As a group, we had many talents; however, being short-winded was not one of them! We had a slew of information to share, and this time boundary would be a challenge for us. After we knew how short our presentation time frame would be, we spent a lot of time preparing for those meetings.

Our strategy was to describe the problem of caregiver abuse and our solution, the REACH registry, in as succinct a way as possible given the complexity of both the issue of abuse and details of the registry. To do this we developed talking points. The first drafts were a summary of the major facts and statistics and an overview of the registry. Realizing that these were too comprehensive and would be more useful during a question-and-answer period, we developed a very precise opening statement with only the most important facts as follows:

- Greetings [tailored to the office representative with whom we were speaking]
- Opening Statement:

  We are here to share with you an important issue regarding public safety and human rights in California. This issue directly affects the 220,000+ individuals in this state who have developmental disabilities and are receiving care in a variety of settings. It also affects the families, friends, professionals, and communities who love and/or support them in this state and across the country. [Review definition of developmental disability if needed.]

- Talking Points:

  1. The incidence of abuse against individuals with developmental disabilities is disturbingly high [referring to the statistics on the fact sheet (Figure 8.1) as needed].

  2. Abuse is most frequently committed by caregivers—ironically, those responsible for the victims' well-being.

  3. Unless they are prosecuted criminally—which is not common—there is no system by which abusive caregivers can be tracked. Therefore, they are moving easily from agency to agency, perpetuating the cycle of abuse. [Share a brief anecdote if appropriate.]

- Solution:

  To address this, we propose the creation of a registry to track unlicensed, direct care workers who are abusing individuals with developmental disabilities. Employers would have access to this vital information when making hires so that they can better protect the individuals for whom they are responsible.

- Closing Statements:

  It is significant to note that registries already exist to protect children and the elderly in California and in all 50 states. Only some states have registries to protect people with developmental disabilities. We believe California belongs at the forefront of any movement to protect people from abuse, particularly those as vulnerable as individuals with developmental disabilities.

> We are looking for a legislator to take our proposal to legislative council and/or to consider authoring the related bill. Would your office be willing to stand up for people with developmental disabilities by taking this on?

Prior to our trip to Sacramento, we researched information about the legislators with whom we would be meeting. Being familiar with their legislative histories and biographies proved to be a great advantage. During the meetings, our team took turns opening and facilitating the sessions. Each group member incorporated her own communication style and used the history of these legislators in an effort to peak their interest. For example, we stressed Assembly Member Benoit's public safety background and Assembly Member Bass's work to protect children in the foster care system.

Overall, the meetings went very well. The individuals we met with were surprised with the severity of the issue and the fact that California was not already tracking these types of abusive incidents. As a group, we answered all questions applying the expertise we had acquired through the advocacy course and our research.

Back home we set up a meeting with the district aide for a local Senator (Christine Kehoe). The meeting was much longer than those we had at the state capitol and very encouraging. The aide told us that because the Senator had changed committees, she probably wouldn't be willing to carry the bill. She would, however, be willing to coauthor the bill, which gave us a lot of encouragement.

Author, Author!

As you are aware from reading Howard's chapter, there is a legislative calendar in California (and, for that matter, in whatever state you reside; see Figure 4.3). This calendar is compiled by the Secretary of the Senate with the Chief Clerk of the Office of the Assembly and establishes specific deadlines with respect to the life of a bill. The last day to introduce new bills for this particular legislative year was February 23, 2007. The countdown of days began!

While we were encouraged by the response during our sessions with various legislators, we did not have a commitment by any of them to author our bill. Several had indicated they would *coauthor*; however, we learned that two or three coauthors does not make an author (seems like it should, doesn't it?). We needed a commitment from one person to author the bill, and the legislative clock was ticking: ticktock, ticktock.

I remember our group looking at the February 23 deadline and feeling daunted. "Wow, how are we going to accomplish this?" I guess you can say *tenacity* became our middle name (or perhaps it was our first).

The days after involved intricate letters to all of the people with whom we met in Sacramento, as well as follow-up phone calls. Our team divided up the list so that no one person would be overwhelmed and we could focus on cultivating the relationships we had begun. We also developed additional materials and engaged our coalition—encouraging supporters to contact members of the legislature.

Encouraging news started rolling in. First, Jessica was informed by the office of Assembly Member Berg that the idea had been taken to legislative council and drafted into legislative language. We also had a spot bill (a bill without any content that is used as a placeholder with the intention to later insert content) from the office of Assembly Member Bass. I was the point person for her office, which meant that I would be following up with Max Espinoza, her legislative aide.

In advocacy, never underestimate the value of relationships. Whether those relationships are internal or external, relationship building is critical to the success of your efforts. When we were in the capitol, we weren't able to get a meeting with Assembly Member Bass and instead met with her aide, Max. Subsequent to our visit, each time I spoke to Max I told him we needed help to move this critical issue along. He continued to be hopeful, although he indicated that Bass's bill plate was getting full. When Max eventually called me to tell us that she couldn't carry the bill, I sensed disappointment in his voice. During our conversation, I told Max that I needed his help once again and asked if he could recommend anyone to whom we could speak in other offices that might be able to assist us. He suggested Assembly Member Noreen Evans.

Phone calls were made immediately. Jessica began contact with Evans's office—she forwarded all of our materials there, and the feedback she received was impressive. However, the legislative clock continued to tick faster, and we still had no commitment.

On the afternoon of February 23, we received a call from Angelica González, the legislative aide for Assembly Member Evans, who told us that the assembly-woman (D-Santa Rosa) introduced AB 1192, sponsored by The REACH Project, which directs the California Department of Developmental Services to establish a registry of care providers with abusive histories and make the information available to groups hiring caregivers. We had an author!

Fireworks were flying over the capitol building in Sacramento! Well, not really, but we did have fireworks in our minds and hearts! The feeling was tremendous. The excitement of our progress was exhilarating; however, the advocacy did not stop here, and there was still much work to be done.

8. Launch a Media Campaign

Once we had an author, our team developed a media timeline (see Figure 9.1) and talking points.

Figure 9.1

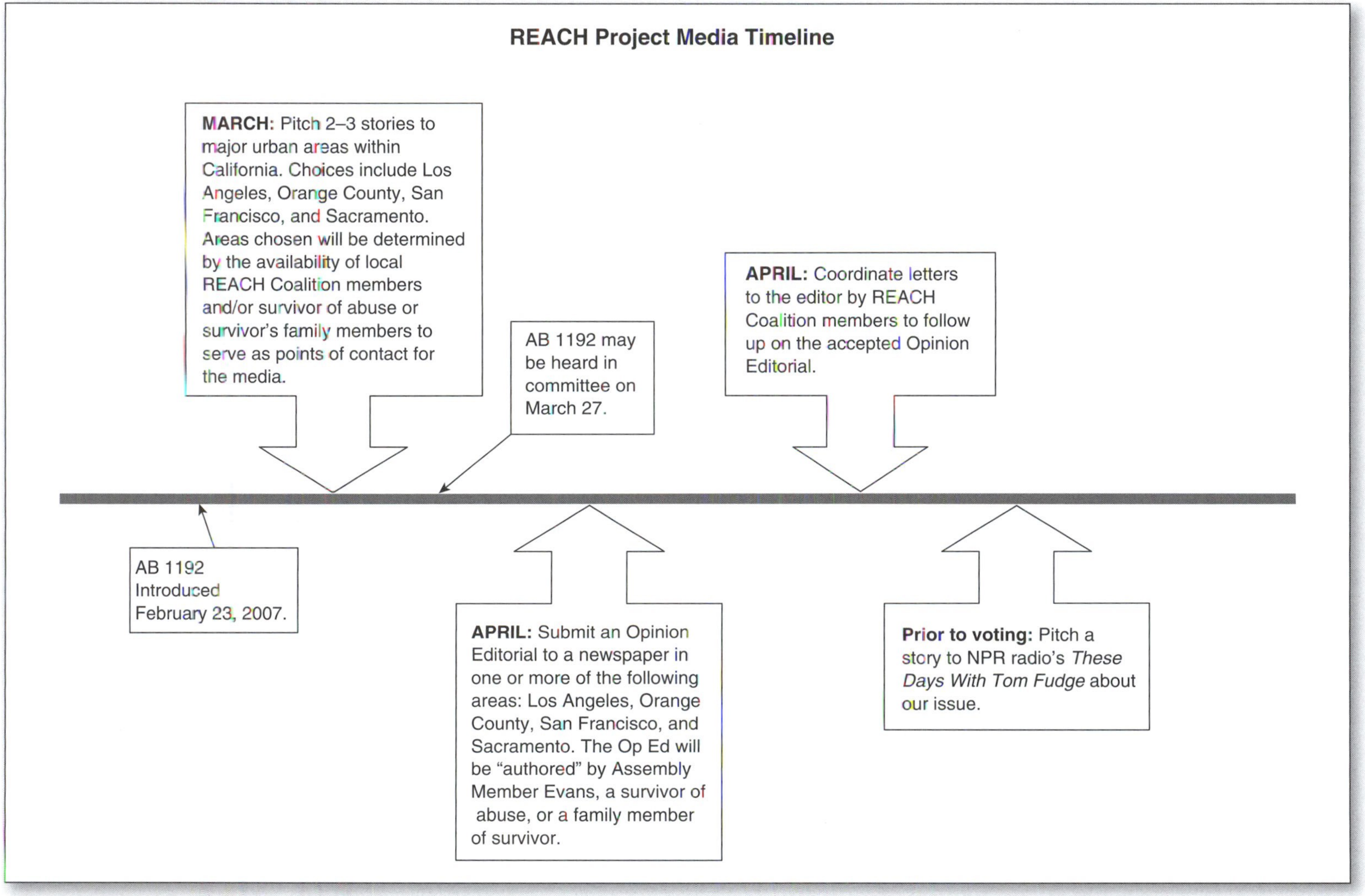

REACH Project Media Timeline

MARCH: Pitch 2–3 stories to major urban areas within California. Choices include Los Angeles, Orange County, San Francisco, and Sacramento. Areas chosen will be determined by the availability of local REACH Coalition members and/or survivor of abuse or survivor's family members to serve as points of contact for the media.

AB 1192 Introduced February 23, 2007.

AB 1192 may be heard in committee on March 27.

APRIL: Submit an Opinion Editorial to a newspaper in one or more of the following areas: Los Angeles, Orange County, San Francisco, and Sacramento. The Op Ed will be "authored" by Assembly Member Evans, a survivor of abuse, or a family member of survivor.

APRIL: Coordinate letters to the editor by REACH Coalition members to follow up on the accepted Opinion Editorial.

Prior to voting: Pitch a story to NPR radio's *These Days With Tom Fudge* about our issue.

TALKING POINTS/MEDIA PITCH

Hi. My name is _____, with The REACH Project. I have a story that you may find interesting. It taps into human rights and public safety issues and has been making its way into the media recently.

First, are you familiar with the term *developmental disability*?

If not, it describes individuals who are severely challenged or lacking in abilities such as self-care, learning, and mobility. This is the result of conditions that arise before the age of 18 and have lifelong implications, such as mental retardation, cerebral palsy, and Down syndrome.

Did you know that people with developmental disabilities are 11 times more likely to be sexually assaulted than you or I? Or that 50% of women with developmental disabilities who are sexually assaulted are assaulted over *10* times?

An equally disturbing fact is that 44% of abusers come into contact with their victims as direct care workers. And the problem is that, between California's strict privacy laws and a lack of tracking measures, abusive caregivers are moving easily from agency to agency, abusing repeatedly. Not enough people even realize this is happening.

However, through REACH's advocacy efforts and sponsorship, Assembly Member Noreen Evans, a Democrat from Santa Rosa, recently introduced AB 1192 into the California Legislature. This bill will create a registry to track abusive caregivers and prevent their rehiring. An interesting thing to note is that similar registries are already in place to protect children and the elderly in California and all 50 states. People with developmental disabilities have been overlooked. Why?

The bill will go to committee in April, and we would like to raise awareness for it. May I send you some materials to inform you further? Also, we have _____ locally who is available to speak with you and share his/her side of the story. Assembly Member Evans and the REACH coalition members are available as well.

Is there anything else you would like to know from me at this point? Is this something you might be interested in pursuing?

Source: Created by Jessica Towne-Cardenas, Paige Simpson, Becky Lee, and Maureen Carasiti. Reprinted with permission.

During one of our advocacy class sessions, a guest speaker spoke about the coordination of advocacy efforts and suggested signing up with Google Alerts. Google Alerts are e-mail updates of the latest relevant Google results (web, news, etc.) based on your choice of query or topic. Some convenient uses of Google Alerts include following a developing news story, keeping current on a competitor or an industry, getting the latest on a celebrity or an event, and keeping tabs on your favorite sports teams.

Becky Lee (Launder) heeded the advice of our class lecturer and queried "abuse to people with developmental disabilities." Through this resource came a wealth of information. Daily, we would receive current local and national stories on the issue. Not only did the horrific accounts breathe fire in our souls and intensify our advocacy even further, but we were able to more effectively engage others and expand our coalition with "real stories." This tool also allowed for further education of the California legislators on the depth and frequency of the issue of abuse with this vulnerable population in the Golden State.

One can only imagine the excitement of The REACH Project group when the following Google Alert was delivered to us on February 25, 2007:

EVANS BILL WOULD EXPAND TRACKING OF ABUSIVE CAREGIVERS

Saturday, February 24, 2007

By David Ryan, *Napa Valley Register* Staff Writer

Assemblywoman Noreen Evans, D-Santa Rosa, introduced a bill Friday to allow the state to track abusive caregivers of developmentally disabled people. "Current safeguards don't prevent caregivers caught or investigated for abuse from moving to another agency providing care," Evans said in a statement. "My bill will help put a stop to this."

Evans said she was inspired to introduce the bill, AB 1192, after hearing disturbing reports as chairwoman of the Assembly Committee on Human Services. "I've heard instances of the developmentally disabled being hurt or dying in suspicious circumstances," she said.

According to the Registry to End Abusive Caregiver Hiring, or REACH, a coalition of developmentally disabled activist groups, there are more than 220,000 people with developmental disabilities in California and they are two to five times more likely to experience abuse than the non-disabled.

According to a UC Irvine study, the developmentally disabled are 11 times at higher risk of being victims of sexual assault and have a higher risk of being re-victimized.

All 50 states have abuse registries for children and the elderly, but only eight have registries for the developmentally disabled.

Developmentally disabled people have many of the same dependencies on caregivers that children and dependent elderly have, according to REACH, including difficulties communicating effectively, tendencies to put more faith in authority figures than is normal, impaired cognitive abilities and dependency on others for their basic needs.

Developmentally disabled advocates maintain California law makes it easy for abusive caregivers who—fired from one agency—simply move to another agency and abuse again, because state privacy laws bar prospective employers from easily getting their hands on potential employees' history of abuse or abuse investigations unless that potential employee is convicted in a formal court of law.

Finding out information on potential caregivers who have merely been investigated is important, studies show, because so much abuse goes unreported and the bar remains high for convicting a caregiver with abuse. One 1992 psychological study found 40 percent of crimes committed against people with mild and mental retardation went unreported to police and 71 percent of crimes against more severely disabled people went unreported.

(Continued)

> (Continued)
>
> Randy Snowden, director of the Napa County Health and Human Services, which serves some developmentally disabled clients through In Home Supportive Services, said the bill sounded helpful.
>
> "It's in line with a move toward trying to bring information and accountability to adult services that have existed for children's services," he said. "For example, we're just moving toward fingerprinting for the In Home Supportive Services program. . . . It sounds as though it's in this same kind of movement recognizing that more people in the community are in need of assistance."

We were making the news!

In addition to the media campaign, Jessica suggested the development of a communication plan for REACH and established a Yahoo! e-mail account. This step was critical because it allowed us as members to be fully informed about all communications to and from The REACH Project with all interested parties, coalition members, legislators, members of the press, and so on. Aside from organizing the coalition members in the account, Becky uploaded all materials for easier accessibility. This facilitated the process of keeping everyone informed.

Paige Simpson and her friend developed a website for The REACH Project (http://www.facebook.com/group.php?gid=159302605400). The website was critical and helped to further build our coalition. Our exposure broadened considerably, and the site denoted a legitimate quality advocacy group. We began to see The REACH Project website linked to others, and we would frequently receive such correspondence from people as "While I was on the Internet I came across your site; how can I support your efforts?" or "I have a child with a disability; thank you for taking on this issue, and please sign me on as a coalition member."

It occurs to me as I am writing this that many readers may be asking, "How long is this advocacy class at the University of San Diego?" Believe me—this was a question our group pondered as well. The fact is the class had ended following our trip to Sacramento; however, as members of The REACH Project we continued to be actively involved in the campaign. We were not students looking for a stellar grade anymore. The class work had morphed us and others into a true grassroots advocacy group. We were and continue to be advocates for people with developmental disabilities. Advocacy doesn't really end. It just becomes a part of you.

If You Build It, They Will Come

By April our coalition had grown to 29 members, all of which were organizations. We decided to expand the coalition to include community members who were interested in our cause. Many family members of children with developmental disabilities joined. This strengthened our voice and extended the coalition throughout the state of California.

AB 1192 was scheduled to be heard in the Human Services Committee on April 24. We were asked by the office of Assembly Member Evans to testify on behalf of the bill. I made the trip up to Sacramento with my sister Patricia Van Natta. As a nursing home administrator, Patricia has a professional interest in our efforts, but, more important, she is deeply committed on a personal level as the mother of Erik, a 15-year-old boy with Down syndrome. Together we prepared our testimonies in preparation for the committee hearing.

When we arrived at the state capitol, there was a tremendous sense of purpose. The committee hearing was long, and we were able to see the process at work prior to actually testifying. It was fascinating! Sitting in the chambers I felt like I could hear history.

When AB 1192 was called, we approached the podiums and were seated in chairs for support. At that time I noticed there were several people sitting in the chairs for opposition. I began to feel overwhelmed and consumed. I was thinking, "Who is opposing?" We did not have any known opposition to this bill. We did our mapping! As it turns out, these people were actually supporters of the bill, and after their testimonies the chairman called forward any more supporters for the bill. I turned around, and there was a line of people extending the full length of the hearing room and out the door. I get goose bumps just recalling this. I do not know where all those people came from, but evidently they were aware of our efforts and wanted to express their voices of support.

The following is the e-mail correspondence we sent to our coalition members informing them of the results from the Human Services Committee hearing:

Dear Coalition Members,

Yesterday Assembly Member Evans presented AB 1192, sponsored by The REACH Project, to the Human Services Committee. AB 1192 moved out of committee *without a single "no" vote!* Patricia Van Natta from Country Hills Health Care Center and I spoke as witnesses. It was a very moving time as many people stepped forward and shared their support for AB 1192. The Chair of the Human Services Committee, Assembly Member Jim Beall (Democrat–24th District), as well as Assembly Member Todd Spitzer (Republican–71st District), asked to be coauthors of the bill. We are moving forward! Please visit our website at http://www.facebook.com/group.php?gid=159302605400 to track the legislation. Once again, continue to share the good news of The REACH Project and AB 1192 with your colleagues. The bigger our coalition, the greater our voice! Thank you for all your support!

Best,

Maureen Carasiti

REACH

Reaching out to protect the developmentally disabled through streamlined, accessible abuse reporting.

Our next committee hearing would be Assembly Appropriations.

May 2007: The Suspense File—A Dark and Dreary Place!

The following is an e-mail the REACH group received on May 2, 2007, from the Legislative Director in the Office of Assembly Member Evans:

> If you haven't already, REACH should send out a letter of support to the Assembly Appropriations Committee. Since I'm sure this bill will be over the threshold of cost, it will most likely be placed on the Suspense File.
>
> I will let you know when it will be heard in Appropriations, but since we will likely waive presentation we don't need anyone to testify.
>
> **Angelica V. González**
> Legislative Director
> *Office of Assembly Member Noreen Evans*

What exactly does this mean? It sounds hopeless, doesn't it? "Suspense File"? "Waive presentation"?

When we received this correspondence, the cell phones were active, and our conversations with each other were hilarious! We remembered one of our professors, Howard Wayne, speaking about the scary Suspense File and what a dark and dreary place it is: "The Suspense File is where bills die"—a horrific fate for advocacy that matters! It was an unacceptable option for an advocacy group whose middle name is *tenacity*.

Once again, The REACH Project members met and strategized on ways to get the bill out of the Suspense File. Remember when Pat talked about Step 6, forming a coalition? I cannot say enough on the importance of this step in our advocacy campaign. By now our coalition had grown, and further outreach efforts were encouraged by engaging colleagues, friends, and families. I believe our coalition became the cornerstone in our success throughout the campaign as we were able to build an influential power base of individuals and organizations that supported the REACH solution for the complex issue of abuse. Our efforts now involved engaging our coalition to contact the Assembly Appropriations Committee members by e-mail, snail mail, phone, fax, and visits, if possible.

And guess what? It worked.

> Jessica,
> I just wanted to let you know that AB 1192 passed off of the Assembly Appropriations Suspense File. They recommended some amendments, which I will be able to review tomorrow. This bill will be brought up on the Assembly floor next week.
>
> **Angelica V. González**
> Legislative Director
> *Office of Assembly Member Noreen Evans*

June 2007: Developmentally Disabled Care Bill Passes Assembly!

> June 1   From committee. AB 1192 ordered to return to second reading.
>
> June 4   Read second time. To third reading.

In California bills passed by committees are read a second time in the house of origin, and then they are assigned for a third reading. The first time a bill is read it is introduced and given a bill number with the name of the author and a general description of what the bill entails.

We learned that prior to the third reading bill analyses are also prepared. During the third reading, the bill is read on the floor by the author. Members have the opportunity to discuss, and then the bill is voted on by a roll call vote.

> June 6   Assembly Bill 1192 read third time.
>
> Roll call vote Ayes 74 Noes 1
>
> AB 1192 Passed onto Senate.

DEVELOPMENTALLY DISABLED CARE BILL PASSES ASSEMBLY

June 8, 2007

By Rachel Raskin-Zrihen, *Vallejo Times-Herald* Staff Writer

The developmentally disabled in California may soon be safer from abusive care givers now that a bill by Assemblymember Noreen Evans, D Santa Rosa, cleared the Assembly on Wednesday. Assembly Bill 1192, which aims to protect the developmentally disabled through creating a registry tracking abusers, passed with strong bipartisan support, according to a statement from Evans' office. The measure now heads to the state Senate for review and will likely be voted on there by late summer.

Our next stop on this advocacy trip was the Senate. In California, once a bill has been approved by the house of origin, it moves to the other house, and the same procedure in terms of readings, committee review, and so on is repeated.

Timing and the Alignment of the Planets

Don't ever underestimate the value of media coverage on your issue. Media coverage keeps your issue alive and draws wider public attention to your campaign.

So here we were the last weekend prior to our deadline struggling with the reality of our bill lying in the Suspense File once again, this time on the Senate side. The legislative clock just kept moving, and I began to lose sleep thinking that we'd come so far we just couldn't let it die now. My wheels began to turn. I tuned into the television in the background and heard the following commentary by news reporter Nancy Grace of CNN:

> Tonight: Caught on video, handicapped patients, unable to even speak, being beaten and slapped, taunted over and over by whom? Oh, no, not some street thug, but by trusted caregivers, men and women working there in the nursing home. Tonight: Thugs busted, caught on videotape. And let me tell you, video doesn't lie.[i]

Wow, talk about timing! I was mesmerized. Videos began airing that depicted the horror of abuse in several states across the nation. One of the incidents showed an abuse case in our own backyard: Anaheim, California. A person who couldn't even speak was being systematically beaten and abused by his health care worker. Another victim. Another example of why change was needed.

As you may know or not, CNN plays its video coverage over and over during its shows.

I sat.

I watched.

My blood pressure rose.

I was tense.

I began to cry.

My heart was beating a million times a minute, and then it occurred to me.

This media coverage was a gift! A gift we would use to help advance our cause and the movement of Assembly Bill 1192!

The planets had aligned.

I slept peacefully.

We were advocates.

August 22, 2007: "Hello, I Have to Talk to Senator Torlakson"

At 8 a.m. I called Senator Torlakson, Chair of the Senate Appropriations Committee:

Maureen Carasiti:	"Good morning. My name is Maureen Carasiti, and I am a member of The REACH Project, sponsor of Assembly Bill 1192. May I please speak to Senator Torlakson?"
Office aide:	"I am sorry, but he is not available. May I take a message?"
Maureen Carasiti:	"Yes, and it is very important that Senator Torlakson get the message today. Is that possible?"
Office aide:	"Yes."
Maureen Carasiti:	"Well, I wanted to make him aware of a Nancy Grace episode that aired last night that depicted abuse to people with disabilities in the state of California. I will forward him the transcript via e-mail as it is available. This is a pervasive problem, and the solution that addresses this concern is sitting in the Suspense File in the form of Assembly Bill 1192. As chairman of the Senate Appropriations Committee I am urging him to pull Assembly Bill 1192 from the Suspense File for review and vote. People with disabilities deserve and have the right to be free from abuse."
Office aide:	"Anything else?"
Maureen Carasiti:	"Yes. My contact information is as follows . . . If he has any questions, please do not hesitate to call. Please be certain Senator Torlakson receives the message today. It is critical. Thank you so much."

E-mails, snail mails, calls, and faxes alike continued throughout the day by The REACH Project and the members of our coalition to all of the Senate Appropriations Committee members. Once again, Becky prepared scripts and letters to facilitate the process. I can't say for certain how many contacts in Sacramento were made, but I know it was a fruitful effort.

The very next day, we received notification that Senator Torlakson had specifically requested AB 1192 from the Suspense File for review, and we were scheduled for presentation to the Appropriations Committee on August 31, 2007.

AB 1192 passed committee unanimously with 17 ayes and 0 noes. Another victory for AB 1192!

We will never know what inspired Senator Torlakson to pull the bill from Suspense. All of us like to believe that it was our action that motivated the movement.

In September 2007, AB 1192 finished its Senate readings and moved back to the Assembly. While in the Senate, there were some amendment recommendations. When amendments are made out of the house of origin, they must be reviewed and concurred by the house where the bill began. The Senate amendments were concurred by the Assembly with a unanimous vote (Ayes 76, Noes 0), and AB 1192 moved to enrollment and to the Governor on September 18, 2007.

Here is our note to the coalition members informing them of our progress:

We are *almost there*! AB 1192 sponsored by The REACH Project has advanced through both the Senate and the Assembly! It passed with unanimous votes! Thank you to all who participated this week in the last-minute advocacy efforts and made contacts in Sacramento. This really does make a difference!

AB 1192 is now waiting for Arnold's signature. Please e-mail Governor Schwarzenegger to support AB 1192. Go to http://gov.ca.gov/interact. Select "Email." Select "Have Comment," enter your name and e-mail address, then select "Disability Issues/Concerns," and then select "Submit." You will be prompted to the next page where you should select your position as "Pro," and then you can enter your text. I've attached a sample letter for your reference. Feel free to use this version or edit as you feel fit.

Forward this e-mail along with our website http://www.facebook.com/group .php?gid=159302605400 to your colleagues, friends, and family and ask them to do the same!

Thank you!

In Advocacy, Maureen, Becky, Jessica, and Paige

REACH

Reaching out to protect the developmentally disabled through streamlined, accessible abuse reporting.

October 2007: "I Said, 'Does Anyone Have a Pen? The Governor Needs a Pen!'"

It is ironic to think that during this entire journey we battled and felt pressured by the deadlines and time swiftly going by. Now we waited and stared at the dreaded clock.

Couldn't time go any faster?

We at The REACH Project used the time since enrollment to make contact with the Governor in various ways and, once again, engaged our coalition. We learned that contacting the Governor is quite simple through the Internet. The Governor had until midnight on October 14 to act on AB 1192. Tick. Tick. Tick.

As of October 9, 2007, AB 1192 was *one* of 596 remaining bills on his desk! Nerve-racking! To date he had signed 354 and vetoed 15 bills. We waited patiently and suspected that our bill would be considered in the final hour. Finally, we heard.

BILL NUMBER: AB 1192
VETOED DATE: 10/14/2007

To the Members of the California State Assembly:

I am returning Assembly Bill 1192 without my signature.

Ensuring the health and safety of California's vulnerable populations is one of my top priorities. To that end, my Administration has increased support for licensing programs, strengthened oversight and sponsored legislation to ensure that potentially dangerous caregivers would be unable to move from one facility to another and continue to have access to children, elderly or disabled individuals in facilities licensed by the State.

While well intended, I am concerned this bill will not provide effective health and safety protections for persons with developmental disabilities and will increase state costs by millions of dollars during a time of budget challenges. This bill does not require that all incidents of substantiated abuse actually be reported to the proposed registry. Second, the bill does not require service providers to actually use the registry. Current law already requires staff of Regional Centers and persons working at community care facilities to report suspected abuse to Adult Protective Services, who in turn is required to investigate these allegations.

Given the flaws in the bill and the fact that developing the proposed registry would require significant financial resources at a time of ongoing budget challenges, I cannot support it. I am directing the Health and Human Services Agency to convene interested stakeholders to identify potential areas where the State can enhance protections for persons with developmental disabilities and improve ongoing efforts to enhance the sharing of information about service providers.

For these reasons, I am unable to support this bill.

Sincerely,

Arnold Schwarzenegger

One can only imagine our disappointment when we learned that our bill was vetoed. We were obviously very upset and surprised! It did not seem feasible that a bill could make it through to the Governor for signature with no known opposition and be vetoed in the final hour!

As we recovered from the initial shock and disappointment, we began to refocus on the work we were able to accomplish thus far. It was extremely heartening to think of the determination and passion that so many people had put into this effort. The REACH team planned a meeting with an advisor to review the message the Governor had provided with his veto and clarify the work ahead. In the meantime, we gained strength from the supportive feedback from our coalition:

> Wow, what a disappointment. I am very sad to hear this news. I wrote an email to the Governor and urged others to do so too. But, I am so encouraged that it made it so very far. Thank you is not strong enough to express my respect for the work you all did to make this happen. Because of your work on this issue, many, many more people are aware of the horrible abuse that often continues for *people with intellectual disabilities*. This is not the end! Let me know if I can support your continued efforts in any way. Take care.

> It doesn't need to end here and it shouldn't. Stay strong and move it forward in the upcoming year! You have all our support!

> Way to go! The job you all did was amazing. I think it was an issue of timing.

Someone once told me that every adversity or failure carries with it the seed of an equal or superior benefit. As I visualized this concept, a new goal began to take shape.

In early November, The REACH Project group facilitated a presentation for the students enrolled in the advocacy course at the University of San Diego. This session was cathartic in a way. As we spoke about our progress, everything felt more composed, and all that had happened had meaning and significance in our legislative journey. Even the veto message seemed easier to read, digest, and accept.

Our team, with the help of new recruits, continued to work on the project, and our work continues to this day. We have met with representatives of seven state agencies in an effort to resolve the issues raised by the Governor, and we continue to organize and inspire our coalition to action.

We learned the legislative process can be long, tedious, complex, and frustrating. Indeed, it is much more difficult to pass a bill than it is to kill one. There are numerous times and places during the legislative process at which a bill can die. Only a very few survive to become law.

We also learned that everyday citizens can make real legislative change. It just doesn't always happen right away.

Chapter Questions

1. Did the REACH story inspire or discourage you?

2. Does lobbying seem easier or more difficult after reading Maureen's story?

3. Would you have the perseverance to work on an advocacy campaign that was meaningful to you or your organization?

4. Do you think there was anything the group could have done differently that would have resulted in the Governor signing the bill?

Endnote

i   Grace, Nancy. (2007, August 21). Caregivers caught on video abusing handicapped patients [Television series episode]. In *Nancy Grace*. New York: CNN.

10

The 10 Steps Strike Again! Breaking the Tire Cycle

A Campaign With International Impact

Ben McCue

U sed automobile tires are a common sight along the U.S.-Mexico border. Referred to as waste tires, they blanket sensitive ecosystems, clog sewage collection systems, exacerbate winter floods, and can serve as vectors for mosquito-borne diseases such as encephalitis and West Nile virus. In the fall of 2008, I and four classmates developed a project for a graduate student class at the University of San Diego called Advocacy Skills and Strategies that was the catalyst to successfully passing state legislation to address the border tire issue.[1] The Breaking the Tire Cycle project is a great case study for how to use the 10 steps to develop and implement an advocacy campaign.

1. Identify an Issue

At the beginning of the semester, our class came up with several potential issues to develop into an advocacy campaign. We weighed each of these against the criteria that our proposed legislation be fiscally neutral, garner broad support from a variety of stakeholders, and address an easily identifiable problem. In sum, we wanted to take an idea to Sacramento that would be politically viable, and that legislators and ultimately the Governor

---

[1]Special thanks to my classmates Adina Veen, Benny Cartwright, Jennifer Martin, and Maureen Guarcello.

would be hard-pressed to reject. Several of our ideas were deemed too difficult to transform into legislation for one reason or another: banning protestors at military funerals—possibly unconstitutional; blocking development projects through state parks—too broad and too contentious; and creating smoke-free apartments—too local. The advocacy idea that we finally took up had a perfect storm of the right elements, and turned out ripe for the political picking.

As a program manager for WiLDCOAST, a binational environmental nonprofit located on the San Diego–Tijuana border and working to conserve coastal ecosystems and wildlife, I was intimately familiar with the challenge of waste tires in the region. I lobbied the class to take on the issue by giving an impromptu slide show presentation. I showed my classmates how the flow of used tires into California from Mexico creates a huge burden on local communities. A legislative "fix," I told the class, had the potential to "break the tire cycle," and reduce the associated economic, public health, and environmental impacts that these tires cause.

My classmates were skeptical but, to give them credit, decided to take on the issue. The more information we uncovered, the more we realized that the issue was perfect for legislative advocacy.

Data show that many of these tires, like much of the solid waste in the Baja California border region, originate in California. Every year, as a way to divert used tires from the state's congested landfills, California exports millions of them across the border to Mexico. In border cities like Tijuana and Mexicali, there is a market for these tires, as they are cheaper than new tires. Most are bought and driven on for six months to a year before they are disposed of. The problem is that Baja California does not have the capacity or infrastructure to deal with the scale of waste tires produced every year, and there isn't a market for used tire products in the state. Some discarded tires are used as an informal building material for hillside stabilization, steps, and even house foundations. Many are simply dumped. While disposing tires into canyons and rivers is illegal in Mexico, enforcement is difficult, and fines are rarely levied. When it rains, thousands of discarded tires are washed further downstream. The creeks and canyons of many Baja California border cities are littered with discarded tires. Many of these make their way back across the border into California with storm water flows (the water flows north). In California they end up in sensitive ecological areas and public recreational parks. Since 2008 WiLDCOAST-coordinated volunteer cleanups have removed over 5,000 tires from the Tijuana River Valley in San Diego. Ironically, the tires that are recovered in California end up in the state's landfills after all.

For every tire that is sold in California, a tire recycling fee is charged by tire retailers and collected in a Tire Fund managed by the California Integrated Waste Management Board (CIWMB). According to a scalding report by the Legislative Analyst's Office (LAO), the CIWMB was underutilizing project funding to divert tires from landfills, and the Tire Fund had a balance of nearly $42 million—an amazing resource given the fact that

California as a state was scrambling to fill a huge budget gap. CIWMB representatives responded that despite these funds they lacked the authority to address the problem at its source in Mexico since their jurisdiction was limited to California's side of the border.

The legislative solution we proposed would authorize the CIWMB to spend Tire Fund monies in Mexico to break the tire cycle. For each tire diverted from the state's landfills through export to Baja California, California would dedicate the disposal fee collected on that tire to assisting Baja California develop a market and infrastructure to support waste tire recycling. This legislation would save California taxpayer dollars spent on tire cleanup and disposal and could draw on existing monies to solve a chronic problem in a cost-effective manner. The proposed legislation would additionally build on previous legislation by Senator Denise Ducheny. The Ducheny legislation, Senate Bill 772, mandated the CIWMB to direct funds to study and develop recommendations relating to the flow of used tires from Mexico into California.

To be politically viable we knew that our bill would have to be structured as a fee rather than a tax. Legislation that is posed as a tax requires a two-thirds majority to pass out of each house while fee legislation can pass with a simple majority. With a critically divided legislature in Sacramento it would be politically impossible to get a two-thirds vote to fall in our favor. The only challenge was that as a fee, the bill would need to successfully create a nexus, or connection, between the Tire Fund monies spent in Baja California and the tire funds collected in California. Essentially we would need to convince the legislators and lawyers that the $1 fee collected on each used tire in California would be spent on the proper disposal of that same tire in Baja California.

2. Research the Issue

Solid research was the foundation of our advocacy campaign. An important part of the process involved conducting formal and informal interviews, both over the phone and in person, with experts on cross-border relations, budget and procedures of the CIWMB, regional environmental concerns, and regional public health concerns. Through these interviews we discovered that some agency officials had been frustrated for years by the insanity of the tire cycle. These individuals had extensive information on the number of tires exported to Mexico from California, the location of tire piles in Mexico, how many tires wash back into California with each rain, and the costs incurred by their agencies to dig them up and eventually dispose of them. All of this information would make a great argument for the legislation we wanted to propose. Yet, these agency officials were actively discouraged from using their information to advocate solutions. Those who dared to take an advocacy position in the past were usually reprimanded or fired.

A key strategy for our advocacy team was to understand this conflict. As the constituent advocates it was our role to collect the information from the agency officials, package it into a coherent argument, and present it to our elected officials.

Our research also involved a careful examination of official CIWMB documents including its Five-Year Plan, a document that was prescribed by Senate Bill 772. The Five-Year Plan and additional documents gave us insight to the CIWMB plans for the future and how progress pointed toward our proposed piece of legislation. These documents also provided statistics and data for our white paper. We identified other relevant documents as well including reports from other government agencies, and academic studies. We also researched and compiled past and recent media reports discussing the tire cycle situation and other cross-border issues as a measurement of the public's awareness of the issue.

We packaged our research into the enclosed white paper (see Figure 10.1). This served as the backbone of our advocacy campaign. Having a well-researched and all-encompassing white paper prepared us to create the rest of the coalition materials. These materials include a fact sheet, a pictorial explanation of the tire cycle, and coalition educational materials.

3. Create a Fact Sheet

In order to create a quick reference document to share with elected officials and potential coalition members, we took some of the most compelling and important pieces of the white paper and constructed a two-sided, full-color fact sheet (see Figure 10.2). Consisting of referenced facts and compelling pictures, this made for a powerful advocacy tool. We included marketing elements to make a stronger case and to grab and hold the reader's attention to our cause. This was one of the most useful tools during our meetings with legislators and community members.

4. "Brand" the Issue

Through our research we knew that the waste tire issue along the border was cyclical. In order to increase the issue's appeal we coined our advocacy campaign "Breaking the Tire Cycle: Pollution Has No Borders" and created an accompanying logo. We also created a flowchart with photos to show how a California tire is exported to Baja California, used for a short period of time, discarded, and carried back across the border (see Figure 10.3). This rendition brought our concerns to life, helping the legislators and prospective coalition members better understand our concerns and how the tire cycle works. The tool also proved very useful during our meetings with elected officials.

Figure 10.1

Contact the Break the Tire Cycle Coalition:
925 Seacoast Drive · Imperial Beach, California 91932
p: 619.929.1363 · f: 619.423.8488 · breakthetirecycle@gmail.com

Breaking the Tire Cycle
White Paper

(Continued)

Figure 10.1 (Continued)

EXECUTIVE SUMMARY

The California Integrated Waste Management Board (CIWMB) exports more than two million waste tires in an effort to divert them from California landfills. In wet-weather months, storm water carries thousands of waste tires every year back across the border from Tijuana into California. San Diego County and the border region have experienced record-breaking rainfall further aggravating an ongoing tire catastrophe that significantly impacts:

- **Economy** – California taxpayers are double and triple paying for tire disposal and the damage that they cause, including mini-dams, large debris that blocks waterways, adding to flood damages.
- **Public Health** – Discarded tires are breeding grounds for mosquitoes, viruses and rodents.
- **Environment** – Thousands of tires lie where storm waters deposit them, including Border Field State Park. The park is located within the Tijuana River National Estuarine Research Reserve, a sensitive habitat for hundreds of bird and wildlife species.

State, local, and federal agencies spend public funds, between $5 and $13, to excavate each tire, which is ultimately deposited in a California landfill. The most efficient and cost-effective way to break this waste tire cycle is to work directly with Baja California agencies investing in and developing cooperative recycling and reuse projects, mirroring the effective waste tire programs in California.

California Integrated Waste Management Board (CIWMB) program examples include:

- Tire Recycling, Cleanup, and Enforcement Grants
- Rubberized Asphalt Concrete Grant Programs
- Tire-Derived Product (TDP) Grants

Despite a surplus of means available in the established fund for these projects, the CIWMB does not currently have the authority to spend money across the border.

The California legislature can help break this tire cycle by amending the Public Resource Code to give the CIWMB the authority it needs to fund tire recycling and reuse projects in Baja California[1]. As these funds are available in surplus, this legislation has a neutral fiscal impact.

I. BACKGROUND

a) California waste tire production, disposal, and recycling

It is estimated that California produces more than **40 million waste tires every year,** the equivalent of 1.1 per resident[2]. In order to reduce the landfill disposal of tires, the

---

[1]Section 42885.5 of the California Public Resources Code

[2]California Integrated Waste Management Board. May 20, 2008 Board Meeting. Agenda Item 7.

Legislature established a statewide recycling program to be administered by the California Integrated Waste Management Board (CIWMB)[3]. A fee of $1.75 per tire is assessed on the sale of new tires, and collected revenue is deposited quarterly into the California Tire Recycling Management Fund (CTRMF). The CIWMB administers the program to encourage the diversion of waste tires from the state's landfills through a number of activities, including conducting/funding research, assessing market demand for waste tire products, and providing grants, and technical assistance to business, state, and local users of waste-tire products. In 2006, CIWMB staff estimated 74% of the waste tires generated were diverted from disposal or stockpiles. However, about 11 million tires are ultimately taken to landfills in California each year.

b) Waste tire export to Mexico

As one way of diverting tires from California landfills, the CIWMB exports more than two million waste tires annually[4]. Many of these waste tires are used in shantytowns, or *colonias*, in Mexican border cities as inexpensive building materials and for attempted erosion control.

c) Return of waste tires to California

Every winter, sewage and trash-laden storm water dislodges and carries thousands of waste tires from Tijuana to California through the Tijuana River channel and open culverts in the border fence. This flow of waste tires represents economic, environmental, and public health challenges to California's border communities.

By obstructing border collection infrastructure, waste tires hinder the capture and treatment of "renegade" wastewater flows from Tijuana, resulting in an increased public health threat for outdoor recreation at downstream parks and beaches. These tires degrade the recreational value of public multi-use trails in the Tijuana River Valley, Estuary, and Border Field State park. Tires create ideal breeding grounds for mosquitoes, rodents, and other vectors of disease, which lead to a potential increase in the incidence of malaria, dengue fever, and encephalitis diseases such as West Nile Virus.

Waste tires from Tijuana blanket the sensitive ecosystems of the Tijuana River Valley, Estuary, and Border Field State Park. They make the removal of sediment from the Tijuana Estuary difficult, as each tire must be excavated by hand.[5] Approximately 80,000 pounds of tires are hand-plucked each year from the river, sediment basins, and the sensitive habitats of the Tijuana River Valley and the Tijuana River National Estuarine

---

[3] The California Tire Recycling Act of 1989 (AB 1843)

[4] California Integrated Waste Management Board. 2007. FIVE-YEAR PLAN FOR THE WASTE TIRE RECYCLING MANAGEMENT PROGRAM. (4th Edition Covering Fiscal Years 2007/08–2011/12) Report

[5] Personal communication with Clay Phillips, Tijuana River National Research Reserve Manager. 11/25/08

(Continued)

Figure 10.1 (Continued)

Research Reserve. Many thousands more are unable to be removed due to limited time and resources. Some of the tires end up being stored creating stockpiles that have the potential to cause great environmental damage in both countries[6]. Tire piles can catch fire and burn for months, emitting noxious fumes and generating liquid wastes that contaminate soil, groundwater, and surface water[7]. Over the next five years Californians will purchase almost 200 million tires increasing the threat that waste tires bring if they are not properly managed.

Categorized as "hazardous waste," tires have high disposal costs and create an economic burden for local government departments and state agencies.

II. BREAKING THE TIRE CYCLE

State agencies acknowledge that funding projects to manage, recycle and reuse waste tires in Baja California is the most efficient solution to keep them from returning to California wetlands and landfills. The California Biodiversity Council's Border Work Group recommended for state waste tire and conservation grant funding to be spent in Mexico to train engineers on how to use waste tires in civil engineering projects including retaining walls, tire-derived aggregate and rubberized asphalt concrete to reduce the number of tires flowing into California.

In recent years, the Legislature has taken the lead by giving statutory direction on the use of the Tire Fund in an effort to address the flow of waste tires from Mexico[8]. In 2005, SB 772 was enacted to require the CIWMB to include in the Five-Year Plan specified border region activities conducted in coordination with the California Environmental Protection Agency. These activities include training programs, environmental education, development of waste tire abatement plan, and a study tracking tire flow across the border.

However, the greatest obstacle to reducing the flow of tires across the border is that the CIWMB does not have the authority to fund projects in Baja California through the established grant program.

III. STATE TIRE FUND SURPLUS

The CIWMB's Tire Fund has carried a persistently large reserve balance of more than $20 million for several years. As of May 20, 2008 this balance was $42 million and was projected to increase to approximately $58 million by Fiscal Year (FY) 2009/10 (this large jump reflects the anticipated repayment of the $17.1 million that was borrowed from the Tire Fund to meet General Fund obligations in FY 2003/04, which is currently set for FY 2008/09).

---

[6]California Biodiversity Council. Biodiversity Along the Border Committee. Final Report. 2007.

[7]EPA 2012 State of the Border Region Indicators Report. (2005)

[8]SB 772 (Ducheny). 2005. An act to amend Section 42885.5 of the Public Resources Code, relating to the environment.

The Tire Fund reserve balance presents the opportunity for the state to increase the waste tire diversion rate from California landfills while reducing the impact of waste tires that flow from Baja California into the Tijuana River Valley and Estuary.

Quotes:

"Preventing tires . . . from entering the Tijuana River and Estuary is a less expensive fix than funding on-going litter removal and recycling programs. California state agencies and local government departments assigned to eradicate tire piles . . . and/or fund projects to do so do not have the authority or the power to spend public funds in Mexico. Yet it is acknowledged that addressing the problem upstream is less expensive than cleaning up the aftermath downstream."

—California Biodiversity Council. Biodiversity Along the Border Committee. Final Report. 2007.

"The amount and proportion of waste tires that are not diverted from landfills is still large . . . the large fund balance presents the board with the opportunity to increase the waste tire diversion rate."

—Legislative Analyst's Office. 2007 report on the California Integrated Waste Management Board.

References

California Biodiversity Council. (2006). *Biodiversity along the border*. San Diego, CA: Author.

California Integrated Waste Management Board. (2007). *Five-year plan for the Waste Tire Recycling Management Program*. Sacramento, CA: Author.

California Integrated Waste Management Board. (2008). *Agenda of May 20, 2008 Board Meeting*. Accessed on November 20, 2008 from http://www.ciwmb.ca.gov.

California Legislative Analyst's Office. (2008). *Analysis of the 2007-2008 budget bill: resources, California Integrated Waste Management Board*. Sacramento, CA: Author.

California Public Resources Code § 42885.5 (2001).

California Senate Bill 772 (2005).

California Tire Recycling Act of 1989, AB 1843 (1989).

Senate Committee on Environmental Quality. (2005). *Analysis of Senate Bill 772*. Accessed on November 20, 2008 from http://info.ca.gov.

State Board of Equalization. (2007). *California Tire Fee* (SBE Publication 91). Sacramento, CA: Author.

United States Environmental Protection Agency, Office of Solid Waste. (2008). *Border scrap tire project action plans*. Washington, DC: Author.

Figure 10.2

SB 167

SB 167 will reduce the public health, environmental, and economic impacts of waste tires along the California-Tijuana border

THE CALIFORNIA - TIJUANA TIRE CYCLE

Border Field State Park, San Diego County on Thanksgiving Day, 2008. Pollution shown in picture is the result of less than one inch of rain which fell in the region the previous day.

The California Legislature can help break this tire cycle by **passing SB 167** (Ducheny) to give the CIWMB the authority to fund waste tire recycling and reuse projects in Baja California. As these funds are available in surplus, this legislation has a *neutral fiscal* impact.

The California Integrated Waste Management Board (CIWMB) exports more than two million waste tires annually in an effort to keep them out of California landfills. In Mexican border cities, waste tires are used in shantytowns, or colonias, as inexpensive building materials and for attempted erosion control. During our annual wet-weather months, storm water carries thousands of waste tires back across the border from Tijuana into California. This creates significant environmental, public health, and economic impacts. State, local, and federal agencies spend public funds to excavate the tires, which are ultimately disposed in California landfills. The most efficient and cost-effective way to deal with this waste tire issue is to work directly with Baja California agencies to support the development and markets for waste tires, and to invest in and develop cooperative reuse projects. Despite a surplus of means available in the established fund for these projects, the CIWMB does not currently have the authority to spend money across the border.

80,000 pounds

Approximately 4,000 tires (80,000 pounds) are hand-plucked each year from the river, sediment basins, and the sensitive habitats of the Tijuana River Valley and the Tijuana River National Estuarine Research Reserve. Many thousands more are unable to be removed due to limited time and resources.

California Biodiversity Council. Biodiversity Along the Border Committee. Final Report. 2007.

Contact the Break the Tire Cycle Coalition at:
925 Seacoast Drive • Imperial Beach, California 91932 • p: 619.423.8665, ext. 208 • f: 619.423.8488
breakthetirecycle@gmail.com

STATE TIRE FUND SURPLUS

Los Laureles, Tijuana - one mile upstream from the US/Mexico border

"The amount and proportion of waste tires that are not diverted from landfills is still large…the large fund balance presents the board with the opportunity to increase the waste tire diversion rate."

-Legislative Analyst's Office. 2007 report on the California Integrated Waste Management Board.

The CIWMB's Tire Fund has carried a persistently large reserve balance of more than $20 million for several years. As of May 20, 2008 this balance was $42 million and was projected to increase to approximately $58 million by Fiscal Year 2009/10.

In recent years, the Legislature has taken the lead by giving statutory direction on the use of the Tire Fund in an effort to address the flow of waste tires from Mexico. In 2005, SB 772 was enacted to require the CIWMB to include in the Five-Year Plan specified border region activities conducted in coordination with the California Environmental Protection Agency. These activities include training programs, environmental education, development of waste tire abatement plan, and a study tracking tire flow across the border.

The greatest obstacle to reducing the flow of tires across the border is that the CIWMB does not have the authority to fund projects in Baja California through the established grant program.

California Integrated Waste Management Board. May 20, 2008 Board Meeting.

SPEAKING OUT TO BREAK THE TIRE CYCLE

"Preventing tires… from entering the Tijuana River and Estuary is a less expensive fix than funding on-going litter removal and recycling programs. California state agencies and local government departments assigned to eradicate tire piles… and/or fund projects to do so do not have the authority or the power to spend public funds in Mexico. Yet it is acknowledged that addressing the problem upstream is less expensive than cleaning up the aftermath downstream."

-California Biodiversity Council. Biodiversity Along the Border Committee. Final Report 2007.

Take Action: What you can do

Contact your California State Senator and Assemblymember and tell them that they can help break this tire cycle by **VOTING YES ON SB 167** to give the CIWMB the authority to support waste tire recycling and reuse projects in Baja California.

Waste tires from Tijuana blanket the sensitive ecosystems of the Tijuana River Valley, Estuary, and Border Field State Park. They make the restoration of the Tijuana Estuary difficult, as each tire must be excavated by hand.

Clay Phillips, Tijuana River National Research Reserve Manager. 11/25/08

SB 167 Bill Supporters:

United States Environmental Protection Agency (USEPA)
American Federation of State, County & Municipal Employees
AFL-CIO
Rubber Manufacturer Association
City of Imperial Beach
Eighth District of San Diego (Benjamin Hueso, Council President)
Heal the Bay
Natural Resources Defense Council
Planning and Conservation League
San Diego Coastkeeper
Southwest Wetlands Interpretive Association
Surfrider San Diego
Tijuana River Valley Equestrian Association
Tijuana River Citizens' Council

Public recreational trail, Tijuana River Valley
County Regional Park - January 9, 2009

SB 167 Bill Sponsors:

WiLDCOAST/COSTASALVAjE and Breaking the Tire Cycle Coalition

Photos courtesy of Ben McCue - WiLDCOAST/COSTASALVjE

Figure 10.3

THE CALIFORNIA - TIJUANA TIRE CYCLE

6.

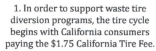

1.

1. In order to support waste tire diversion programs, the tire cycle begins with California consumers paying the $1.75 California Tire Fee.

2. More than two million waste tires are exported from California annually.

3. Waste tires are used as inexpensive building materials and for attempted erosion control in Mexican border cities.

4. Storm water carries thousands of waste tires back across the border from Tijuana to California posing environmental, health and economic threats.

5. More than 80,000 pounds of waste tires are removed, by hand, from the sensitive habitats of the Tijuana Estuary annually.

6. Costing the state between $5 and $13 per tire removed, the waste tires ultimately end up in California landfills.

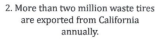

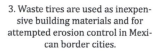

2.

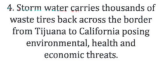

5.

California
Mexico

California
Mexico

4.

3.

BREAKING THE TIRE CYCLE
pollution has no borders

Reducing the public health, environmental, and economic impacts of waste tires along the California-Tijuana border

We also developed letterhead, an e-mail address, and labels for campaign material folders, and branded our existing fact sheet and white paper with this new brand identity.

_____ 5. Map Out Possible Supporters and Detractors

Figure 10.4 shows the positional map we developed before we engaged in research on supporters and detractors. The map became a living document since we didn't know who would be opposed to the issue.

As we researched organizations and other stakeholders that would support and oppose our efforts, we started with the groups closest to the issue. These included municipal and county governments in San Diego that were paying to dig up and dispose of tires in the Tijuana River Valley; environmental organizations like WiLDCOAST that organized volunteer cleanups to remove discarded tires; state agencies; and the tire manufacturer and sales associations that are required to pay into the state's Tire Fund.

It was pretty easy to place the municipal and county agencies, along with the environmental groups in the supporter category since they would directly benefit from the legislation. Categorizing the other stakeholders was more difficult.

No government agency likes being told what to do by legislators. We assumed the CIWMB would not be any different. We felt that CIWMB officials would dislike this legislation because it would essentially mandate that they grant their funds in a certain way. It was a sensitive issue that we wanted to handle in a delicate manner. Opposition from the CIWMB would pose a significant obstacle to our efforts.

We thought that the Governor's office might oppose our legislation because of the state's severe financial shortfall. We were not necessarily concerned about the Governor being opposed to the spirit of the legislation, but by drawing attention to this large pot of unused money, the Governor could find more pressing alternative uses for the funds. Tire Fund monies had been loaned to the General Fund in the past, and the current economic situation of the state was so dreary that another fund raid was possible.

Tire sales associations would most likely oppose our efforts because of their dislike of the CIWMB's tire program. They were actively lobbying to reduce or cut the program entirely. If our legislation allowed the CIWMB to use Tire Fund monies in Baja California to successfully address a real need, their argument for dissolvement of the fund would be weakened.

The biggest surprise for us was that the Rubber Manufacturers' Association, an industry trade group, joined as a strong supporter of the legislation. In our research we found that this association had supported previous legislation, as well as work by the Environmental Protection Agency, to deal with the tire cycle.

BREAKING THE TIRE CYCLE: POLLUTION HAS NO BORDERS

POSITIONAL MAP

OPPOSITION	NEUTRAL	PROPONENTS

CA INTEGRATED WASTE MANAGEMENT BOARD

GOVERNOR'S OFFICE

DEPARTMENT OF HOMELAND SECURITY

TIRE INDUSTRY

IMPERIAL BEACH SCHOOLS

HOSPITAL SYSTEMS

MINUTEMEN

CHICANO GROUPS

TIJUANA RIVER VALLEY EQUESTRIAN ASSOCIATION

TIJUANA RIVER CITIZENS' COUNCIL

AUDUBON SOCIETY

HUMANE SOCIETY

SIERRA CLUB

FAMILY HEALTH CENTERS OF SAN DIEGO

SAN DIEGO STATE UNIVERSITY

SURFRIDER FOUNDATION

COASTKEEPERS

NATIONAL BORDER PATROL COUNCIL: LOCAL 1613

SCRIPPS INSTITUTION OF OCEANOGRAPHY

LOCAL HEALTH CLINICS

CITY OF SAN DIEGO

CITY OF CHULA VISTA

CITY OF IMPERIAL BEACH

CITY OF CORONADO

COUNTY OF SAN DIEGO

I LOVE A CLEAN SAN DIEGO

WILDCOAST

UNITED STATES NAVY

_____ **6. Form a Coalition**

Our next step was to contact the potential supporters of our legislative idea to enlist as coalition members. As our group began researching organizations and other stakeholders that might sign on to our coalition, the obvious choices were environmental organizations. We brainstormed a list of the environmental organizations that we thought would support our idea: WiLDCOAST, the Surfrider Foundation, San Diego Coastkeeper, the Sierra Club, and I Love a Clean San Diego.

We also wanted to expand our coalition to some unusual suspects, including city officials, educational institutions, and labor unions. Following is a list of possible coalition members that came from "outside the box": Scripps Institution of Oceanography; Imperial Beach Schools; Tijuana River Citizens' Council; National Border Patrol Council: Local 1613; Tijuana River Valley Equestrian Association; City of San Diego; City of Chula Vista; City of Imperial Beach; City of Coronado; County of San Diego; San Diego State University; California Environmental Protection Agency; and the California Integrated Waste Management Board.

As we continued to research our issue and narrow down the framework of our legislative idea, we found it was difficult to get coalition members to sign on for support without a bill number. Nevertheless, we came up with language that could be used before and after our idea became a bill.

We created and circulated a support letter to show legislators the diverse support we had garnered through our "Breaking the Tire Cycle" coalition (see Figure 10.5).

Our eventual coalition included quite a diverse and powerful group of organizations and agencies, including the U.S. Environmental Protection Agency; the American Federation of State, County and Municipal Employees; the American Federation of Labor–Congress of Industrial Organizations; the Rubber Manufacturers' Association; the City of Imperial Beach; the Eighth District of San Diego (Benjamin Hueso, Council President); Heal the Bay; the Natural Resources Defense Council; the Planning and Conservation League; San Diego Coastkeeper; the Southwest Wetlands Interpretive Association; the Surfrider Foundation, San Diego Chapter; the Tijuana River Valley Equestrian Association; and the Tijuana River Citizens' Council.

It was also critical to enlist influential allies in our efforts to push through the legislation. Rather than playing a public role as official coalition members, these individuals supported our efforts behind the scenes. One critical ally was an ex-elected official who, as a member of the CIWMB, could not play a public role in our advocacy efforts. Through a family contact I was able to communicate with him the importance of our legislative efforts and to request that he assist us. He agreed and was able to give us a better understanding of the opposition that the CIWMB staff had to our bill. He was also able to apply pressure from within the Sacramento machine by communicating to the Governor's office that, as a member of the CIWMB, he supported the bill.

Figure 10.5

 Border Environment Cooperation Commission

Comisión de Cooperación Ecológica Fronteriza

C10560/ADM2009
April 17, 2009

Serge Dedina, Ph.D.
WiLDCOAST Executive Director
925 Seacoast Dr.
Imperial Beach, CA 91932, USA

Dear Doctor Dedina:

The Border Environment Cooperation Commission (BECC) would potentially be able to assist the California Integrated Waste Management Board through the certification of viable bi-national projects to deal with the appropriate disposal and management of waste tires along the California-Mexico border. The BECC is an international organization created pursuant to the Agreement between the government of the United States of America and the United Mexican States concerning the Establishment of a Border Environment Cooperation Commission and a North American Development Bank, signed November 16 and 18, 1993, and amended through Protocol of Amendment signed November 25 and 26, 2004.

The purpose of the BECC is to help preserve, protect and enhance the environment of the border region in order to advance the well being of the people of the United States and Mexico. The border region is defined as the area in the United States that is within 100 kilometers of the international boundary between the United States and Mexico, and the area in Mexico that is within 300 kilometers of the international boundary between the United States and Mexico.

Over the last 15 years BECC has acquired specific insight of the environmental and human health problems of the Border Region. With the cooperation of United States and Mexican Federal agencies and in partnership with state and local authorities, BECC has been able to confront many of the environmental issues affecting the Border Region. BECC is permitted to provide technical assistance for the development of environmental infrastructure projects along the border region to local and state agencies and governments, as well as to authorize non-governmental entities. By developing water, wastewater, solid waste, air quality and alternative energy infrastructure projects, among others, BECC has been able to contribute to solving environmental problems with Trans-boundary effects, and as a result improve the border region environment. As a requirement of the development of these projects BECC ensures that all regulatory requirements and standards, as established by each agency, are fulfilled.

In order to carry out its purpose, BECC is authorized to administer funding from both nations, and currently manages several bi-national programs and grants funded by the United States Environmental Protection Agency (USEPA). As such, BECC is interested in associating with other entities, including the State of California, on projects to improve the environment of the US-Mexico border.

The BECC appreciates your commitment to improve the welfare of the border region through the conservation, protection and improvement of the environment in a sustainable manner.

Sincerely,

Daniel Chacón Anaya
General Manager

Cc.   Maria Elena Giner, General Deputy Manager, BECC
Cc.   File

Blvd. Tomás Fernández 8069   Fracc. Los Parques   Cd. Juárez, Chih. C.P. 32470   •   P.O. Box 221648   El Paso, TX 79913-4648
www.cocef.org

7. Develop Educational Materials

We used our fact sheet, along with photo documentation of tires along the border, to develop educational materials. The photos we used in the advocacy campaign were powerful. We made sure that they demonstrated the scope of the problem, along with the human and cross-border elements. Certain photos were blown up and printed on mat board to use during committee hearings. I am still convinced that during my testimony, the Senate Environmental Quality Committee paid more attention to the photos than to me.

Photo 10.1.   Waste tires from Tijuana blanketing Border Field State Park in San Diego County after less than 1″ of rain on Thanksgiving Day, 2009.

Photo 10.2.   Thousands of residents in Tijuana live without basic infrastructure. Waste tires are often used as building materials to create stairs, retaining walls, and house foundations. March 2009.

Photo 10.3.   A public hiking trail in San Diego County completely blocked by tires and debris from Tijuana. January 2009.

Photo 10.4.   A house in Los Laureles Canyon, Tijuana. Tires in this canyon are dislodged by heavy winter rains and carried downstream to Border Field State Park in San Diego County. March 2009.

Photo 10.5.   Two young volunteers help with a WiLDCOAST-sponsored clean-up in San Diego's Tijuana River valley.

8. Launch a Media Campaign

The media were a key tool in our advocacy campaign. We knew that by framing and pitching the story correctly, television and print articles would amplify our message, and the resulting exposure would support our advocacy efforts in Sacramento. We framed the issue and created a hook that combined the intrigue of the U.S.-Mexico border, nightmarish visuals of environmental pollution, and the irresistible spice of government mismanagement of public funds.

When we contacted the media we discovered that *The San Diego Union-Tribune*'s environmental reporter, Mike Lee, had researched the issue in the past and was interested in covering it. The timing was perfect. One week to the day before we left for Sacramento, Mike Lee's article "Tire Trouble Knows No Borders" ran in the December 29 edition of the *Union-Tribune*. The story was expertly researched and written and had been picked up by media across California, including *Rough & Tumble*, a favorite of Sacramento legislators. We included copies of the article in the advocacy packets we created for our legislative meetings (see Figure 10.6).

Figure 10.6

SignOnSanDiego.com
THE SAN DIEGO UNION-TRIBUNE

PRINT THIS

🖨 Click to Print

SAVE THIS | EMAIL THIS | Close

Watchdog report: Tire trouble knows no borders

Allegedly recycled material ends up piling up as waste

By Mike Lee

2:00 a.m. December 29, 2008

Ben McCue of Wildcoast inspected debris that flowed from Tijuana to San Diego after a storm. (John Gibbins / Union-Tribune) -

REUSE OPTIONS

Old tires can be turned into:

- Rubberized asphalt

- Fuel for cement kilns

- Erosion-control products

- Athletic tracks and fields

- Playground covers

- Doormats

- Fuel for power production

- Retread tires

REDUCING WASTE TIRES

- Maintain proper air pressure in tires

- Buy tires that promise higher mileage

- Purchase retread tires

- Buy other products made from the rubber of old tires

TIRE DISPOSAL: BY THE NUMBERS

44 million: Waste tires generated annually in California

33 million: Tires recycled or reused per year

300,000: Tires sent to local landfills each year

0: Tire-recycling facilities in San Diego County

(Continued)

Figure 10.6 (Continued)

SOURCES: *California Integrated Waste Management Board; San Diego County*

When rains pound Tijuana, thousands of tires fill the torrents of sewage and trash that stream north across the international border.

Most of the tires are from California, where residents pay more than $60 million a year for safe disposal and recycling. Still, countless numbers land in Mexico through legal and illicit channels.

Federal and California waste officials blame each other, poor research and financial constraints for the cross-border tire mess.

An investigation by The San Diego Union-Tribune has found they aren't doing nearly enough to fix a problem that mainly affects middle-class and low-income residents who live far from most of the decision-makers.

"It's a lot easier to point the finger at Mexico, which doesn't solve the problem at all," said Oscar Romo, who teaches urban studies at the University of California San Diego.

Through interviews and documents, the Union-Tribune identified many flaws in the system. They include:

▪ San Diego County's lack of a tire-recycling facility, even though tire disposal problems have been known for at least 20 years.

▪ A state tire-recycling fund that has grown to $42 million while potential solutions lack money.

▪ California's ban against spending tire-recycling money in Mexico, even when such funding ultimately would benefit the state by reducing tire piles that fuel large fires or become breeding grounds for mosquitoes.

▪ Ineffective rules targeting illegal tire exports from California and spotty enforcement of those rules that leave regulators fuzzy about how many tires are sent to Mexico.

Both the United States and Mexican governments could devote more resources to the tire issue, said Christina Buchanan at San Diego's Local Enforcement Agency, which regulates solid waste in the city.

"Millions of waste tires . . . are accumulating along the Mexican border because of inadequate infrastructure for their regulation, recycling or disposal," Buchanan said.

California residents discard an average of more than one tire per person each year – about 44 million in all.

Roughly three-quarters of those tires go toward what regulators call productive uses, such as making rubberized asphalt, creating erosion-control products or covering landfill garbage. This recycling rate is more than twice what it was in 1990, but it is much lower than the national rate of 87 percent.

The remaining 11 million tires a year are destined for dumps, vacant lots or illegal export.

Air-pollution rules and public opposition to tire burning have limited California's ability to reuse tires as fuel. Nationwide, about half of the discarded tires become feedstock for industrial boilers and similar uses.

Many old tires from San Diego County are hauled to Los Angeles County for recycling, only to be trucked back through the region to Baja California for legal or unlicensed resale.

Tires from the United States are valued because they tend to have more tread left on them than old tires used only in Mexico.

Californians send about 800,000 tires annually to Mexico through legal channels. Waste experts suspect that hundreds of thousands more are exported illegally.

"People know that they can get a good price for them in Mexico. . . . Apparently, they are not that hard to smuggle," Buchanan said.

She singled out Otay Mesa, where auto-dismantling shops routinely hand off tires to shadowy figures who skirt the law by taking small loads to Mexico. California only requires registration and other documentation from people who transport 10 or more tires, a provision that Buchanan said benefits illegal haulers.

She and other regulators inspect tire-handling and hauling businesses to see whether they are meeting codes.

State waste officials acknowledge gaps in their supervision. In a report last year, they said that "effectively addressing all enforcement issues . . . continues to be a concern."

Despite major shortcomings in the tire-recycling system, federal and California officials touted their border cleanup accomplishments in August.

The U.S. Environmental Protection Agency announced that thanks to cooperation between U.S. and Mexican agencies, 4 million tires had been removed from the border region since 2003. Regulators from both countries agreed to consider more steps for further reducing waste tires.

"The solutions will come if there are laws and regulations and funding on the Mexican side," said EPA waste expert Emily Pimentel.

In California, tire-recycling efforts have languished despite the tens of millions of dollars that residents pay each year when they replace old tires.

Consumers pay a state-mandated $1.75 per new tire that's commonly listed as a disposal or recycling fee. That description is only partly accurate.

The state's Air Resources Board collects 75 cents from each fee to fight air pollution. The rest goes to the state's Integrated Waste Management Board for clearing piles of waste tires, researching ways to reuse old tires, developing markets for tire scrap and regulating tire storage and hauling.

(Continued)

Figure 10.6 (Continued)

The fee doesn't directly cover the cost of recycling tires that customers leave at shops. Some vendors charge an additional $2 or more in the name of doing so.

"Almost all tire shops will tell you it's a recycling fee. . . . But at least in San Diego County, at least half of those (tires) are going to end up in landfills," Buchanan said.

In recent years, the state's waste board has collected millions more in tire fees than it has spent. The result: The fund has ballooned to roughly $42 million from less than $1 million in fiscal 2001, when fees were increased.

The current balance doesn't include a $17 million loan that the waste board made to the state's general fund in fiscal 2004. The money is supposed to be repaid by mid-2009, but it Is unclear if that will happen because of California's budget crisis.

Last year, the nonpartisan Legislative Analyst's Office raised questions about the tire fund.

"The waste tire program appears to be in a holding pattern," it said. "Despite large initial gains in waste tire diversion, in recent years, both the diversion rate and the number of waste tires deposited into the state's landfills . . . have remained relatively constant."

Waste board officials said the fund has grown because the Legislature has limited how much the agency can spend regardless of what it collects. Jordan Scott of the waste board wouldn't say whether the board is aggressively seeking to free up more money.

California's large tire-fund reserve frustrates local waste and environmental officials who want more dollars spent on turning old tires into useful products.

"I would like to see that money, on a percentage basis, come back to San Diego County. That is just a reasonable thing," said Wayne Williams, a recycling coordinator for the county.

The recycling options include grinding up tires and adding them to asphalt, making what local road officials said is a quieter and more durable surface. In San Diego County, about 37 miles of road have been paved with rubberized asphalt and 23 more miles are in the works.

Several waste experts said the region's top need is a tire-recycling facility.

Bonsall entrepreneur David Willis is trying to win state grants and obtain final approvals for what would be the county's first such plant.

The facility would be housed in an existing industrial building in Vista. Willis hopes that by late spring, he will be shredding about 1.1 million tires a year and selling the material mainly for paving local roads.

The startup process has been arduous, he said, because the business needs multimillion-dollar machines and numerous permits.

In the nonprofit sector, the environmental group Wildcoast in Imperial Beach is battling the recurrence of tires washing up in the border region after each storm.

In June and October, Wildcoast volunteers helped to collect tons of tires from the Tijuana River Valley County Park. The tires were stored on county land, where they remain while park officials seek a state grant to pay for their removal.

After a storm during Thanksgiving week, the spot that Wildcoast and other groups had cleaned became waist-deep in debris – including more tires.

Ben McCue, a Wildcoast activist, wants the state to start spending money to reduce the waste-tire problem from the Tijuana end. McCue is talking with local legislators about proposed programs such as teaching residents how to prevent the tires that they use to build retaining walls and home foundations from washing away during storms.

It could be a tough sell in California's budget-weary Capitol. McCue remains hopeful that he can convince politicians they can save money and help the environment by short-circuiting the waste-tire cycle.

"It's just a matter of if it's the right time or if we have to wait a little longer," he said.

Mike Lee: *(619) 542-4570; mike.lee@uniontrib.com*

Find this article at:
http://www3.signonsandiego.com/stories/2008/dec/29/1n29tires012827-tire-trouble-knows-no-borders/?uniontrib

🖨 Click to Print   SAVE THIS | EMAIL THIS | Close

☐ Check the box to include the list of links referenced in the article.

9. Approach Elected Officials

Through research on the California Assembly and Senate websites we were able to determine which committees would most likely hear our bill. With guidance from our professors and staff in Assembly Member Lori Saldaña's office we decided to schedule meetings with the chairs and vice chairs of the Senate Environmental Quality Committee and the Senate Natural Resources and Water Committee. We also requested meetings with Assembly Members and Senators from the San Diego delegation. Once we made contact with the Sacramento offices we were asked to send a written request through e-mail. At this point our group decided it would be best to create a Gmail account for the coalition to receive e-mail correspondence on our issue. This e-mail account not only portrayed a more professional presence than a personal e-mail account, but it will also come in handy as our coalition grows. This is how breakthetirecycle@gmail.com was created.

We sent requests to eight different legislators, which resulted in five meetings—four in Sacramento (our state capital) and one in San Diego. We also met with the California Environmental Protection Agency (Cal/EPA). Since Cal/EPA is Sacramento's lead on environmental border issues with Baja California, we knew that its support of our legislative idea would be critical to getting the bill authored and passed through committee and floor votes. If our bill got through to the Governor, we knew that he would consider the position of his appointed staff at Cal/EPA before signing anything. We left Sacramento with two aces: Senator Ducheny, the San Diego representative of the border region and Chair of the Budget Committee, was interested in introducing our bill this session, and Cal/EPA was 100% behind our efforts. In fact, all of our meetings were well received. Our meeting with Cal/EPA expanded on our legislative idea and gave us a number of leads for key stakeholders to include in our coalition.

After a long day in Sacramento, our meetings were not over. The next day we met with Policy Director Deanna Spehn in the office of our local Senator Christine Kehoe. Meeting with her was the perfect next step. We had a possible author and supporters in state agencies, and now all we needed was key contact information for other agencies and organizations that would be vital to our coalition. Not only did the Legislative Director confirm that our positional map was on the right track, but she added other key agencies we needed to contact and get on-board. She also helped us get our foot in the door for these agencies and elected officials. We found the hardest part of calling offices like these was knowing exactly who we needed to ask for, and she solved that problem.

Immediately following our visits we sent out personalized thank-you e-mails to all the staff and legislators with whom we met (even one to our tour guide of the capitol).

10. Monitor Progress on the Issue

Through this process, one of the most critical steps for us was the last. Once our issue got taken up by Senator Ducheny, we maintained constant contact with her staff. As the bill sponsor, we played a critical role. We provided language for the bill to the Senator, assisted with committee testimony in Sacramento, and recruited local supporters in San Diego. As Senate Bill 167 made its way through committees and floor votes, we were constantly working to drum up more support.

Figure 10.7 (see p. 250) shows the history of the legislation as it worked its way through the process.

In the end our hard work paid off. On October 11, 2009, Governor Arnold Schwarzenegger signed SB 167 into law.

Using the 10-step advocacy process as a guide, our graduate school team successfully advocated for California legislation to address a historical environmental challenge along the California–Baja California border. Not only did we learn how to navigate the legislative process, but we came to a greater understanding of the relationship between constituent advocates, government agencies, and elected officials.

Figure 10.7

```
COMPLETE BILL HISTORY


BILL NUMBER  : S.B. No. 167
AUTHOR  : Ducheny
TOPIC   : Solid waste: waste tires.

TYPE OF BILL :
                Inactive
                Non-Urgency
                Non-Appropriations
                Majority Vote Required
                Non-State-Mandated Local Program
                Fiscal
                Non-Tax Levy

BILL HISTORY
2009
Oct. 11 Chaptered by Secretary of State.  Chapter   333, Statutes of 2009.
Oct. 11 Approved by Governor.
Sept. 28   Enrolled.  To Governor at   1 p.m.
Sept. 10   In Senate.  To enrollment.
Sept. 9 Read third time.  Passed.     (Ayes 48. Noes 28. Page  3228.)  To
        Senate.
Aug. 31 From committee:  Do pass.     (Ayes 12. Noes  5.)  (Heard in
        committee on August 27.)  (Received by desk on August 28 pursuant to
        JR 61(a)(11).)  Read second time.  To third reading.
July 8  Set, first hearing. Referred to  APPR. suspense file.
June 23 From committee:  Do pass, but first be re-referred to Com. on  APPR.
        (Ayes  7. Noes  2.)  Re-referred to Com. on  APPR.  (Heard in
        committee on June 22.)
May 28  To Com. on  NAT. RES.
May 14  In Assembly.  Read first time.  Held at Desk.
May 14  Read third time.  Passed.  (Ayes 25. Noes  9. Page   888.) To
        Assembly.
May 5   Read second time.  To third reading.
May 4   From committee:  Be placed on second reading file pursuant to Senate
        Rule 28.8.
Apr. 24 Set for hearing May  4.
Apr. 22 Read second time.  Amended.  Re-referred to Com. on  APPR.
Apr. 21 From committee:  Do pass as amended, but first amend, and re-refer
        to Com. on  APPR.  (Ayes  6. Noes  1. Page   585.)
Mar. 24 Set for hearing April  20.
Mar. 9  To Com. on  EQ.
Feb. 15 From print.  May be acted upon on or after  March  17.
Feb. 14 Introduced.  Read first time.  To Com. on RLS. for assignment.  To
        print.
```

11

Fighting for Justice in Cyberspace

The Role of Technology in Advocacy

John McNutt

I n this chapter, we will look at the technology available, how it fits into a strategy for advocacy, how it relates to more traditional advocacy techniques, and what types of skills you are going to need to use it effectively. The approach here is that simple technology can be effective when integrated with traditional advocacy techniques. We will start with a discussion of four processes that define technology and advocacy. We will then look at how technology and advocacy strategy work together. Then we will look at some of the technology tools that are available to advocates. Finally, we will explore some of the skills that you will need to use technology within your advocacy practice.

Technology and Advocacy

In the past two decades technology has become a major component of advocacy efforts in the United States and much of the world (McNutt & Menon, 2008). From a very modest beginning in the mid-1990s, technology has emerged as a major asset to those who are committed to social justice and a better society. Advocates now find themselves with a range of tools that can improve on their best efforts and help them reach goals that were unattainable just years before. This has changed the paradigm for issue advocacy and political campaigns.

What can technology do for advocates? It can extend their range, allowing them to affect more people over a greater distance; it can cut the costs of advocacy; and it can help advocates reach audiences in new and effective ways. It can also allow advocates to reach new populations and build larger and more effective constituencies (see Hick & McNutt, 2002). All of these great reasons mean that advocates will want to make use of the wonderful technology resources available to them. Specifically, some of the things that advocates can do with technology include the following:

- Use an online newsletter to inform and educate people about an issue. This could link to a website or a blog that can provide greater detail.
- Use an interactive online map to demonstrate groundwater pollution in a town or county. Let participants find their home, their children's school, or another important address.
- Put up a Facebook page to help raise awareness of a cause or an issue such as world hunger. Also use the same page to raise money for the cause and recruit supporters.
- Use a website to raise money to support a cause or an organization that you believe in. You can develop a page easily and without advanced technology skills at Google Sites.
- Use e-mail or text action alerts to mobilize your supporters to write letters or attend a rally or meeting.
- Create an online petition to encourage decision makers to act on a cause like protecting children or animals.
- Conduct research on an issue or a problem. Help the public understand the dimensions of the issue and its consequences.

These are just some of the things involving technology that real advocates in many fields are doing to address the issues they currently care about. Many more ways to use technology in advocacy are being developed every day. One of the important things to be aware of is that you can take almost all of these actions *now*. They generally require little knowledge of technology, and most of them are free. Many student social action groups make very good use of these technologies in advocating for their causes such as fair wage campaigns (Biddix & Park, 2008), sweatshop reforms, and university disinvestment.

Technology has reached the point where exciting things are happening. The election of President Barack Obama was due in no small part to his campaign's excellent use of technology (Cornfield, 2004; Smith, 2008). Obama for America and My Barack Obama were two excellent innovations that involved many citizens in a new political movement (see Smith, 2008). Most of those who seek political office today would not think of running without a website and a Facebook page (Gueorguieva, 2008). In fact, technology is often one of the first parts of a new campaign.

On the issue advocacy side of politics, the same processes are at work. MoveOn (http://www.moveon.org) developed from a small protest about the impeachment of President Clinton to the largest advocacy organization in the world. Aside from MoveOn, many traditional advocacy organizations have invested heavily in technology to make their advocacy work more effective. Well-known organizations such as the Sierra Club (http://www.sierraclub .org/), PETA (http://www.peta.org/), the Children's Defense Fund (http:// www.childrensdefense.org/), and so forth have interesting websites and well-developed online advocacy efforts. Transnational organizations are especially invested in creating technology efforts that can prosper in the international environment (Clark & Themudo, 2006; McNutt & Flanagan, 2008; Shumate & Pike, 2006).

The Four Processes

Technology is used differently in advocacy than it might be used in other fields such as education, business, or government. Understand, however, that for the most part it is the same technology. It is often better to think of technology as part of a process rather than a tool on its own. There are really two parts of this: what the technology is and how you use it in the context of an activity like advocacy. This usually means using several technologies together to conduct a single set of activities. To simplify how this works, it is often easier to talk about a series of recurrent processes than technology or task (see McNutt & Menon, 2008; McNutt & Penkauskas, 2000). In this context, technology contributes to nonprofit advocacy in four ways: (1) issue research and information gathering, (2) educating and informing the public, (3) coordinating and organizing, and (4) applying pressure. Each of these processes is used over and over again during the progress of an advocacy campaign.

Issue Research and Information Gathering

The considerable power of the Internet allows for gathering and presenting information quickly and effectively. Information is critical to any advocacy effort. Campaigns need many types of information. First, they need information on advocacy issues and social problems. The vast quantities of statistics, primary and secondary sources, and opinion pieces available online make this type of research faster and less time-consuming than in the past. The types of research that advocates use in implementing their campaigns include issue research, opposition research, and research to track and follow campaigns. Learning about issues is an important prerequisite to advocacy. The theories, statistics, resources, and so forth are easily available online. As the advocacy debate evolves, different information might be needed to counter arguments made by the opposition. The ability of Internet-based tools to gather and analyze information quickly can be invaluable during fast-moving campaigns.

Looking at our opponents is also useful (Bovee, 1998). Background information about individuals and groups is readily available online, and many things that took months to develop can be collected quickly. Even free search systems like ZabaSearch (http://www.zabasearch.com) and Pipl (http://www.pipl.com) provide a lot of information about individuals. Information on political contributions can be found at the Federal Election Commission (http://www.fec.gov) and the Center for Responsive Politics (http://www.opensecrets.org). You can get information about nonprofit organizations from GuideStar (http://www.guidestar.org). Opposition research is a highly technical field with many specialized resources. You will be surprised by how many things you can find out with very simple tools. You can find, for example, previous addresses, birth dates, criminal convictions, and lawsuits. In addition to help in gathering information, technology also makes it easier to analyze, present, and disseminate information. Social bookmarking sites, such as Delicious (http://www.delicious.com/), and content sharing sites, such as SlideShare (http://www.slideshare.net/), can also be used in the research process.

Educating and Informing the Public

A vast range of new and traditional technologies makes it easier to reach, educate, and persuade people to understand and take action on important issues. At a very simple level, an e-mail-based newsletter can inform stakeholders of new issues and actions. If you use every opportunity to create a list of e-mail addresses (a database program like Access is good for this) from those who are interested in your cause, then an online newsletter can be as simple as creating a document that is attractive and interesting and mailing it to your fans. You can also put your newsletter on the organization's website, Facebook page, or blog and send an invitation by e-mail to your supporters. More extensive resources (like pictures, video, or audio) can be provided that help people understand the issue. A website or blog can provide space to offer documents and videos of discussions and other informative programming. The development of online video (consider YouTube) means that video productions are no longer beyond the reach of even the smallest groups.

Coordinating and Organizing

Familiar tasks for advocates, coordinating and organizing are also tasks that technology can be remarkably helpful with. Technology can not only coordinate the activities of many people at the same time; it can also bridge distance and create new opportunities for interaction. At a very simple level, e-mail and texting can help bring people together and point them in the right direction. Social networking sites, such as Facebook and NING, also allow the capacity to coordinate and organize. Blogs, both internal and external, work well here. Finally, websites and discussion lists can help coordinate and plan events and campaigns.

Applying Pressure

At the end of the day, advocacy is about influencing decision makers. Technology can play an important role here as well. There are essentially two ways that technology can pressure decision makers: directly and indirectly. Direct pressure means that the technology works directly with the decision maker. Examples are e-mail campaigns and electronic petitions. These techniques can be supplemented by techniques that get others to intervene with decision makers such as action alerts for direct contact or raising funds for direct contributions.

Throughout the course of an advocacy effort, these processes will be used again and again. Consider the processes like building blocks of your work for social justice online. Each consists of a set of tasks and activities coupled with a number of technologies. These processes, along with any technology you might use, have to be contained within a carefully worked-out strategy to have a chance of being effective.

Involving Technology in Your Strategy

Strategy is the key to winning any campaign—online or off. Using all the relevant tools is important, but they must be tightly integrated into a working strategy. The 10 steps in the strategy process can be augmented by the use of technology, and technology can be guided by a well-developed strategic vision. In this section we will briefly look at how technology can be used in each step of the advocacy process.

The first three steps (identifying an issue, researching the issue, and creating a fact sheet) can make exceptional use of the power of technology to harness and disseminate information. This is clearly part of the "issue research and information gathering" process but moves into the process in the third stage. A whole range of research technologies can be used here. Discussion lists and e-mail can help identify an issue as can web searchers and databases. New technologies like social bookmarking and document sharing sites can be useful in gathering the information that can help define and evaluate a policy issue. The fact sheet can be enhanced through technology provided by desktop publishing, graphics, and links to a video, blog, or website.

The next step ("branding" the issue) can make use of the Internet's ability to educate and inform the public. Tools such as blogs and websites can help spread the message. This can help shape ideas and perceptions about the issue. Technology can also create the images that help to convey a coherent brand.

Moving on to the fifth step (mapping out possible supporters and detractors) means looking at the players in the arena, both organizations and individuals. This is, again, the first process at work, and technology can support opposition research and other types of explorations. Web searches and alerts (such as Google Alerts) can be used to establish positions of various players in the process. Database and online searches for newspaper articles, blog posts, voting records, and other materials can help fill in the gaps when trying to characterize positions. When we take this information and use it in Step 6 (forming a coalition), we move into the third process, organizing and coordinating. This is one of the Internet's great strengths because it reduces the costs of keeping the coalition moving in the right direction. E-mail, discussion lists, blogs, wikis, and related technologies can help schedule meetings, monitor task completion, and facilitate the development of shared documents. While considerable nontechnology effort still is needed to make a coalition successful, the tools available can greatly facilitate this effort.

After the coalition is developed, we move on to the seventh step (developing educational materials). The technology available from instructional and distance education technology can make the effort more successful. This is part of the "educating and informing the public" process. Presentation software, such as PowerPoint, Prezi, and Camtasia, can promote more effective educational programming.

Step 8 (launching a media campaign) is also part of the "educating and informing the public" process. Traditional media still has an important part of the advocacy scene, but, more and more, the technology front affords new and exciting possibilities. The growth of online video, particularly on YouTube, has made serious inroads in traditional media, and blogging is well on its way to becoming a legitimate form of media. Bloggers can have a large audience of readers, and some blogs (like the Daily Kos and the Drudge Report) can be highly influential.

When we reach the next step (approaching elected officials), technology plays more of a role as a consequence of the growth of e-democracy efforts. Most officials have e-mail and a website, and many have invested in social networking sites, Twitter, and so forth. While not taking anything away from personal face-to-face contact, new avenues for electronic contact are available and should be used frequently.

Finally, the tenth step (monitoring progress on the issue) is important. Many legislative victories become policy defeats because implementation is poorly conducted. Technology can make oversight and monitoring easier and more accurate with online surveys and other data collection measures.

Strategy has an important role to play in developing the relationship between traditional advocacy methods and technology. It is also important in helping technology to reach its full potential as an advocacy tool.

It is clear that technology has a role to play in advocacy. As technology develops, that role will increase.

Technology

Technology is an ever-expanding resource and one that offers wonderful opportunities for advocacy and social change. This section will give you a brief "cook's tour" of technology. Earlier technology, which is still quite useful today, is generally considered part of the Web 1.0 world. It is less interactive and less capable for organizing and coordinating. The past 10 years saw the rise of Web 2.0 technology, sometimes called social media or social software (see Bryant, 2006; Fine, 2006; Germany, 2006; Kanter & Fine, 2010; McNutt, 2007). This is technology that is much more interactive, builds networks, allows users to create their own content, and fuels the sharing of ideas and intelligence. It also operates at the level of the Internet rather than on individual machines. These newer technologies are a real gift for advocates and organizers. They work in a very similar fashion to the way that organizing and advocacy work.

Earlier Technologies

The techniques that advocates have used for the last two decades do not share some of the advantages that the newer technologies have, but they are still a solid choice for advocacy work. They are well-understood technologies that are generally dependable, and most people know how to use them.

Electronic Mail

By far the most useful of the older technologies, electronic mail, or e-mail, has been around for many years and is a very useful tool for making inquiries, coordinating and organizing, conducting pressure campaigns, and so forth. The primary advantages are that it's easy and fast and, for the most part, free. E-mail also has some disadvantages. The biggest disadvantage is that spam has created a situation where much e-mail is deleted prior to reading, and there is also a federal law making spam illegal. E-mail can also be easily forwarded, which means that it can be sent to the opposition. These problems aside, it is a first-rate technique for the advocate.

An emerging issue with e-mail is that decision makers are having a harder and harder time dealing with the amount of e-mail that they receive (Congressional Management Foundation, 2005). Various systems are being created to process the flood of e-mail that the government deals with. This may weaken e-mail's effectiveness in this particular role.

E-mail can be made more effective when combined with other technologies. Bulk mailing programs can provide the ability to send out many e-mails at one time. Having a database of e-mail addresses can be incredibly useful in an advocacy campaign. Even a simple database program will work. Make sure that every contact that you make provides you with an e-mail address. It is also important to collect e-mail addresses on your website and to make available the organization's e-mail address at every opportunity. E-mail can ask supporters to do things (like attend a meeting or call a legislator) or donate money to a cause. Organizing for America (the successor to Obama for America) regularly uses its extensive e-mail list to contact supporters to take action.

Discussion Lists

One of the more popular extensions of basic e-mail is the discussion list, popularized by LISTSERV (the first software application of this type). These lists can provide an opportunity for discussion, and such discussions can build cooperation and ensure that everyone is in the same place. Discussion groups can be easily created with a number of free services including Yahoo! Groups (http://groups.yahoo.com) and Google Groups (http://groups.google.com).

If you want to just send things to people and do it efficiently, you need a distribution list. This type of list is like a discussion list, but the traffic is only one-way. It is a good choice for action alerts or for an e-mail newsletter. In general, these are set up the same way that discussion lists are with the discussion feature turned off.

Websites

In advocacy today, you almost have to have a website. The creation of websites was once an arcane art requiring coding and other sophisticated skills. No longer. Creating a website is relatively easy and can even be done automatically. Free websites are also available, although some come with built-in ads. Many organizations are moving beyond a simple webpage to one run by a content management system, which organize and change content within an entire website. While content management systems seem to imply a larger and more costly site, free blogging systems can also be used as a content management system for more modest needs. Websites are natural places to share general orientations about the problem, statistics, copies of legislation, white papers and other documents, advocacy tips, and so forth, and they can provide a platform for organizing other types of technology, such as video and blogs. The principal disadvantages of websites are their static nature and their lack of flexibility. People must come to a website. It has no way of reaching out. In the past few years the development of RSS (Really Simple Syndication) has made it easy to subscribe to a website. You just click on the RSS symbol (an orange square with a white circle and two white curved lines) and follow the instructions. Page updates will come to you.

Traditional Online Fund-Raising

Raising money is important in all types of political action. Websites and other systems allow you to raise money over the Internet. It can be as easy as creating a link, on your website, to an e-commerce provider that accepts the money for you. Another way of raising money over the Internet is to use a "shop for a cause" approach. Major online retailers often are willing to donate to your organization if you help drive traffic to their site. You place an icon on your webpage, which is a link to their site, and each time a customer comes via that link the company makes a donation. Newer technologies, such as Facebook, also offer ways to raise funds online. Federal and state laws on contributions must be followed here (see Chapter 2), and other rules apply if we are collecting money for an electoral campaign. It is also important to distinguish between deductible and nondeductible contributions.

Text Messaging and SMS

Text messaging provides a surprisingly useful way to alert supporters and coordinate activity. The widespread availability of cell phones and smart phones has made this technology even more effective.

Online Petitions

Traditional petitions have taken on a high-technology look. There are several ways to create an online petition, which include using an e-mail sign-on, posting a petition on an organization's website, and posting a petition on a site like e.thePeople (http://www.e-thepeople.org/) or Care2's petition site (http://www.thepetitionsite.com/). Each of these has pros and cons. E-mail sign-on means that you send a carefully crafted statement in an e-mail to potential signatories. With a website-based petition, you must use some other mechanism to get people to come to the site. On balance, e-mail petitions may fall victim to spam filters.

While these technologies became popular in the 1990s, they are still useful and widely employed in advocacy campaigns (McNutt & Barlow, 2008). The newer technologies offer a lot of additional capacity and can be used in concert with the older technologies and many nontechnology advocacy methods.

Newer Technologies

In the days following the turn of the new millennium, a new set of technologies began to emerge. Eventually, these innovations were referred to as Web 2.0, social media, or even social software. As was said earlier, these technologies allow for sharing, networking, pooling of ideas and expertise, and the creation of content by users. They also use the Internet as a platform.

New Web 2.0 technologies are being constantly developed through the process of creating mash-ups. A mash-up is a combination of two or more existing technologies. At the present time, however, some of the more popular include the following.

Blogs

Weblogs, or blogs, are online journals that readers can comment upon. The author writes a post and then adds it to the blog. People who read it are encouraged to make comments about what the author has said. Blogs are very good for sharing ideas and news and can be used to coordinate activities as well.

Blogs have risen from an obscure technology to a major form of media (Davis, 2005). Bloggers have received journalist credentials at major political conventions. Maintaining relationships with bloggers is important, and political campaigns and advocacy organizations often take care to make sure that relationships are positive.

Internal blogs can be used to coordinate activity and share information. They can also be used to give everyone access to information.

Blogs are easy to create and generally free. Blogger (http://www.blogger .google.com) is a free Google product, and WordPress (http://wordpress.org/) is also generally free. Many of the social networking systems also offer a blog-like ability. In order to be effective, a blog needs new material and consistent care. This is not something you can start and forget.

Wikis

A wiki is a website that can be edited by anyone or by anyone with permission. Wikipedia (http://www.wikipedia.org/) is the best-known wiki, but there are many others. A wiki can provide you with the ability to provide your supporters with a variety of shared documents. Lists of assignments can be posted, documents can be created cooperatively by many users, and directories can be updated by any member of the team. Wikis can be easily created via many online providers. Many of these providers offer a free version of their wiki software.

Social Networking Sites

Social networking sites like Facebook (http://www.facebook.com/), Myspace (http://www.myspace.com/), Friendster (http://www.friendster.com/), NING (http://www.ning.com/), and others are not only popular forms of entertainment; they are first-rate organizing tools. In general, each of these sites has a central site for each member or organization, and this central site provides access to a suite of organizing and networking tools. This allows users to search for other users; post notices, events, and ideas; upload video and images; and link to other pages. A recent wrinkle is the incorporation of geographic information. Foursquare (http://foursquare.com/) popularized this trend, and Facebook Places (http://www.facebook.com/places/) brings this into the Facebook world. Many of the social networking sites can also be used for marketing and fundraising, which makes them even more useful for advocacy.

Facebook is probably the most frequently used social network for advocacy efforts. You can create a page for your organization or cause. Many potential tools are available from Facebook or other providers. A manual on Facebook activism is available from DigiActive (Schultz, 2008), and many other helpful resources are available on the web.

Twitter

Twitter is a form of microblogging. Messages, or tweets, are limited to 140 characters and can contain links to images, documents, or websites. Twitter users can follow other users and can join lists that include a number of different users. Twitter is great for getting the word out about events, good for educating the public, and very useful for staying abreast of new developments. If you subscribe to newspapers, magazines, think tanks, and other news sources, there are often daily tweets that have links to articles and reports. Twitter is also an excellent organizing tool that allows for quick coordination of events. A manual on Twitter activism is available from DigiActive (Jungherr, 2009).

Podcasting

Podcasts are downloadable audio files that can be played on an iPod or a similar device. They are relatively easy to create and can be used for influencing and educating the public. They are also useful for training your campaign workers and other supporters.

Social Bookmarking

Social bookmarking is a terrific research tool that can give you access to the judgment of many similar researchers when you look for information on the web. When you go to search, you log into your social bookmarking program and then search as always. When you find something good, you bookmark it. The site pools all of the recommendations and recommends the sites that people who search for a given topic recommend. In this way you benefit from the collective knowledge of all of the searchers. Probably the most popular of all of these sites is Delicious (http://www.delicious.com/). Easy to use and relatively intuitive, it has a lot of features that make social bookmarking more productive.

Content Sharing Sites

Content, including user-generated content, is critical on the Internet, and content sharing sites offer users access to many resources that traditional providers do not offer. This can be specialized reports, illustrations of local conditions, unofficial analysis, and so forth. The major types of content sharing sites are image sharing sites, video sharing sites, and document sharing sites. Sometimes these are free-floating sites, and sometimes they are combined with other types of technology. Image sharing sites, such as Flickr (http://www.flickr.com/), allow users to upload and share images such as photos and graphics. Pictures of a rally or an album that illustrates a problem condition can be a powerful tool to bring people together. Video sharing sites, such as YouTube (http://www.youtube.com/) and Google Videos (http://video.google.com/), allow users to upload movies to a site and share them with other users. Users can also create channels and subscribe to content providers that they like. Document sharing sites, including Scribd (http://www.scribd.com/) and SlideShare (http://www.slideshare.net/), allow users to share documents and presentations. These tools are great for involving the public, building morale, and conducting advocacy research.

Google Tools

Some terrific organization and coordination tools are offered by Google. They include Google Docs (for documents, spreadsheets, and presentations), Blogger, Google Calendar, Google Sites, Google Groups, and Gmail. All of these applications can be accessed from anywhere online. No additional software is needed (aside from a browser), and many people can work on a shared document like a report, a spreadsheet, or a presentation. Shared calendars can help in organizing an event. The different applications are designed to work seamlessly together. Most of the applications are available from the "More" tab on the Google search page.

Meetup

Meetup (http://www.meetup.com) is an application designed to arrange face-to-face meetings via the Internet. It was one of the major technologies used in Howard Dean's primary campaign in 2004 (Sanders, 2005; Teachout & Streeter, 2008; Trippi, 2004) and has blossomed into a first-line political technology. Meetup organizers schedule a meeting, and people who are looking for a group in their area respond and send an RSVP to the organizers. There is a group page where members of the local group can communicate and share.

This technology is especially effective when face-to-face meetings are essential and many of the participants are strangers. The meetings are reinforced by the group technology features on the website.

Setting up a Meetup site is fairly straightforward. Meetup is a fee-based service, so a subscription is needed. The directions for setting up and managing a site are fairly comprehensive.

Online Mapping

While computer mapping has a long history in technology, a new wrinkle has developed. Individuals can now use online systems to create their own maps from data that an organization makes available online. This allows people to see the data on a map that they generate and how these data apply to their life. For example, pollution data can be overlaid on a map that lets users see how close a chemical waste dump or another noxious facility is to their home or to their child's school. Google Earth and Google Maps offer the opportunity to customize online maps. The Natural Resources Defense Council (http://www.nrdc.org) provides visitors with the opportunity to download a file (http://www.nrdc.org/reference/maps.asp) that will allow them to explore environmental issues around the world on Google Earth. The Tactical Technology Collective (http://www.tacticaltech.org/) has some excellent resources on mapping and advocacy.

Virtual Worlds

Virtual worlds are simulated realities that allow for interaction and role playing. Second Life (http://secondlife.com/) is by far the most popular product of this type, but there are certainly others. You can build a site that simulates any situation or forum (the House of Representatives has a site), and you can interact with other users via an avatar.

Virtual worlds give you the opportunity to try out different things virtually before you try them in real life. They also allow you to demonstrate different possibilities and receive feedback. PETA (www.peta.org) uses Second Life (http://www.peta.org/b/thepetafiles/archive/tags/second+life/default.aspx) to show visitors to its website about the organization's efforts to prevent cruelty to animals.

New technology is constantly developing, and it is often a race to keep up with the new developments in the field. The question is not what the latest technology is but rather what technology works best for the task at hand. Newer technologies often come with a cost. They are unfamiliar, which means that it takes more time to learn how to use them. In addition, most new technologies don't work perfectly in the beginning. Technology gets better because users find the flaws, and the software developers fix those defects. The longer a technology is in use, the better chance it has to be reliable.

Security and privacy are serious issues in technology. It is important to safeguard your organization's information. You can lose critical strategic advantages if your confidential information is compromised. This goes as well for your personal information. Having basic protection from malware is part of this protection, but guarding passwords, protecting access, and understanding the various privacy protections are also important.

Regardless of what technology you decide to use, it is important that it be dependable, that your people know how to use it, and that you provide adequate technical support. Technology that doesn't work is nobody's friend. It frustrates your colleagues and supporters, damages your cause, and makes your efforts less successful. You also need training. No matter how often the advertising literature uses terms like *intuitive* and *easy-to-use*, there is still a learning curve. This doesn't necessarily mean that you need a formal course; sometimes a book, website, tutorial, or trusted friend is enough.

Building Skills for Electronic Advocacy Practice

Just knowing how to use the technology will not make you a capable online advocate. In order to be good at that, you first need to understand advocacy and policy change. Second, you need to have a comfortable understanding of technology. Third, you need to understand how the two processes fit together. This is not as easy or as obvious as it sounds. As we noted earlier, technology and advocacy technology are different because of how you use the technologies involved.

Understanding advocacy is critical to the process. This allows you to anticipate the points in the process where your interventions will do the most good and at what point other interventions might be a better idea. Some of the things that make great technology sense are really not called for in an advocacy situation. You clearly need to understand both the federal and state regulations for advocates. They often differ, sometimes significantly. Having an understanding of the full range of advocacy options and the characteristics of the decision-making bodies you are dealing with greatly facilitates designing an effective online effort.

It is also essential to understand technology and some of the emergent technological trends. This is an ever-moving target, and many of today's hot technologies were unknown even three years ago. Basic information about databases and networking and a little about programming, as well as an understanding of how to use a standard office suite, are probably the minimum needed to be effective as an online advocate. It goes without saying that a general familiarity with technology is also required. The more that you know about technology, the better the advocate you can be.

You also need organizing and management skills. Such skills as allocating resources, creating and enforcing schedules, managing budgets, coordinating different people's contributions, and getting everything to work when it needs to are critical to attaining a good outcome. You need a vision, a plan, and a monitoring system. You need systems for coordinating resources and developing new ones. Like most other things in an organization, effective advocacy requires effort, inspiration, and good management.

Very few people begin a career in online advocacy with all of the skills that they will eventually need. Experience, classes, websites, and other resources will help you fill the gaps. More and more cities have groups of advocates who meet regularly to share their online techniques. These can be very rewarding sessions.

The Future

Online advocacy has a bright future, and many nonprofit organizations are creating positions for people who can deal with their needs in the area of advocacy technology. It is a sure bet that technology will develop, becoming more capable and responding to more issues. Hardware will become smaller and smaller yet more powerful.

Many advances are being made in the less technological aspects of online advocacy. We know a great deal more about who uses the Internet, for what, and what roles they fulfill in the online world. This knowledge has allowed us to create online systems for advocacy. One example is the online influential work conducted by PoliticsOnline.

One of the more important trends is the evidence-based practice techniques that have been carefully developed, rigorously evaluated, and carefully revised (Bergan, 2009; McNutt, 2006). This aims at the development of better and more reliable techniques. So far the fruits of these efforts have been modest, but as the field matures, the possibility of evidence-based online advocacy presents itself.

Electronic and online advocacy is an emergent practice. A product of the past three decades, it has the potential to both enrich and revolutionize the quest for social justice. This is an exciting time to be involved in online advocacy.

Chapter Questions

1. What kind of technology do you use in your life and your work? What do you use most often? Which technologies make you more successful?

2. Have you ever used technology to promote a cause or an issue? What technology did you use? Did you feel that it was a success?

3. Do you have a blog, a website, or a page on Facebook or Myspace? Have you ever used it to draw attention to a cause or an issue that you care about?

4. Have you ever contacted a public official online? How was the contact made? What was the issue? How satisfied were you with the content?

5. Have you ever been part of an online electoral or issue campaign? How were you involved? What happened?

References

Bergan, D. E. (2009). Does grassroots lobbying work? A field experiment measuring the effects of an e-mail lobbying campaign on legislative behavior. *American Political Research, 37*(2), 327–352.

Biddix, J. P., & Park, H. W. (2008). Online networks of student protest: The case of the living wage campaign. *New Media and Society, 10*(6), 871–891.

Bovee, J. (1998). How to do opposition research on the Internet. *Campaigns and Elections, 19*(9), 48–52.

Bryant, A. (2006). Wiki and the Agora: "It's organizing Jim, but not as we know it." *Development in Practice, 16*(6), 559–569.

Clark, J. D., & Themudo, N. S. (2006). Linking the web and the street: Internet based "dotcauses" and the rise of the "antiglobalization" movement. *World Development, 34*(1), 50–74.

Congressional Management Foundation. (2005). *Communicating with Congress: How Capitol Hill is coping with the surge in citizen advocacy.* Washington, DC: Author.

Cornfield, M. (2004). *Politics moves online*. Washington, DC: Brookings.

Davis, R. (2005). *Politics on-line: Blogs, chat rooms and discussion groups in American democracy*. New York: Routledge.

Fine, A. (2006). *Momentum: Igniting social change in the connected age*. San Francisco: Jossey-Bass.

Germany, J. B. (Ed.). (2006). *Person to person to person: Harnessing the political power of on-line social networks and user generated content*. Washington, DC: The Institute for Politics, Democracy and the Internet, George Washington University.

Gueorguieva, V. (2008). Voters, Myspace, and YouTube: The impact of alternative communication channels on the 2008 election cycle and beyond. *Social Science Computer Review, 26*, 288–300.

Herrnson, P. S., Stokes-Brown, A. K., & Hindman, M. (2007). Campaign politics and the digital divide. *Political Research Quarterly, 60*(1), 31–42.

Hick, S., & McNutt, J. (Eds.). (2002). *Advocacy and activism on the Internet: Perspectives from community organization and social policy*. Chicago: Lyceum Press.

Jungherr, A. (2009). *The DigiActive guide to Twitter for activism*. Retrieved March 21, 2011, from http://www.digiactive.org/wp-content/uploads/digiactive_twitter_guide_v1-0.pdf

Kanter, B., & Fine, A. (2010). *The network nonprofit*. San Francisco: Jossey-Bass.

McCaughey, M., & Ayers, M. D. (Eds.). (2003). *Cyberactivism: On-line activism in theory and practice*. New York: Routledge.

McCullagh, K. (2003). E-Democracy: Potential for political revolution. *International Journal of Law and Information Technology, 11*(2), 149–161.

McNutt, J. G. (2006). Building evidence based advocacy in cyberspace: A social work imperative for the new millennium. *Journal of Evidence Based Practice, 3*(2/3), 91–102.

McNutt, J. G. (2007). Web 2.0 tools for policy research and advocacy. *Journal of Policy Practice, 7*(1), 81–85.

McNutt, J. G., & Barlow, J. (2008). *Building civil society for children in cyberspace: A longitudinal study of political technology use by nonprofit child advocacy organizations*. Paper presented at the 2008 Meeting of the Association for Research on Nonprofit Organizations and Voluntary Action, Philadelphia, November.

McNutt, J. G., & Boland, K. M. (1999). Electronic advocacy by non-profit organizations in social welfare policy. *Non-Profit and Voluntary Sector Quarterly, 28*(4), 432–451.

McNutt, J. G., & Flanagan, M. (2008). *Transnational nonprofit advocacy organizations and the social networking technology revolution: Patterns of adoption across organizational fields*. Paper read at the Eighth International Conference of the International Society for Third Sector Research, Universitat de Barcelona, Barcelona, Spain, July 9–12.

McNutt, J. G., & Menon, G. M. (2008). Cyberactivism and progressive human services. *Families and Society, 89*(1), 33–38.

McNutt, J. G., & Penkauskas, K. (2000). *Electronic advocacy*. Presentation at Getting Wired: Advocacy in Cyberspace: The First Boston College Conference on Electronic Advocacy in Social Work Practice, Chestnut Hill, MA, April 14.

Rigby, B. (2008). *Mobilizing Generation 2.0: A practical guide to using Web 2.0*. San Francisco: Jossey-Bass.

Sanders, T. H. (2005). *E-Associations? Using technology to connect citizens: The case of meetup.com*. Paper presented at the Annual Meeting of the American Political Science Association.

Schultz, D. (2008). *A DigiActive introduction to Facebook activism*. Retrieved March 21, 2011, from http://www.digiactive.org/wp-content/uploads/digiactive_facebook_activism.pdf

Shumate, M., & Pike, J. (2006). Trouble in a geographically distributed virtual network organization: Organizing tensions in continental direct action network. *Journal of Computer-Mediated Communication, 11*(3), article 8. Retrieved March 23, 2011, from http://jcmc.indiana.edu/vol11/issue3/shumate.html

Smith, A. (2008). *From BarackObama.com to Change.gov: Those active in the Obama campaign expect to be involved in promoting the administration*. Retrieved March 23, 2011, from http://pewresearch.org/pubs/1068/post-election-voter-engagement

Teachout, Z., & Streeter, T. (Eds.). (2008). *Mousepads, shoeleather and hope*. Boulder, CO: Paradigm Publishers.

Trippi, J. (2004). *The revolution will not be televised: Democracy, the Internet and the overthrow of everything*. New York: Reagan Book/HarperCollins.

Chapter 11 Appendix

Websites and Other Helpful Resources

Technology

Idealware: http://www.idealware.org/

Jayne Cravens & Coyote Communications: http://www.coyotecom.com/

Technology for the Nonprofit and Philanthropic Sector, Deborah Elizabeth Finn: http://blog.deborah.elizabeth.finn.com/blog

TechSoup: http://home.techsoup.org/pages/default.aspx

Advocacy and Activism

DigiActive: http://www.digiactive.org/

Electronic Advocacy: http://www.policymagic.org/electron.htm

e.politics: http://www.epolitics.com/

Groundwire: http://groundwire.org

Movements: http://www.movements.org

NetCentric Advocacy: http://www.network-centricadvocacy.net/

NetSquared: http://www.netsquared.org

New Organizing Institute: http://neworganizing.com

PoliticsOnline: http://www.politicsonline.com/

Tactical Technology Collective: http://www.tacticaltech.org/

Wellstone Action: http://www.wellstone.org/

Recommended Reading

Delany, C. (2008). *On-line politics 101*. Washington, DC: e.politics.

Feld, L., & Wilcox, N. (2008). *Netroots rising*. Westport, CT: Praeger.

Hick, S., & McNutt, J. G. (Eds.). (2002). *Advocacy and activism on the Internet: Perspectives from community organization and social policy*. Chicago: Lyceum Books.

Kanter, B., & Fine, A. (2010). *The network nonprofit.* San Francisco: Jossey-Bass.

Policy Link Institute. (2008). *Click here for change: Your guide to the E-Advocacy revolution.* Oakland, CA: Author.

Rigby, B. (2008). *Mobilizing Generation 2.0: A practical guide to using Web 2.0.* San Francisco: Jossey-Bass.

Shirky, C. (2008). *Here comes everybody: The power of organizing without organizations.* New York: Penguin.

12 So Now You Have a Law

What Do You Do With It?
Monitoring Progress on the Issue

Howard Wayne

By this time you have put a lot of effort into your campaign, and you have had success. A bill has been passed by the legislature and signed by the Governor. But the battle is not over. In this chapter I want to talk about hurdles that may need to be overcome even after you have accomplished enactment. It's not time to rest on your laurels.

Fighting Repeal

If you had a particularly controversial bill, you had to overcome many obstacles to get it passed. But that does not mean the opposition is finished. Just as there are no final defeats in public affairs, there are also no final victories. There is still much to be done.

An example of just how extensive such a postenactment battle can be will be seen with the Affordable Care Act (national health care). The Republicans opposed President Obama's bill and made opposition to it a major issue in the 2010 election. They recaptured the House of Representatives, made gains in the Senate, and are interpreting (or spinning) those victories as a mandate for repeal. Of course, the wish may be the father of the thought. Polling showed that voters in 2010 were about equally split on the Affordable Care Act, and some polled as opposing it did so on the basis it did not go far enough.

A direct effort to repeal the health care law is not likely to be successful in 2011–2012. While the House passed repeal, the Senate is likely to reject the House's bill. Even if repeal cleared the Senate, the President would veto it. So the issue is likely to be preserved into the 2012 election. After that—who knows?

In the interim, indirect efforts at repeal are likely. These will take at least three forms: not funding implementation (e.g., refusing to fund the rulemaking process needed to create the rules that will govern national health care), litigation, and the refusal of some states to implement key provisions such as setting up the insurance exchanges provided for by the Affordable Care Act.

At the time of this writing a number of state attorneys general have filed actions attacking the constitutionality of provisions of the law, and at least one federal judge has invalidated the keystone mandate for everyone to purchase health insurance.

Repeal by litigation was a tactic employed against early New Deal legislation in the 1930s. A conservative U.S. Supreme Court, in *Carter v. Carter Coal Company,* invalidated regulation of the mining industry on the basis that mining was not commerce within the meaning of the Commerce Clause of the Constitution,[1] and threw out the Agricultural Adjustment Act that sought to regulate the production of crops. That led to the famed effort by President Franklin Roosevelt to "pack the court" by increasing the number of justices so he could appoint justices more amenable to his positions.

Although Roosevelt lost the battle, he won the war. The Supreme Court began deferring to congressionally passed legislation. From the late 1930s until the mid-1990s the Supreme Court seldom invalidated congressional legislation. However, this has begun to change. An energized conservative court has once again demonstrated judicial activism by invalidating acts of Congress. Notable examples include *United States v. Lopez*[2] (gun control) and *United States v. Morrison*[3] (Violence Against Women Act). Since both of those cases utilized a narrow reading of the Commerce Clause, and the Affordable Care Act is premised on the Commerce Clause, the Supreme Court may be prepared to declare national health care unconstitutional.

Funding

As you can see from above, even if you get your bill enacted, you may have another battle in being sure it is funded. Most things worth doing will cost money, and in these fiscally tight days that alone can stop your campaign.

The efforts of The REACH Project, detailed earlier in this book, failed to achieve its goal because the Governor vetoed the bill out of concern for its costs. Subsequent efforts to pass REACH failed in the California State Assembly because of fiscal concerns in the Appropriations Committee.

When I succeeded in having AB 411 signed into law, as described in Chapter 4 of this book, I had to also make sure there were funds in the budget to pay for creating the regulations required by the law. After that, I had

---

[1]Article I, Section 8, Subdivision 3 of the Constitution grants Congress the power to regulate commerce "among the several states."

[2]514 U.S. 549 (1995).

[3]529 U.S. 598 (2000).

to work to have the testing program funded in the state budget (remember, that was part of the compromise I had negotiated to get the bill signed. Please see AB 411, Section 1, Subdivision (h), as shown in Figure 4.8).

Beach water testing was popular and not terribly expensive. Testing began in 1999 and was funded every year, and I left the legislature in 2002. The line item continued in the budget in the ensuing years. That is, until 2008. Given how difficult the state finances were, the legislature reduced the funding for testing by 10%. The Governor vetoed even that reduced expenditure. No money = no testing.

However, AB 411 had many friends. Following passage of the bill I was responsible for inserting $87 million for beach water quality in a state bond measure that passed in 2000. When the Governor vetoed the beach testing money, supporters sought to utilize funds from the state bond to cover the costs of testing until the state's finances improved. Their efforts were initially successful, but a complication arose. In San Diego County, the Board of Supervisors stepped up to the plate and advanced the money for beach water testing.

How long that will continue is problematic, given the severe recession the nation is experiencing. But the point is clear. If you succeed in having your law passed, you also have to secure funding, and you may have to fight years later to have the funding continued.

The Regulatory Process

With many laws, the work does not end with the Governor signing the bill, and that includes work on the substance of the law created by the bill. Often the important details need to be fleshed out through the regulatory process by what is called rulemaking. In rulemaking, an administrative body acts as an unelected legislature in enacting laws, called regulations (in the parlance "regs"), and the process is described as quasilegislative.

AB 411 is an example of this. Section 2, Subdivision (a) of the bill provided that the "department [of Health Services] shall by regulation, in consultation with local health offices and the public, establish minimum standard for the sanitation of public beaches . . ." The implementing regulations were not promulgated until mid-1999, about 21 months after the bill was signed. They appear in the California Code of Regulations at Title 17, Chapter 5, Subchapter 1.5, Group 10, Sections 7958, 7961, and 7962.

The Administrative Procedure Act (APA)[4] governs the rulemaking process at the national level. Many states have their own version of the APA, often based on a Model Act. The process is called Notice and Comment.

Just like with AB 411, some statutes will delegate rulemaking to an agency. Agency staff, in consultation with experts in the field and the agency's

[4]For those of a legal mind, or who simply want to delve into it, the APA can be found at 5 U.S.C. Section 55, *et seq.* The California version appears at Government Code Section 11370, *et seq.*

attorneys, will propose a regulation. The proposed regulation will be published in the Federal Register along with a reference to the legal authority under which the rule is proposed.[5]

Upon publication, the public has the opportunity to comment in writing and sometimes orally on the proposed rule, including offering amendments to it. Understandably, most people do not peruse the Federal Register each morning over their cornflakes (and just after reading the sports page). But those involved in the legislative process with an interest in a particular field are reviewing the proposed rules, advising their interest group clients, and sending in comments.

Agencies are required to consider the public comments in formulating the final version of a rule. The agency, not the Congress, adopts the rule, which then appears in the Code of Federal Regulations (CFR). Adopted rules are subject to being challenged in court, such as by a claim that the rule is inconsistent with the statute from which it is supposedly derived.

California has added an extra step to the rulemaking process. Before a rule can be adopted by an agency, it has to be reviewed by the Office of Administrative Law. The OAL is required to determine whether the proposed regulation is consistent with the underlying statute, is not inconsistent with the statute, and is reasonably necessary to affect the purpose of the statute.[6]

What this means for the advocate is that the effort to implement your proposal can continue on from the legislature to the administrative agency charged with working out the details of your law. Watch out for "agency capture." Many agencies need highly specialized staff with expertise that can only be obtained from the industry the agency was created to regulate. There is often a revolving door between the agency and the industry, and relationships develop over a period of time as agency staff members repeatedly deal with the same people on the regulated side. As an agency "matures," it may even view the regulated industry as its customer (particularly when it is dependent on funding from fees charged to the regulated businesses). Thus there is a risk that the agency will be "captured" by the very businesses it was created to regulate.

Hence, if your bill seeks to affect regulated businesses and you must go through the regulatory process, beware the staff. They may take away what the legislature has granted, and they often can outwait the legislator who is your champion (particularly in this term-limited era).[7] Of course, you might want to avail yourself of the remedy of litigation.

---

[5]The California equivalent is called the California Regulatory Notice Register.

[6]For the Office of Administrative Law, see Government Code Section 11340.2, *et seq*.

[7]Also there is the possibility of effective capture, when the agenda of the appointing power (such as the Governor or President) leans against aggressive enforcement of the law. The National Labor Relations Board under Bush II is a sad example of that, as is the failure to regulate financial markets by the Securities and Exchange Commission during that era.

Litigation

This is something you should be thinking about when you draft your law. How do you plan to have it enforced? There are generally three means of enforcement, and they need not be mutually exclusive: public prosecution, agency proceedings, and private lawsuits. You should consider which remedies you want available. Remember that remedies count, as demonstrated more than 200 years ago in the landmark case of *Marbury v. Madison*.[8] There the outgoing Federalist president John Adams appointed William Marbury to a judicial position, but the appointment papers were not delivered before Adams left office. The new Democratic-Republican Secretary of State James Madison refused to deliver the appointment papers, and Marbury filed suit in the U.S. Supreme Court for an order (called writ of mandate or *mandamus*) to compel Madison to deliver the papers. The Supreme Court found that Marbury had a right to the appointment papers, but did not have a remedy of having the Supreme Court issue a writ of mandate.

Each means of enforcement has its advantages and disadvantages. For public prosecution (either criminally or by an organization such as the Attorney General), major advantages include public attention and consistency in bringing actions. But in a down budget time, there may not be funding to bring an action, and the decision to file or not file could be guided by political factors.

Agency procedures, essentially administrative enforcement, can mean a more expeditious action. However, because agencies can be captured, the very entity you wish to regulate can block enforcement. Moreover, even the agency may be subject to fiscal constraints and political considerations.

Finally, there is enforcement by private lawsuits. Those who are injured may vigorously enforce the law and receive compensation. However, if a person has only a small loss, there is little incentive for injured parties to act or for their attorneys to initiate litigation. Hence, there is the risk there will be no enforcement.

Let's take an example in federal law. Title IX (20 U.S.C. Section 1681) provides that "no person in the United States shall, on the basis of sex, be excluded from participation in, be denied the benefits of, or subject to discrimination under any education program or activity receiving Federal financial assistance." The plaintiff, a woman, was denied admission to a medical school that received federal financial assistance on the basis of her sex, and she sued under Title IX. The Supreme Court noted that the statute did not expressly authorize a private lawsuit for a person injured by its violation. Instead, the Court found that a provision of Title IX established a procedure for the termination of federal financial support for sex discrimination and concluded that Congress intended that remedy to be the exclusive means of enforcement.[9]

---

[8](1803) 5 U.S. (1 Cranch) 137.

[9]Eventually the U.S. Supreme Court, by highly convoluted reasoning, concluded Congress must have intended to have a private right of action. See *Cannon v.*

Or suppose a person injured in an automobile accident sues the vehicle's manufacturer in federal court on the theory the accident was caused by a vehicle defect that violated a standard set by the National Highway Traffic Safety Administration. The injured person is likely to lose because the act did not provide for an individual to sue, only for the agency to establish standards and bring enforcement actions in its own name when an automaker failed to comply with the standards.

In my own work as a Deputy Attorney General I sued an insurance company for setting rates in violation of an insurance reform initiative. In an unfortunate ruling the California Supreme Court held that the Department of Insurance, not a law enforcement agency, should have the first crack at determining if the insurance company's rate setting factors violated the law.[10]

So, if you have spent all that effort in establishing a right, be certain that your bill also provides a remedy to vindicate that right, and that it is the remedy you desire. Otherwise, you might find yourself with little to show for your efforts.

Oversight

Another means of ensuring enforcement of your statute is legislative oversight. This is when the legislature calls the executive (or administrative body) to task in the way it has carried out (or failed to carry out) the law. While oversight is one of the most important things the legislative branch can do in our system of checks and balances, it is one the "bill factory" gets to last and upon which it usually spends little energy.

In a system of checks and balances, the legislature's power to enact policy includes the obligation to monitor compliance with previously adopted laws. It is a way the legislature can hold the executive branch accountable for whether and how it administers current law. By focused inquiry the legislature can realign an agency's priorities to be consistent with the legislature's intent in passing the law.

A near universal complaint is that legislatures don't devote enough time or attention to oversight. Critics say that is because it is hard work, not terribly rewarding and not something for which legislators can easily take credit. Academic work by two political scientists, Matthew McCubbins and Thomas Schwartz, as well as University of California Professor Bruce Cain, divides oversight into police patrol oversight and fire-alarm oversight.

University of Chicago (1979) 441 U.S. 677. Later in that same year, the Supreme Court essentially eliminated imputing a private right of action when a remedy by a private party was not provided for in the statute. See *Touche Ross & Co. v. Redington* (1979) 442 U.S. 560.

[10]Again, for those of a legal mind, the Supreme Court invoked the doctrine of primary jurisdiction. See *Farmers Insurance Exchange v. Superior Court* (1992) 2 Cal. 4th 377.

Police patrol oversight is the routine work of "patrolling" the executive branch looking for problems in program implementation. It is usually centralized in an audit or program review committee with a staff that evaluates the performance of executive agencies.[11]

Fire-alarm oversight of executive programs occurs when interest groups complain about how programs are administered, the media expose waste or abuse, or constituents report problems with governmental services that reveal flaws in program design or implementation. It requires outside actors to "sound an alarm" and therefore is less systematic than police patrol oversight.

Critics who complain about lack of attention to legislative oversight usually are complaining about police patrol oversight. In fact, legislators devote considerable effort to fire-alarm oversight because it provides media attention and credit-taking opportunities. Consequently,

> The widespread presumption that Congress has neglected its oversight responsibility is a widespread mistake. Congressional scholars have focused their attention on police patrol oversight. What has appeared to many of them to be neglect of oversight is really a preference—an eminently natural one—for fire-alarm oversight. That a decentralized, incentive-base control mechanism has been found more effective, from its users' point of view, than direct, centralized surveillance should come as no surprise.[i]

My experience in the California Legislature was the most consistent and effective means of oversight was done in the budget process. Executive agencies are compelled to come before the budget subcommittees to justify their financial requests. Committee members questioned them about the administration of programs for which the agencies are responsible. Often a budget bill would require agencies to prepare detailed reports to the budget committee for the following session. If the reports were not prepared, or if they were inadequate, the budget committee could penalize the agency by reducing or withholding its requested funding.

One of the funnier stories that illustrate how the budget process can be used to affect agency actions involved then Assembly Speaker Willie Brown. Brown lived in San Francisco and would commute to Sacramento by driving at breakneck speeds. On one of those trips to the capitol he was stopped and given a ticket by a California Highway Patrol officer who was unacquainted with Brown and his influence. Brown continued to the capitol, walked in a budget hearing, and in the legislative parlance "zeroed out" (i.e., reduced to nothing) the Highway Patrol's budget. Ultimately the budget item was

---

[11]In California the Joint Legislative Audit Committee (JLAC) often does this type of oversight. Created by statute in 1956, JLAC oversees the work of state agencies and the programs they administer. Both independently and through the state auditor, JLAC investigates public entities to ensure programs are achieving their legislative intent. To a lesser extent, in its periodic reports on state government, the Legislative Analyst's Office also performs oversight.

restored, and along the San Francisco–to–Sacramento corridor the Highway Patrol circulated photos of Brown (and probably his car) with a note not to stop him.

Conclusion

Many laws are not self-executing but instead require follow-up to be sure their purposes are achieved. The fact you may have gotten a law enacted is not the end of your journey. There are many steps you may need to take afterward—in some cases many years afterward—to achieve the goals for which you have already fought so hard.

Chapter Questions

1. What do you believe should be the role of the Supreme Court in reviewing measures enacted by Congress pursuant to the Commerce Clause? Why?

2. If you were a legislator advocating a new program, what steps would you take to ensure continual funding for that program?

3. Does your state use a version of the Administrative Procedure Act? If not, what does it use?

4. In your state legislature, can you find instances of patrol oversight? What entity or entities perform that function?

5. Is it legitimate to deny funding for an enacted program in order to indirectly repeal it? Why or why not?

6. What does *quasijudicial* mean in the administrative process?

7. In your state, where can you find regulations adopted by notice and comment? Where can you find the notice for those proposed regulations?

8. Does your state have a version of the Office of Administrative Law? If so, what is it called?

9. Can you find a good example of agency capture at the federal level? How about in your state?

Endnote

i   McCubbins, M. D., & Schwartz, T. (1984, February). Congressional oversight overlooked: Police patrols versus fire alarms. *American Journal of Political Science, 28*(1), 165–179.

Addendum

Understanding the Difference Between Full-Time and Part-Time State Legislatures

Brian Becker

Among the 50 state legislatures, 10 are clearly full-time. Not surprisingly, most of them are among the most populous states. These legislatures operate nearly year-round and require work that is full-time, or in many cases much more. In addition to their own direct work, legislators typically manage a large legislative and support staff. Though pay levels vary and may or may not be commensurate with the quantity and scope of the required work, many legislators in these states derive much of their regular income from their jobs as legislators. In most cases, even when underpaid, they have little time for other employment.

For example, in Massachusetts the legislature was officially in session for 98% of the business days in 2009. The legislature meets every year. Elections are held every two years in both houses, generating much ongoing work fund-raising and campaigning. There are approximately five staff members for each legislator to manage and receive support from. Legislators are paid $58,237.15 a year in base pay and receive per diem based on how far their district is from Boston. Of Massachusetts lawmakers, 57.7% consider their public office as their full-time profession.

Another 22 legislatures can be generally called part-time. Most of these legislatures govern states with smaller populations. These legislatures meet much less frequently. A handful meet only biennially (every other year). Some meet every year but maintain tight restrictions on session length and have a general culture of limiting other activities.

Idaho operates a part-time legislature. The legislature was in session for just a third of the business days in 2009 even though no limit to session length is prescribed by statute or the state constitution. Idaho also meets annually and holds elections every two years for both houses, but legislators from less populated states represent far fewer constituents on average. There are just 1.4 staffers for each legislator, and many of those only work when the legislature is in session. Idaho legislators are paid $16,166 annually, and 2.6% of them list politics as their full-time profession.

The remaining 18 legislatures fall into a gray area of part- and full-time hybrids. Legislators in these typically midsized states likely spend around three quarters of their work time on state business. The legislators in these states are often paid much less than a full-time wage. The state likely intends to maintain a part-time legislature composed of "working citizens" rather than "career politicians," and indeed many legislators do maintain another line of work. Even if they have little time for it, they need to remain personally financially solvent. These three-quarters-time hybrid legislatures maintain on average 5.5 staff members for each legislator. There is wide variance in staffing levels by state in this category; depending on the size of the state government, more professional staffers are required to compensate for maintaining a "citizen legislature."

Arizona is an example of a three-quarters-time legislature state. The legislature was in session for 64% of the working days in 2009. The legislature meets annually and holds elections every two years for both houses. State Senators represent about 215,000 constituents each. There are 7.8 staffers for each legislator to manage. Only 11.2% of Arizona legislators consider themselves full-time professional politicians. They are paid $24,000 a year for their service.

Conflict of interest—is it really a citizens' legislature when people have to "work"?

While there are some structural similarities among state legislatures, there is just as much variance. While there is a common purpose for state legislatures, there is no common rule establishing the number of legislators or the size of their staffs. Even within the full-time, three-quarters-time, and part-time categories there is tremendous variance on session length and how special sessions are to be called, rates of remuneration, and so on. Some who attempt to categorize the legislatures place them in these three categories, others in five or six. They are so difficult to measure with regard to workload that it is nearly impossible to place them into two categories.

Furthermore, the work of a legislator is difficult to quantify. Legislators are often researching legislation, conferring with staff and one another, connecting with constituents, working on their behalf, and participating in political activities that are well outside the legislative session. These activities may take place inside or outside the statehouse, and nobody counts the hours; from budget negotiations to Fourth of July parades, it all just comes with the job. Research on this is particularly difficult because it is based on unreliable self-report data. Often in the same legislature one member reports a high percentage of his or her time is spent on government work, and another reports a low percentage.

In 1971 the Citizens Conference on State Legislatures published a book called *The Sometime Governments: A Critical Study of the 50 American Legislatures*. This first-of-its-kind study compared and rated legislatures objectively for their ability to be functional, accountable, informed, independent, and representative. This was part of a groundswell movement discouraging the "sometime" governance of very part-time legislatures. State governments began to see legislatures professionalize, extend and add sessions, increase salaries, adjust composition, and generally move toward full-time in order to become coequal to the executive and judicial branches, both of which work full-time for better pay and with significant staffing. Of particular importance to the movement was not only effective lawmaking but the provision of thorough oversight of the state executive branch as state governments continued to grow. There is an inverse relationship between the power of the executive and the power of the legislature.

Most citizens are unaware of the complexity of such oversight. In large states, the annual budget alone is often hundreds or thousands of pages of complicated detail with serious consequence. States must accurately project revenues while the economy is in flux. The U.S. Constitution does not allow states to accumulate operational debt—so the budget must be balanced. Legislatures have sometimes approved budgets that they had insufficient time and staffing to review, debate, and amend due to operational, staffing, and time limitations. Over time, states have worked to mitigate this undue risk. In 2007 the *Lawrence Journal-World* reported that complaints over budget problems led to discussion of a more full-time legislature. The Kansas Legislature already holds longer sessions than many small states, but its budget has grown dramatically. "State government didn't have its first $1 billion budget until its 1974 fiscal year, and the budget still was less than $6 billion in fiscal 1993. When lawmakers finish their work this year, the fiscal year 2008 budget will be between $12.5 billion and $12.6 billion" (Hanna, 2007).

According to the National Conference of State Legislatures (Brenda Erickson, NCSL, personal communication, May 25, 2010), in 1960 only 19 states met every year. The rest of the states met every other year. Today only five states still meet biennially, and they are an endangered breed. Arkansas, Connecticut, Louisiana, North Carolina, Maine, and Wyoming still meet in abbreviated session on the even numbered years. The session is limited for either length, scope, or both. In most cases, the even-year session focuses on the annual budget. A two-year budget is just too unwieldy to approve and lacks agility in an unpredictable economy. In order to facilitate adequate oversight of the budget and other executive branch functions, many legislatures also now have the ability to call themselves into special session rather than requiring the Governor to do it.

No state in modern legislative history has ever moved significantly from a full-time to a more part-time legislature. At times session lengths are limited modestly, or the number of legislators is adjusted up or down, but no state has moved from an annual session to a biennial. No state has aggressively cut the size and function of the legislature—the trend has been exactly the opposite (Brenda Erickson, NCSL, personal communication, May 25, 2010).

This does not stop citizens, advocates, and the press from arguing for a move to part-time, particularly in large states with the largest and costliest legislatures. Citizens do not always have a high impression of legislatures, and especially in recessionary times when legislatures are cutting budgets there is often pressure for the legislature itself to be cut back. Paradoxically, budget constriction is among the most strategic and challenging jobs a legislature undertakes. Furthermore, the cost to operate even the most costly legislatures is only 0.53% of general state government expenses (Brenda Erickson, NCSL, personal communication, May 25, 2010). While legislative operating cost may be one indicator of effectiveness, the effective operation of the state government is of paramount concern, and governance needs vary by state. Cost is best measured on a per-capita basis (see Figure A.1).

Figure A.1

State	Ft – 3/4t – Pt	Legislators	Staff Per Legislator	Legislator Base Salary	Per Capita Expenditure
Alabama	Part-Time	140	3.9	$10/day	$7.94
Alaska	Part-Time	60	7.7	$50,400/year	$57.72
Arizona	¾ Time	90	7.8	$24,000/year	$7.34
California	Full-Time	120	17.6	$95,291/year	$9.19
Texas	¾ Time	181	13.2	$7,200/year	$5.18
Pennsylvania	Full-Time	253	11.5	$78,315/year	$25.40

There have been calls for a unicameral legislature (like that of Nebraska) in recent years in both Maine and Minnesota, but initiatives have not gotten far. In 2007 there was a movement in Michigan to move to part-time because of budget issues, even though the legislature cost residents $10 per capita (Citizens Research Council of Michigan, 2007). In 2010 in Pennsylvania the Commonwealth Foundation called for a part-time citizen legislature with term limits due to cost and alleged corruption.

California moved to a true full-time legislature in 1967, approved by a strong majority of voters in 1966 as Proposition 1A. In 2004 in California, Governor Arnold Schwarzenegger first publicly called for a shift back to a part-time legislature over bills that he considered inconsequential and frivolous (Murphy, 2004). Ever since, he and several other Republican political leaders in the state have repeatedly raised the issue. Low public opinion of the California Legislature undoubtedly helps give the issue some traction in the press and with the public. The Governor's own political struggles with even his own party's caucus in the legislature are also well known. In 2010 the issue failed to be placed on the ballot due to insufficient funding to acquire 694,354 required signatures from registered voters in the state (Marelius, 2010).

Aside from cost, another major argument for a part-time legislature is that as a "citizens' legislature" most of the time legislators are working normal jobs and living a normal life in the community. This populist notion still resonates with the American idea—with a rejection of European elitism. In some of the least populated states, it may be true that legislators spend more time on other things than their elected public office. Yet this system favors elite professionals who have the privilege of leaving their regular jobs (with or without pay) for several weeks or months a year. Most citizens do not have that luxury. Many legislators who curtail their work temporarily are business owners with others to do the work in their stead, rather than average citizens.

An argument against part-time legislatures is the concern over conflict of interest. When a full-time doctor is also a part-time legislator, she may be responsible for legislation that regulates or benefits her own industry. Yet this may be true to some degree for all legislators, even career politicians. What is most important is the level of established conflict-of-interest policies and procedures in each statehouse and the enforced consequences when they are broken.

Another argument against part-time is that as legislators have less time to work on lawmaking and listening to public testimony in committee, political power is increased for the executive branch, insider lobbyists, and legislative staff. The Texas Legislature meets in general session only biennially. Yet lawmakers meet for committee work and study legislation on the off years. They also manage large staffs. Aside from biennial sessions and low pay, Texas lawmakers work more than part-time. Yet only the wealthy or retired citizens likely can afford to work for so little.

At any given time several states are talking about expanding toward a full-time legislature, and a few among the 10 with full-time legislatures are talking about cutting back to part-time. The reality is far more complex than the labels indicate. While no state has effectively moved from full-time to part-time in at least the last 80 years, it is important that legislatures continue to look for ways to become more effective carrying out the people's business as state budgets grow far larger than our ancestors ever anticipated. Whether in

California, where the budget (and its complexities and conflicts) dwarfs most nations on earth, or in Wyoming, where the entire population is just slightly more than the constituency of one California Assembly Member, the legislature is a vital and representative branch of our three-part democracy.

The map in Figure A.2 and the chart in Figure A.3 will help you determine how your legislature functions.

Figure A.2

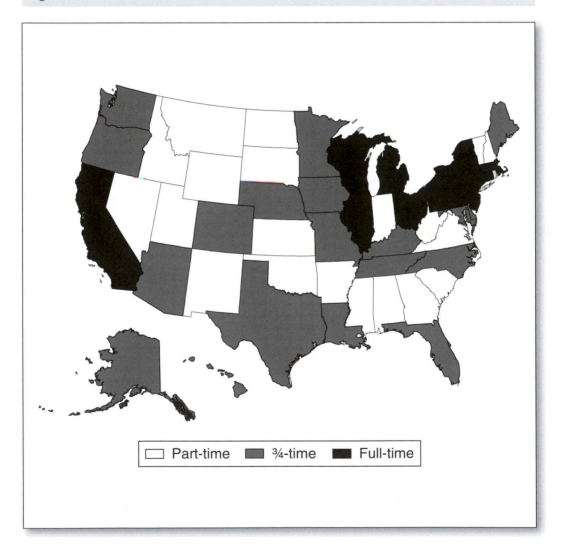

Part-time   ¾-time   Full-time

Figure A.3

State	FT/PT Legislature	% of Working Days in Session (2009)	Gen Sess Annual or Biennial?	Lower Chamber	No. of Legislators(L)	Term Length (Years)	Upper Chamber	No. of Legislators(U)	Term Length (Years)	No. of Staff Per Legislator	% of Self-Declared FT Legislators (2009)	Legislator Base Salary (2010)	State Population (2008) (in Thousands)	Legislative Branch Expenditures (2008) (in Thousands)	Per Capita Legislative Branch Expenditures (2008)	Notes
Wyoming	PT	15%	Annual	House of Representatives	60	2	Senate	30	4	1.4	2.2%	$150/day	533	$5,823	$10.92	40 days in odd years, 20 days in even years, not more than 60 days every two years, special sessions excluded
Vermont	PT	34%	Annual	House of Representatives	150	2	Senate	30	2	0.5	3.4%	$636.62/week	621	$9,941	$16.01	
North Dakota	PT	32%	Biennial	House of Representatives	94	4	Senate	47	4	0.7	1.4%	$148/day	641	$7,867	$12.27	
Alaska	3/4T	25%	Annual	House of Representatives	40	2	Senate	20	4	7.7	13.3%	$50,400/yr	688	$39,709	$57.72	
South Dakota	PT	27%	Annual	House of Representatives	70	2	Senate	35	2	1.0	0.0%	$12,000/2 yr term	805	$4,805	$5.97	
Delaware	3/4T	45%	Annual	House of Representatives	41	2	Senate	21	4	2.0	17.7%	$41,680/yr	876	$12,432	$14.19	
Montana	PT	31%	Biennial	House of Representatives	100	2	Senate	50	4	1.6	8.7%	$82.64/day	968	$12,354	$12.76	
Rhode Island	PT	48%	Annual	House of Representatives	75	2	Senate	38	2	3.9	0.0%	$13,089.44/yr	1,054	$28,238	$26.79	
Hawaii	3/4T	30%	Annual	House of Representatives	51	2	Senate	25	4	9.3	36.0%	$48,708/yr	1,287	$29,150	$22.65	

(Continued)

Figure A.3 (Continued)

State	FT/PT Legislature	% of Working Days in Session (2009)	Gen Sess Annual or Biennial?	Lower Chamber	No. of Legislators(L)	Term Length (Years)	Upper Chamber	No. of Legislators(U)	Term Length (Years)	No. of Staff Per Legislator	% of Self-Declared FT Legislators (2009)	Legislator Base Salary (2010)	State Population (2008) (in Thousands)	Legislative Branch Expenditures (2008) (in Thousands)	Per Capita Legislative Branch Expenditures (2008)	Notes
Maine	PT	53%	Annual	House of Representatives	151	2	Senate	35	2	1.1	2.1%	$13,526/yr	1,320	$23,399	$17.73	Additional $9,661/yr for 2nd special session
New Hampshire	PT	49%	Annual	House of Representatives	400	2	Senate	24	2	0.4	0.5%	$200/2 yr term	1,322	$14,316	$10.83	
Idaho	PT	33%	Annual	House of Representatives	70	2	Senate	35	2	1.4	2.9%	$16,116/yr	1,528	$13,368	$8.75	
Nebraska	3/4T	44%	Annual	N/A	0	NA	Senate	49	4	5.0	6.1%	$12,000/yr	1,782	$15,834	$8.89	
West Virginia	PT	33%	Annual	House of Delegates	100	2	Senate	34	4	3.1	0.0%	$20,000/yr	1,815	$25,833	$14.23	
New Mexico	PT	19%	Annual	House of Representatives	70	2	Senate	42	4	6.1	0.0%	$0	1,987	$22,590	$11.37	Term is 1/2 length in odd numbered years
Nevada	PT	31%	Biennial	Assembly	42	2	Senate	21	4	9.5	0.0%	$146.90/day	2,616	$47,418	$18.13	1 week special session in off year
Utah	PT	21%	Annual	House of Representatives	75	2	Senate	29	4	2.1	1.0%	$117/day	2,727	$12,226	$4.48	
Kansas	PT	40%	Annual	House of Representatives	125	2	Senate	40	4	2.4	1.8%	$88.66/day	2,797	$21,419	$7.66	
Arkansas	PT	31%	Annual	House of Representatives	100	2	Senate	35	4	4.0	2.2%	$15,362/yr	2,868	$37,676	$13.14	Short fiscal session on even years
Mississippi	PT	42%	Annual	House of Representatives	122	4	Senate	52	4	1.2	1.7%	$10,000/yr	2,940	$22,126	$7.53	

State	FT/PT Legislature	% of Working Days in Session (2009)	Gen Sess Annual or Biennial?	Lower Chamber	No. of Legislators(L)	Term Length (Years)	Upper Chamber	No. of Legislators(U)	Term Length (Years)	No. of Staff Per Legislator	% of Self-Declared FT Legislators (2009)	Legislator Base Salary (2010)	State Population (2008) (in Thousands)	Legislative Branch Expenditures (2008) (in Thousands)	Per Capita Legislative Branch Expenditures (2008)	Notes
Iowa	3/4T	29%	Annual	House of Representatives	100	2	Senate	50	4	2.5	12.8%	$25,000/yr	2,994	$31,285	$10.45	
Connecticut	FT	79%	Annual	House of Representatives	151	2	Senate	36	2	3.3	26.5%	$28,000/yr	3,503	$61,367	$17.52	Slightly shorter session on even numbered years
Oklahoma	PT	32%	Annual	House of Representatives	101	2	Senate	48	4	2.7	9.5%	$38,400/yr	3,644	$37,790	$10.37	
Oregon	3/4T	46%	Biennial	House of Representatives	60	2	Senate	30	4	5.3	10.1%	$21,612/yr	3,783	$36,496	$9.65	Committee work takes place between sessions
Kentucky	3/4T	25%	Annual	House of Representatives	100	2	Senate	38	4	4.9	3.7%	$186.73/day	4,288	$45,213	$10.54	Term is 1/2 length in odd numbered years
Louisiana	3/4T	17%	Annual	House of Representatives	105	4	Senate	39	4	6.0	7.9%	$22,800/yr	4,452	$60,156	$13.51	
South Carolina	PT	43%	Annual	House of Representatives	124	2	Senate	46	4	2.7	5.9%	$10,400/yr	4,503	$53,544	$11.89	
Alabama	PT	31%	Annual	House of Representatives	105	4	Senate	35	4	3.9	5.0%	$10/day	4,677	$37,137	$7.94	
Colorado	3/4T	33%	Annual	House of Representatives	65	2	Senate	35	4	3.5	14.0%	$30,000/yr	4,935	$23,430	$4.75	
Minnesota	3/4T	36%	Annual	House of Representatives	134	2	Senate	67	4	3.6	11.1%	$31,140.90/yr	5,231	$57,422	$10.98	Flexible biennial schedule: 120 days total

(Continued)

Figure A.3 (Continued)

State	FT/PT Legislature	% of Working Days in Session (2009)	Gen Sess Annual or Biennial?	Lower Chamber	No. of Legislators(L)	Term Length (Years)	Upper Chamber	No. of Legislators(U)	Term Length (Years)	No. of Staff Per Legislator	% of Self-Declared FT Legislators (2009)	Legislator Base Salary (2010)	State Population (2008) (in Thousands)	Legislative Branch Expenditures (2008) (in Thousands)	Per Capita Legislative Branch Expenditures (2008)	Notes
Wisconsin	FT	97%	Annual	Assembly	99	2	Senate	33	4	4.8	54.6%	$49,943/yr	5,628	$59,482	$10.57	
Maryland	3/4T	25%	Annual	House of Delegates	141	4	Senate	47	4	3.9	11.7%	$43,500/yr	5,659	$68,305	$12.07	
Missouri	3/4T	39%	Annual	House of Representatives	163	2	Senate	34	4	2.6	0.0%	$35,915/yr	5,956	$33,513	$5.63	
Tennessee	3/4T	43%	Annual	House of Representatives	99	2	Senate	33	4	2.5	6.1%	$19,009/yr	6,240	$34,005	$5.45	Flexible biennial schedule: 90 days total
Indiana	PT	36%	Annual	House of Representatives	100	2	Senate	50	4	2.5	6.7%	$22,616.46/yr	6,388	$36,429	$5.70	
Arizona	3/4T	64%	Annual	House of Representatives	60	2	Senate	30	2	7.8	11.2%	$24,000/yr	6,499	$47,690	$7.34	
Massachussetts	FT	98%	Annual	House of Representatives	160	2	Senate	40	2	4.5	57.7%	$58,237.15/yr	6,544	$56,910	$8.70	
Washington	3/4T	29%	Annual	House of Representatives	98	2	Senate	49	4	5.8	18.4%	$42,106/yr	6,566	$80,733	$12.30	
Virginia	PT	13%	Annual	House of Delegates	100	2	Senate	40	4	5.4	1.4%	$18,000/yr	7,795	$43,263	$5.55	$18K/yr senate, $17,640/yr house
New Jersey	FT	97%	Annual	Assembly	80	2	Senate	40	4	8.2	21.9%	$49,000/yr	8,663	$76,545	$8.84	
North Carolina	3/4T	54%	Annual	House of Representatives	120	2	Senate	50	2	3.8	2.4%	$13,951/yr	9,247	$45,498	$4.92	Flexible biennial schedule: even year short session
Georgia	PT	23%	Annual	House of Representatives	180	2	Senate	56	2	3.3	3.4%	$17,342/yr	9,698	$37,770	$3.89	

State	FT/PT Legislature	% of Working Days in Session (2009)	Gen Sess Annual or Biennial?	Lower Chamber	No. of Legislators(L)	Term Length (Years)	Upper Chamber	No. of Legislators(U)	Term Length (Years)	No. of Staff Per Legislator	% of Self-Declared FT Legislators (2009)	Legislator Base Salary (2010)	State Population (2008) (in Thousands)	Legislative Branch Expenditures (2008) (in Thousands)	Per Capita Legislative Branch Expenditures (2008)	Notes
Michigan	FT	97%	Annual	House of Representatives	110	2	Senate	38	4	6.6	56.5%	$79,650/yr	10,002	$102,252	$10.22	
Ohio	FT	99%	Annual	House of Representatives	99	2	Senate	33	4	3.5	39.7%	$60,584/yr	11,528	$47,971	$4.16	
Pennsylvania	FT	99%	Annual	House of Representatives	203	2	Senate	50	4	11.5	77.5%	$78,314.66/yr	12,566	$319,212	$25.40	
Illinois	FT	97%	Annual	House of Representatives	118	2	Senate	59	4	5.8	47.2%	$67,836/yr	12,843	$71,482	$5.57	
Florida	3/4T	23%	Annual	House of Representatives	120	2	Senate	40	4	9.8	5.7%	$29,697/yr	18,424	$174,930	$9.49	
New York	FT	98%	Annual	Assembly	150	2	Senate	62	2	13.0	58.9%	$79,500/yr	19,468	$216,339	$11.11	
Texas	3/4T	37%	Biennial	House of Representatives	150	2	Senate	31	4	13.2	1.7%	$7,200/yr	24,304	$125,997	$5.18	
California	FT	107%	Annual	Assembly	80	2	Senate	40	4	17.6	80.0%	$95,291/yr	36,580	$336,170	$9.19	
Total		**47%**				**2.2**			**3.52**	**4.8**	**15.4%**			**$57,297**	**$11.62**	
Total full-time legislatures	10															
Total 3/4 time legislatures	18															
Total part-time legislatures	22															
Total annual general sessions		45														
Total biennial general sessions		5														

References

Benefield, N. A., & Bryan, E. (2010, February). The case for a citizen legislature. *Policy Brief from the Commonwealth Foundation*. Retrieved March 22, 2011, from http://www.commonwealthfoundation.org/docLib/201003111_PB2204 CitizenLegislature.pdf

Citizens Conference on State Legislatures. (1971). *The Sometime Governments: A Critical Study of the 50 American Legislatures*. Toronto; New York: Bantam Books.

Citizens Research Council of Michigan. (2007, June). *Legislative term limits and full-time and part-time legislatures*. Retrieved March 22, 2011, from http://www.crcmich.org/PUBLICAT/2000s/2007/note200703.pdf

Gudrais, E., & Gregg, K. (2007, March 26). Political scene: Proposal for full-time legislature resurfaces. *Providence Journal*. Retrieved March 22, 2011, from http://www.projo.com/news/content/political_scene_26_03-26-07_GR4PLFK .2718184.html

Hanna, J. (2007, April 30). Budget complaints spur discussion of full-time legislature. *Lawrence Journal-World*. Retrieved March 22, 2011, from http://www2 .ljworld.com/news/2007/apr/30/budget_complaints_spur_discussion_fulltime_ legisla/

Keefe, W., & Ogul, M. (2010). *Annual versus biennial legislative sessions*. National Conference of State Legislatures. Retrieved March 22, 2011, from http://www .ncsl.org/default.aspx?tabid=17541

Marelius, J. (2010, March 1). Critics seek a part-time California Legislature. *San Diego Union-Tribune*. Retrieved March 22, 2011, from http://web.signonsandiego.com/ news/2010/mar/01/group-seeks-a-part-time-legislature-is-proposed/

Murphy, K. (May 14, 2004). *Is the grass greener for part-time legislatures?* Retrieved March 22, 2011, from http://www.stateline.org/live/ViewPage.action?siteNode Id=136&languageId=1&contentId=15648

National Conference of State Legislatures. (2009, June). *Full and part-time legislatures*. Retrieved March 22, 2011, from http://www.ncsl.org/default.aspx?tabid=16701

Schneider, M. B. (2010, January 4). Part-time legislators, full-time duties. *Indianapolis Star*. Retrieved March 22, 2011, from http://www.indy.com/posts/part-time-legislators-full-time-duties

Index _____

About the Editor _____

Pat Libby, Clinical Professor, created and directs the Institute for Nonprofit Education and Research (INER) at the University of San Diego, which comprises a master's program, a research center, a doctoral specialization, and community education programs focused on the third sector. INER was developed in 2001 through a comprehensive environmental scanning process that involved interviews, focus groups, and surveys of hundreds of actors in the nonprofit, philanthropic, and academic communities. Its pedagogy has a unique emphasis that interweaves theory with applied learning. Since the institute's inception in fall 2002, INER students have completed hundreds of applied projects for nonprofit organizations.

A Boston native, Pat has served as a senior executive, board member, and consultant to numerous nonprofit organizations since 1978. Prior to becoming an academic and consultant, she devoted her career to nonprofits serving economically disadvantaged people and communities in Massachusetts and California. Her last executive management position was as President/CEO of the Massachusetts Association of Community Development Corporations (MACDC), which she developed into a nationally recognized model for community development trade organizations. Under her auspices, MACDC leveraged hundreds of millions of dollars in public and private investment for affordable housing, commercial development, and small business lending in economically distressed areas. Her experiences there led Pat to develop the strategic framework that she uses to teach students local and state lobbying as described in this book.

Pat holds a BA in sociology from Tufts University and a graduate degree in urban planning from MIT. She lives in San Diego, California, with her husband, Mike Eichler, and dog, Frank.

About the Contributors _____

Brian Becker is a political advocacy student of Pat Libby. He serves as the Director of International Ministries at Point Loma Nazarene University in San Diego, California, and is a master's student in the Nonprofit Leadership and Management Program at the University of San Diego. He is married to Kelly. They enjoy living amidst amazing cultural diversity in City Heights, San Diego, and are actively engaged in immigrant and refugee communities and issues of social justice.

Maureen Carasiti has a significant record of accomplishment supporting individuals with developmental disabilities and has passionately advocated on their behalf for over 28 years. Currently, she is the Associate Director for Developmental Services Continuum, Inc., a nonprofit in San Diego, California. She is deeply connected within the local provider community and is an active participant on state initiatives that stand to impact people with developmental disabilities. Maureen holds an MA in nonprofit leadership and management from the University of San Diego and a BA in education from Long Island University in New York.

Elizabeth Heagy has led nonprofit organizations and programs at both the national and state levels for over 15 years, including as Managing Director of Strategic Partnerships in support of federal environmental policies at the Environmental Defense Fund, as President and CEO of the Center for Lobbying in the Public Interest, and as Executive Director of the Virginia Campus Outreach Opportunity League. In each case, she has created, implemented, and evaluated clearly articulated strategic plans with critical public policy components. Liz is an attorney with a JD from Temple University Beasley School of Law and a BA from the University of Mary Washington. She was a Visiting Fellow at Georgetown Public Policy Institute's Center for Public & Nonprofit Leadership.

Ben McCue is the Conservation Director for WiLDCOAST, a binational U.S.-Mexico nonprofit that works to conserve coastal and marine ecosystems and wildlife. In 2008, he was influential in convincing federal legislators to allocate $100 million to upgrade the South Bay International Wastewater Treatment Plant in San Ysidro, California, to meet Clean Water Act standards. His 2009 journey to pass state legislation to address the flow of waste automobile tires across the California-Baja California border is chronicled in this book. Ben holds an MA in nonprofit leadership and management from the University of San Diego and a BS in ecology, behavior, and evolution from the University of California–San Diego.

John McNutt is Professor in the School of Public Policy and Administration and Coordinator of the nonprofit concentration in the MPA program at the University of Delaware. He has coauthored or coedited four books and many articles, book chapters, and other works on advocacy, the digital divide, volunteerism, community development technology and nonprofit organizations, and technology and public participation. He regularly presents at national and international conferences and is also a member of the editorial boards of several scholarly journals. John earned a BA at Mars Hill College, an MSW from the University of Alabama, and a PhD from the University of Tennessee.

Howard Wayne represented the south coastal area of San Diego County from 1996 through 2002 in the California State Assembly. As a legislator he authored more than 60 bills that were signed into law, chaired the Natural Resources Committee and the Environmental Safety Committee, and was a member and Chair of the California Law Revision Commission. He is a cum laude graduate of the University of San Diego School of Law, where he was an editor of the *Law Review*. For more than 30 years Howard has served as a California Deputy Attorney General. He has argued six cases in the California Supreme Court and was the lead counsel in more than 30 published appellate opinions. In 1994 he was a Supreme Court Fellow with the National Association of Attorneys General. In addition, he teaches an advocacy course at the University of San Diego with Professor Pat Libby and a course in legislation at Thomas Jefferson School of Law.

SAGE Research Methods Online
The essential tool for researchers

Sign up now at www.sagepub.com/srmo for more information.

An expert research tool

- An **expertly designed taxonomy** with more than 1,400 unique terms for social and behavioral science research methods
- **Visual and hierarchical search tools** to help you discover material and link to related methods

- Easy-to-use navigation tools
- Content organized by complexity
- Tools for citing, printing, and downloading content with ease
- Regularly updated content and features

A wealth of essential content

- The most comprehensive picture of quantitative, qualitative, and mixed methods available today
- More than **100,000 pages of SAGE book and reference material** on research methods as well as editorially selected material from SAGE journals
- More than **600 books** available in their entirety online

Launching 2011!

⑤SAGE research methods online